PRACTICAL PROGRAM DEVE
USING JSP

COMPUTER SCIENCE TEXTS

COMPUTER SCIENCE TEXTS

Practical Program Development using JSP

A Manual of Program Design using the Design Method developed by M. A. Jackson

RALPH STORER

MA, Dip. Ed.
Department of Computer Studies
Napier Polytechnic
Edinburgh

OXFORD

BLACKWELL SCIENTIFIC PUBLICATIONS

LONDON EDINBURGH BOSTON

MELBOURNE PARIS BERLIN VIENNA

It is better to be **unborn than untaught**, for ignorance is the root of misfortune.

PLATO

Ignorance, when voluntary, is criminal, and a man may be properly charged with that evil which he neglected or refused to learn how to prevent

SAMUEL JOHNSON

© 1987 by
Blackwell Scientific Publications
Editorial offices:
Osney Mead, Oxford OX2 0EL
25 John Street, London WC1N 2BL
23 Ainslie Place, Edinburgh EH3 6AJ
3 Cambridge Center, Cambridge
  Massachusetts 02142, USA
54 University Street, Carlton
  Victoria 3053, Australia

Other Editorial Offices:

Arnette SA
2, rue Casimir-Delavigne
75006 Paris
France

Blackwell Wissenschaft
Meinekestrasse 4
D-1000 Berlin 15
West Germany

Blackwell MZV
Feldgasse 13
A-1238 Wien
Austria

First published 1987
Reprint with updates 1991

Printed and bound in Great Britain by
Hollen Street Press Ltd

DISTRIBUTORS

Marston Book Services Ltd
PO Box 87
Oxford OX2 0DT
(*Orders*: Tel: 0865 791155
            Fax: 0865 791927
            Telex: 837515)

USA
Blackwell Scientific Publications, Inc.
3 Cambridge Center
Cambridge, MA 02142
(*Orders*: Tel: (800) 759–6102)

Canada
Oxford University Press
70 Wynford Drive
Don Mills
Ontario M3C 1J9
(*Orders*: Tel: (416) 441–2941)

Australia
Blackwell Scientific Publications
(Australia) Pty Ltd
54 University Street
Carlton, Victoria 3053
(*Orders*: Tel: (03) 347–0300)

British Library
Cataloguing in Publication Data
Storer, Ralph
    Practical program development using
    JSP: a manual of program design
    using the design method developed by
    M. A. Jackson.—(Computer Science
    Texts)
    1. Jackson structured programming
    I. Title   II. Series
    005.1'13   QA76.6

    ISBN 0-632-01545-4 Pbk

Library of Congress
Cataloging in Publication Data
    Storer, Ralph
    Practical program development using
    JSP.
    (Computer science texts)
    Bibliography: p.
    Includes index.
    1. Jackson structured programming.
    2. Electronic digital computers—
    Programming. I. Jackson, M. A.
    II. Title. III. Series.
    QA76.6.S77 1987   005'.1   86-26368

    ISBN 0-632-01545-4

Contents

Preface, vii

Acknowledgment, xi

1 Introduction, 1

1.1 Software engineering, 1; 1.2 Overview of JSP, 13.

2 Drawing Data Structures; 25

2.1 Data components, 25; 2.2 Elementary components, 27; 2.3 Sequence components, 28; 2.4 Selection components, 30; 2.5 Iteration components, 35; 2.6 Data analysis, 41; 2.7 Exercises, 44.

3 Designing Simple Programs, 46

3.1 Design procedure, 46; 3.2 Elementary examples, 51; 3.3 The read-ahead principle, 62; 3.4 Further examples, 69; 3.5 Exercises, 80.

4 Coding and Testing Programs, 82

4.1 Varieties of code, 82; 4.2 Coding constraints, 90; 4.3 Program design languages, 94; 4.4 HOST, 97; 4.5 Testing, 105; 4.6 Exercises, 113.

5 Correspondence, 114

5.1 Multiple data sets, 114; 5.2 Programs which process two data sets, 116; 5.3 Programs which process three data sets, 122; 5.4 Matching data sets, 125; 5.5 Limitations of the correspondence technique, 136; 5.6 Exercises, 138.

6 Direct-Access Data Sets, 141

6.1 Direct-access files, 141; 6.2 Tables, 145; 6.3 Database,153; 6.4 Exercises, 162.

7 Backtracking, 164

7.1 Condition evaluation problems, 164; 7.2 Hamish goes for a walk, 168; 7.3 Backtracking with no side-effects, 171; 7.4 Using favourable side-effects, 178; 7.5 Handling intolerable side-effects, 194; 7.6 Exercises, 203.

8 Inversion, 206

8.1 The technique of inversion, 206; 8.2 Programs which process two sequential data sets, 209; 8.3 Programs which process three sequential data sets, 232; 8.4 Process scheduling, 238; 8.5 In praise of inversion, 240; 8.6 Exercises, 244.

9   Structure Clashes, 245

9.1 Introduction, 245; 9.2 Ordering clash, 246; 9.3 Boundary clash, 249; 9.4 Interleaving clash, 255; 9.5 In praise of parallel inversion, 265; 9.6 Exercises, 269.

10   Jackson System Development, 270

10.1 Introduction, 270; 10.2 The JSD procedure, 272; 10.3 Retrospect, 288.

Appendices, 293

A. Operations in COBOL and BASIC, 293; B. Operations and conditions checklists, 294; C. Component labels, 296; D. Coding rules, 299; E. Large diagrams, 307; F. Outline sample solutions, 309.

References, 335

Index, 336

Preface

This book is about program development. The starting point of the development process is taken to be a program specification which describes the inputs to the program, the outputs from the program and the processes by which the inputs are transformed into outputs. The end point of the development process is an implemented program.

The development process traditionally consists of intuitive coding followed by arbitrary testing, producing programs which are unreliable and unmaintainable. As a result the software industry lurches from one crisis to another, forever failing to meet deadlines and budgets and rarely giving users exactly what they require. The panacea of structured programming, widely touted for the past fifteen years, has failed to produce the goods. Like modular programming before it, it is open to all sorts of abuse in practice. What constitutes a module? Which is the best structure?

It is the thesis of this book that only by concentrating on program design, and only by basing that design on the structure of the data to be processed, will programs of the necessary quality be developed. Data which is input to and output from a program is always structured in one form or another, and if the structure of the program which processes this data is derived from the structure of the data, then it will be obtained without intuition, will be open to inspection and verification, and will be simple to amend should processing requirements change. Moreover, it is the author's view that such data-driven program design is the *only* method of program design which can be taught and learned.

Much of the pioneering work in data-driven program design was done by M. A. Jackson, and it is his method, called Jackson Structured Programming (JSP) which this book expounds. It should be stressed, however, that while acknowledging an enormous debt to Jackson the author takes sole responsibility for the views presented here, which on occasion differ from Jackson's (where this occurs it is noted in the text).

Although JSP is a program design method, it has important ramifications for the steps in the development cycle which follow it: coding, testing and implementation. Coding: an important by-product of using JSP is that coding becomes a facile task which can be automated—see Chapter 4. Testing: JSP facilitates the specification of test data in a methodical manner—see Chapter 4. Implementation: by using the technique of inversion it is possible to design batch and online programs in the same way and choose the implementation at a later date—see Chapter 8. Therefore, although the book will concentrate on program design, it will also have important things to say about other areas of the development process.

The text is aimed primarily at the programmer who must produce a working program from a given specification, but systems analysts and managers will also find many issues which will be of interest to them. It is a teach-yourself text which requires no prior knowledge of modular programming, structured programming or program design. As such it is ideal for trainee programmers and students, even though it is probably 'experienced' programmers who have most to learn from it.

The JSP method is presented both theoretically and practically, using many fully documented worked examples, from simple non-computing examples through to the design of multi-user real-time programs. All the examples are commercial application oriented, and a knowledge of the terminology of commercial data processing (DP) is assumed (e.g. data validation, updating, direct-access).

The most widely used commercial computer languages are COBOL (on mainframes and minis) and BASIC (on micros), and therefore all coding examples are given in COBOL (COBOL 74, with notes on COBOL 85) and (Microsoft) BASIC. However, JSP is a language-independent design method and a knowledge of these languages is not necessary in order to use the book as a self-teaching program design text. As with any learning process, the reader will become proficient in JSP only by using it. Exercises are provided at the end of every chapter, and backup from experienced JSP users (colleagues, tutors, consultants) will increase confidence and reduce the learning curve.

There are ten chapters. Chapter 1 discusses the software crisis in DP and the need for JSP, ending with an overview of the design method. Chapters 2 to 4 present the basic design method: Chapter 2 shows how to represent the structure of data diagrammatically, Chapter 3 explains how to build program structures from data structures, and Chapter 4 discusses the coding and testing issues involved.

Chapters 5 to 9 extend the design method to increasingly complex DP problems. Chapter 5 deals with programs which process multiple data sets, and Chapter 6 with direct-access files and databases. Chapter 7 deals with problems concerning the evaluation of conditions. Chapters 8 and 9 introduce the technique of inversion, which enables uniformity of design of batch programs, online programs and whole systems of programs. Chapter 10 extends the principles of JSP into the realm of systems analysis and design and presents an overview of Jackson System Development (JSD).

The field of computing should be non-sexist, and all references in the text to 'he' should be taken as meaning 'he or she'.

A book of this nature which is heavily biased towards the practical solving of real-life problems could not have been possible without the support of colleagues in the practical application of the principles advocated herein. I owe a particular debt to Michael Jackson, who showed me the light. The staff of John Menzies (Holdings) Ltd. supported my first steps in the practical application of JSP. The Jackson Method Computer Aids Development Working Party has provided (and continues to provide) a lively forum which has catalysed many of my ideas.

The staff and students, both past and present, of Napier College, Edinburgh have supplied ideas for this book (sometimes unwittingly), and have prompted me to improve upon its content and presentation. My thanks go to all of them, especially my colleagues Shirley Gibbs, Rob Kemmer and Jim Murray for their support and advice. Finally, apologies and thanks to all those colleagues and friends who have for too long had to tolerate more than the usual amount of inconsideration during the evolution of this book.

Ralph Storer

Acknowledgment

The following acknowledgment is reprinted from *American National Standard Programming Language COBOL,* X3.23-1974 published by the American National Standards Institute, Inc.

COBOL is an industry language and is not the property of any company or group of companies, or of any organization or group of organizations.

No warranty, expressed or implied, is made by any contributor or by the CODASYL Programming Language Committee as to the accuracy and functioning of the programming system and language. Moreover, no responsibility is assumed by any contributor, or by the committee, in connection therewith.

The authors and copyright holders of the copyrighted material used herein

FLOW-MATIC (trademark of Sperry Rand Corporation), Programming for the UNIVAC® I and II, Data Automation Systems copyrighted 1958, 1959, by Sperry Rand Corporation; IBM Commercial Translator Form No. F 28-8013, copyrighted 1959 by IBM; FACT, DSI 27A5260-2760, copyrighted 1960 by Minneapolis-Honeywell

have specifically authorized the use of this material in whole or in part, in the COBOL specifications. Such authorization extends to the reproduction and use of COBOL specifications in programming manuals or similar publications.

PROBENCH is a registered trademark of
Systems Computer Management Ltd,
Templeton Business Centre, Templeton Street,
Glasgow G40 1DA.

Chapter 1

Introduction

This chapter examines the software crisis in the Data Processing industry and advocates a software engineering approach to its resolution. Jackson Structured Programming is introduced as a software engineering technique, and an overview of its premises, procedure and merits is presented.

1.1 SOFTWARE ENGINEERING

Jackson Structured Programming (JSP) is a method of program design which has arisen within the field of commercial Data Processing (DP) as part of a whole new approach to systems development. This new approach has become necessary because traditional methods of systems development simply do not work, giving rise to a situation commonly referred to as the 'software crisis', in which many systems are characterized by late delivery, costliness, unreliability, unmaintainability and unusability.

This is a blunt and damning indictment of the DP industry, yet anyone familiar with DP would be able to cite numerous instances of software failure in one form or another. In his book *Software Reflected* [1], Baber devotes over thirty pages to listing typical systems problems and concludes that they are the rule rather than the exception. The term 'crisis' is no exaggeration, and before moving on to examine the way forward and the role of JSP, it is perhaps worth taking a closer look at the major characteristics of the software crisis.

Lateness

The failure to deliver a system by a pre-determined deadline is commonplace and has several causes: project managers are notoriously bad at deadline estimation, system enhancements are allowed to prolong development time, inadequate development techniques which are not susceptible to rigorous measurement are used.

1

Costliness

The popular image of diminishing computer costs caused by better and cheaper hardware bears little relationship to the reality of systems development, where typically 80% of the total budget goes on software and staff salaries [4, reprinted in 23]. Software costs are ever-increasing and more than counterbalance plummeting hardware costs.

Unmaintainability

If there is one factor which differentiates DP programs from all others it is their subjection to constant change—from users, managers, trade unions, government legislation, etc. For example, a user may demand an alteration to a report, a trade union may negotiate a new pay structure, the governement may decide to decimalize (decimalization in the 1970s was one of the largest exercises ever undertaken by the UK DP industry).

The process of keeping a program up-to-date is known as maintenance, and the degree of ease with which a program can be maintained is known as its maintainability. To a programmer unfamiliar with DP, the amount of maintenance required in a DP environment will come as a shock. In the early 1970s an average of 50% of a DP department's budget was spent on maintenance [3]; more recent studies give figures of 80% plus with some installations having no time at all to spend on new developments [14]. It follows that anything which can be done to ease maintenance and make programs more maintainable must have a high priority, and this includes making programs easy to read, understand and change.

Unreliability

The problem of maintenance is closely connected with that of reliability: unreliable systems require more maintenance and are less easy to maintain—it is no coincidence that the more errors a system contains the more difficult it is to understand and change it. Unreliability has become such an accepted part of implemented systems that there has even arisen the notion of the inevitability of error, enshrined in Lubarsky's Law of Cybernetic Entomology: 'There's always one more bug'.

Evidence in support of this is provided by the fact that no less than 54% of all system errors detected are not detected until after implementation [8]. During the initial weeks of implementation programmers are commonly required to be on 24-hour standby for emergency fixes.

Moreover, it has been shown that after an initial glut of software errors detected by live processing, the volume of errors detected decreases, without ever reaching zero, but then begins to climb again as new errors are introduced by maintenance itself [22]. Not in vain has maintenance been defined as the substitution of one set of errors by another. After the system has been patched so many times it becomes an unwieldy beast with which programmers meddle at their peril.

Unusability

It might be supposed that despite the above problems it would at least be possible to give the user what he wants, but not so. Sometimes the user does not know what he wants in the first place, being unaware of the possibilities of computerization or simply misunderstanding the system specification to which he agrees. Sometimes it is not possible to meet the specification by the stated deadline and trade-offs have to be made. Sometimes the user's requirements turn out to be not cost-effective once system design gets under way, and again a compromise is effected. Whatever the reason, the situation is unsatisfactory.

What is to be done about the software crisis? It will be apparent that a way forward will emerge only from an attack on a broad front. The skills required in the development of programs and systems are many and varied, and we should not expect to find a single panacea which will cure all the ills of DP. Here are just a few of the abilities required during the systems development life cycle:

—The ability to estimate how long it will take to produce a working program from a given specification.

—The ability to estimate how much it will cost to develop a system.

—The ability to produce program code which is understandable and maintainable by others.

—The ability to produce system and program documentation which is understandable and maintainable by others.

—The ability to produce programs which contain no errors.

—The ability to understand user problems and translate that understanding into computerized solutions.

—The ability to coordinate and manage the man-machine resources required during the development life cycle.

This list of skills is by no means complete. Systems development is a complex business, and the complete answer to the software crisis will involve improved skills, techniques and methods in a number of quite independent areas. However, it would be useful if there were an overall, integrated approach to systems development into which each of these improved techniques could be slotted, and it may be productive to step back from the DP morass for a moment and consider another kind of project whose end product should also be on time, economical, maintainable, reliable and useful—an engineering project.

Consider the civil engineering of a bridge. After construction we would not expect the bridge to collapse under use, now or at any point in the future. We would expect it to be robust enough to withstand wind of a specified velocity. We would expect to be able to carry out maintenance such as repainting or resurfacing without interfering with its function. Why should we expect less of a computer system?

Consider the mechanical engineering of a car. We would expect a design which easily permitted modification according to user requirements, such as the addition of fog lamps, the replacement of the carburettor or the removal of the back seat to enable the carrying of large loads. After delivery we would expect the car to be reliable and not break down the first time it was driven over 30 mph. We would expect it to be delivered on time. We would expect it to be secure from thieves. Why should we expect less of a computer system?

Consider the electrical engineering of a lighting system. After installation we would expect the system to be user-friendly, with sockets conveniently sited. We would expect the result of depressing a switch to be predictable. Why should we expect less of a computer system?

We expect less because we have become accustomed to less through years of haphazard approaches to systems development, but why should the expectations and principles of engineering projects not be applied to software projects? Why should software not be engineered?

The term 'software engineering' refers to the application of principles of engineering to the development of software. Of course the analogy between a software project and an engineering project is not a direct one.

The problems of software development are far more intransigent than those of engineering, because a software product is limited not by the laws of physics but solely by the imagination of the producer.

Nevertheless, there is no reason why the methodological experience of engineering should not be usefully applied to the process of software development. In other words, the process by which a user problem evolves into a computerized system could be directed by a formal step-by-step procedure similar to that used within the engineering industry (see Fig. 1.1).

The four steps of software engineering	
Step 1	Problem definition
Step 2	Solution design
Step 3	Solution implementation
Step 4	Solution verification

Figure 1.1

Step 1   Problem Definition

Step 1 involves the identification of a problem and its formulation in terms of inputs, processes and outputs. In traditional systems development this step results in a system specification which is written in verbose and ambiguous English narrative, is incompletely understood by the user, is often machine-dependent, always contains inaccuracies and inconsistencies and often presupposes the computer solution.

The software engineering approach, on the other hand, attempts to provide a clear, concise definition of the problem as it exists in the user's real-world environment; it presupposes no solution and is entirely intelligible to the user. One method adopting this approach is Jackson System Development (JSD) [13], which uses entity life-history diagrams to describe entities within the user's environment and show how actions affect them over time (see Chapter 10). JSD is rigorous, proven and teachable, producing a problem definition in diagrammatic form which is communicable to the user, machine-independent and capable of being input directly to Step 2.

Step 2   Solution Design

Step 2 involves the search for and evaluation of alternative solutions to the problem and the production of a solution specification. Traditionally this step is intuitive, minimal and often preordained by elements of the system specification. Often the solution design does not evolve from the problem definition at all but from previous solution designs of which the designer has experience. Any extra design required may be done by flowcharting—if the charting of procedural flow can be called design.

In the traditional approach Steps 1 and 2 are hopelessly confused, but in the software engineering approach they are rigorously separated. Solution design involves the definition of system processes and connections between them (e.g. data streams, direct accesses). The resulting logical solution specification is documented in JSD in the form of a system specification diagram and program structure diagrams.

JSD is a complete system design method, but this manual is concerned primarily with program design, and it is to the area of program design that JSP addresses itself. JSP is a program design method which takes a program specification as its starting point and by a rigorous step-by-step procedure produces a logical solution specification (i.e. a program design) in the form of a program structure diagram or a program design language which is clear, concise and capable of being input directly to Step 3.

Step 3   Solution Implementation

Step 3 involves the transformation of the logical solution specification into a physical implementation. At the system level it involves the transformation of system processes into program load modules and the transformation of their connections into data stores (e.g. files, databases). At the program level it involves the transformation of programs into source language code, a task traditionally left as an artistic exercise for programmers, with some design decisions still to be made. In software engineering, however, there is no place for such artwork, and coding becomes a simple process of applying standard transformation rules to the solution specification. In JSP and JSD Step 3 can be almost completely automated, including such traditional 'design' issues as to whether to implement the solution physically as batch or online.

Step 4   Solution Verification

Step 4 is traditionally carried out by testing, using a strategy based on intuition in which quantity of test data replaces quality. The software engineering approach is more qualitative, building up a test specification from the documentation produced by previous steps, and using concepts such as path testing and sampling theory to build up test cases (see Section 4.5).

Moreover, one of the great merits of the software engineering approach is that less testing is required because fewer bugs get into a system in the first place. It is a sobering thought that bugs get into a system only because analysts and programmers put them there. By concentrating on correct problem definition and solution design JSD and JSP ensure that fewer bugs are generated than during traditional systems development methods, and consequently testing assumes less importance. Some installations using JSP have even suggested that in many cases the testing of JSP programs is no longer cost-effective.

To summarize the relationship of JSP to the software engineering approach, it is to the area of solution design that JSP addresses itself, and more specifically to the level of program rather than systems design. In addition, the rigour of JSP has a great impact on solution implementation, especially in making coding open to automation, and on solution verification, especially in making testing clearer and open to automation. JSP is not the whole answer to the software crisis, but it is an important improvement in the area which it addresses, and the reason for this becomes apparent when one considers the nature of the program development task.

The kinds of program required in the world of DP are of a different order from those produced on a home computer in BASIC by a whizz-kid with an IQ of 200. A whizz-kid may fail to become even a competent DP programmer, because DP programs require more than intellectual virtuosity:

—DP programs must be maintainable. They must be written in a way which enables other programmers to read and understand them easily, otherwise the maintenance iceberg may sink the whole DP department.

—DP programs involve sophisticated processing of varied data sets, and must be written in a programming language suited to such applications, e.g. COBOL.

—DP programs are relatively large, often running to thousands of lines. The larger programs take months to develop, and the programmer must keep to a systematic plan if he is to produce a working program on schedule.

—DP programs do not exist in a stand-alone environment isolated from all other programs. They must be capable of interfacing with others in a suite of programs and of executing alongside others in a multipro-gramming environment.

—DP programs must be reliable. If a micro-based games program contains a bug it is likely to cause nothing more than irritation; if a payroll system, a chemical process control system or a hospital's patient-monitoring system contain a bug results are likely to be more far-reaching.

The fact that a program works is therefore an insufficient criterion of a good DP program. A good DP program will achieve many other objectives besides and will suffer from none of the failings which characterize the software crisis and which have been outlined at the beginning of this chapter. Yet the traditional approach to program development does not aid in the production of good programs. Tradition-ally, programming has been regarded as a form of personal art, requiring a creative ability somewhat akin to that required for the writing of poetic works. In this approach the main criterion of a good program is efficiency, stemming from the early days of computing when it was hardware not software which consumed the greater part of systems development costs. The good programmer was then the 'clever' programmer who could code a routine using less statements than his colleagues.

Such an approach resulted in very clever, complex and obscure programs which no-one but the author could understand or maintain. There was no attempt at any logical construction of the program, which was simply an amorphous mass of code whose logic flow has been likened to a bowl of spaghetti. Because it was complex it was full of errors, and so the programmer rushed through the design process in order to leave time to test the program and correct the errors he had made by rushing through the design process. It is a sad fact that you can still occasionally hear this strategy advocated as desirable, that it is better not to think too much about program design, it is better to begin coding straightaway so that more time can be devoted to testing.

In this traditional approach the only design aid used was the flowchart, but often the flowchart was not used as a design aid at all but merely as a means of documenting 'spaghetti'. The 'clever' programmer wrote the program first and then drew the flowchart. Such an approach to programming soon became outmoded. As software costs became greater than hardware costs, the efficiency criterion on which it was originally based became less important than other objectives such as readability, understandability and reliability. As long ago as the late 1960s this was becoming widely recognized within the DP industry, but in the 1980s something of a backward step was taken as a result of the micro revolution, in which sudden access to computing power by a host of unsophisticated users resulted in a resurgence of 'spaghetti'.

To reduce complexity it is necessary to adopt a clearer and more methodical approach to the construction of a program, and in the 1970s this led to a view of a program as a network of functional subroutines or modules. 'Modular programming' became a vogue in DP in the early 1970s, but in practice the gains were negligible because there was no well-defined basis on which the decomposition of a program into modules could be undertaken. Exactly how is a program to be decomposed? What goes into one module as opposed to another? At what point does decomposition end? How are modules to interface with each other? Without answers to these questions program design could only remain personal, intuitive and artistic, and any reduction in complexity remained a hope rather than an achievable aim.

In an attempt to overcome the problems of modular programming DP turned to a parallel movement which had been growing within European academic establishments since the early 1960s—the structured programming movement. Structured programming was a collective term for a set of ideas about what characterized good programs, although which ideas formed part of the canon and which did not varied from one advocate to another (see, for example, the range of ideas propounded in *Classics in Software Engineering* [23]). At base, however, structured programming included two rules of program design which soon became *de rigueur* in DP circles: restricted control structures and top-down design.

Restricted Control Structures

Control structures describe the relationships among the instructions of a program. A program can be viewed as consisting of two kinds of building block:

1 operations, which describe *what* the program is to do (e.g. instructions to input, output or calculate data),

2 control stuctures, which describe *how* it is to do it (i.e. describe the relationships among the operations).

Structured programming restricts control structures to three: sequence, selection and iteration.

A sequence consists of two or more operations which occur, once each, in order. Sequence is normally specified by the order in which operations are written, e.g.

Input a number.
Add number to total.

A selection consists of two or more operations of which one, and only one, occurs once. One way of specifying a selection is to use an IF... ELSE... control structure, e.g.

IF number <10
    Add 1 to units total
ELSE
    Add 1 to tens total.

An iteration consists of an operation which occurs zero or more times. One way of specifying an iteration is to use a DO... UNTIL... control structure, e.g.

DO Add-number-to-total UNTIL number =99.

It is also possible to nest sequences, selections, and iterations within each other in hierarchical form, e.g. a sequence of sequences. There is also a fourth control structure, the branch or GOTO, which is a common feature of traditional program design but which is avoided by structured programming for a number of reasons.

GOTOs are a primary source of spaghetti-bowl logic, because a GOTO can direct the flow of logic to any other point in the program without restriction and without ever returning. Sequence, selection and iteration, on the other hand, are closed constructs which do not allow transfer of control to another part of the program without returning. When reading a program containing GOTOs it is necessary to follow the logic flow around the program in order to understand it. But if programs are hierarchically structured as nests or blocks of sequences, selections and iterations, the relationship of one part of the program to another is more visible and comprehensible.

For example, the statement 'DO Add-number-to-total UNTIL number=99' iterates the procedure Add-number-to-total a number of times, following which control is returned to the statement following the DO statement. The relationships of the DO statement to the procedure Add-number-to-total is completely comprehensible, and it is not necessary to examine the procedure in order to understand the program structure. If the branch instruction 'GOTO Add-number-to-total' is used to invoke the procedure, however, it is necessary to examine the content of the procedure in order to determine what happens next. Control may return, but it may not.

The iteration construct is a much more powerful, sophisticated and problem-oriented construct that the GOTO. GOTOs have nothing to do with real world problems. It is possible to have a sequence of customers, a selection between employees, an iteration of transactions, but not a GOTO. The GOTO is a primitive machine instruction concerned solely with logic flow and the computer implementation of a problem solution. Control structures should be used which allow us to describe the solution not the computer implementation.

It has been demonstrated mathematically [5, reprinted in 23] that any program can be written without a GOTO, and therefore there is no need for the GOTO to form part of any modern high-level problem-oriented language. In short, the GOTO is best avoided, and this conclusion is borne out by a number of psychological experiments which have shown that programs which do not use GOTOs are indeed easier to understand and amend [20]. JSP does not use GOTOs.

Top-down Design

Top-down design (also known as stepwise refinement, functional decomposition and hierarchical decomposition) is a method of modularisation which begins with a general statement of a program's function (e.g. OUTPUT FILE TOTALS) and successively refines that statement into increasingly greater levels of detail until source language statements are

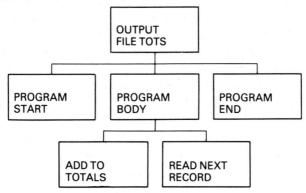

Figure 1.2

reached. For example, OUTPUT FILE TOTALS may be refined into the three modules PROGRAM START (Open file, Read first record), PROGRAM BODY and PROGRAM END (Output totals, Close file); PROGRAM BODY may be further refined into the modules ADD TO TOTALS and READ NEXT RECORD. What results is a hierarchical modular structure which resembles an inverted tree, with the root at the top (see Fig. 1.2).

In this diagram each box represents a module and lines connecting boxes represent module links (e.g. a COBOL PERFORM or a BASIC GOSUB statement). The diagram is incomplete (see Figs 1.7 and 1.8 for a complete version of the program) but serves to illustrate the fundamental flaw in the top-down design strategy. Top-down design may be an excellent design principle for a known solution, but program design is all about solution design, i.e. *finding* a solution.

An analogy of the program design task which is commonly used to demonstrate the top-down design strategy is the task of designing a stool. The designer of a stool subdivides the task into two—the design of the seat and the design of the legs; then he joins the seat and legs together. The joining can even be automated.

The flaw in the analogy is that the stool designer must have foreknowledge that a stool consists of a seat and legs in order that he can subdivide the task in the first place. Such knowledge may be available to him because a stool is a known quantity, but the designer of a computer program has no such foreknowledge of the composition of his program. Program design is all about *finding* the best way to compose a program from its constituent parts (i.e. its instructions).

Top-down design requires the designer to subdivide one abstract unknown quantity (e.g. OUTPUT FILE TOTALS in Fig. 1.2) into increasingly detailed and known quantities, but if the original quantity is an unknown, on what basis is that subdivision to take place? The answer is intuition, experience and trial and error. The designer is forced to make important design choices (the most important ones first) among a number of possible functional designs, without any effective criteria for making those choices, in the hope that his decisions will not be invalidated by lower-level refinements of the design. This is a difficult task for experienced programmers, an almost impossible one for students and trainee programmers and one which varies from person to person.

Top-down design is as individual and variable as any modular design and therefore does not improve upon the situation. Moreover, when coupled with the concept of restricted control structures and the need to avoid GOTOs, the arbitrary set of modules produced by top-down design spawns interfaces, a rash of programmer-invented switches and deeply nested conditional statements which are difficult to follow.

In essence the advocacy of top-down design as a method of program design arises out of a confusion between results and the process by which these results are obtained; a good descriptive method does not necessarily make a good prescriptive method. An example of the inadequacy of top-down design is given later in this chapter (see Figs 1.7 and 1.8).

Despite the problems of top-down design DP was quick to adopt it alongside the principle of restricted control structures in an attempt to bolster modular programming. The turning point came around the end of 1973 when the DP journal *Datamation* devoted a whole issue to structured programming, including an article entitled 'Revolution in Programming' [17, reprinted in 23]. Soon every programmer had to pay at least lip service to structured programming, but because of the innate difficulties with top-down design the way out of the growing software crisis remained elusive.

In the past few years an attempt has been made to impose some rigour on the top-down design process by defining the desirable characteristics of a module and automating modularization. Yourdon and Constantine's Structured Design method [22], for example, suggests that a module should undertake only one function and have as few links with other modules as possible, and Hamilton and Zeldin's Higher Order Software [15] automates module linkages. Such refinements may help to improve the situation, but they do not and cannot overcome the fundamental flaw in the process of top-down design.

Top-down design simply cannot help the programmer decide how to break up a program into a correct set of modules, correct in the sense that the program then achieves all the objectives of DP program design. Automating the implementation of the wrong set of modules is not a recipe which will help resolve the software crisis. It was this that was recognised by Michael Jackson and which prompted him to develop a radically different approach to program design: Jackson Structured Programming.

1.2 OVERVIEW OF JSP

JSP does not begin with an abstract function which is refined into more detailed functions. JSP begins with the real world of the problem environment. The real world contains real entities such as customers and accounts which are to be modelled on the computer. The intial premise of JSP is that the relationships among real world entities should be reflected in the computer model of the real world. In other words the sequences, selections and iterations of the real world should be reflected in the data structure of whichever data set is to be used to describe them in the computer model.

A program structure is formed by combining the data structures for all data sets processed by the program. It then becomes a simple matter to allocate functional operations to their logical and correct place in the program structure. In contrast to the top-down design approach, which can be categorized as a functional method, JSP is a data-driven method of program design. It begins with data analysis and modelling and forms a skeletal program structure on which the flesh of functional operations can then be hung. Rather than following a process of decomposition, it advocates a process of composition, in which a program structure is composed from data structures.

The standard JSP procedure consists of 3 steps:

Step 1   Define the structure of the data to be processed by the program, by drawing a data structure diagram for each data set.

Step 2   Form a program structure diagram from the data structure diagram(s).

Step 3   List and allocate operations and conditions, i.e.

        Step 3.1   List the functional components (operations) of the program and allocate them to the program structure diagram.

        Step 3.2   List the conditions which determine each selection and the end of each iteration and allocate them to the program structure diagram.

This procedure (with extensions) is suitable for all DP programs from simple batch print programs to complex multi-user real-time systems. Here is a preliminary example of the design of a simple sequential file processing program. It is presented merely for purposes of illustration, and you should not expect to be able to follow it completely at this stage.

Example 1.2.1

A bank maintains a file of the transactions of its customers. A customer may have a number of accounts. An account consists of an account header record containing account information, followed by a number of transaction records, where a transaction is either a deposit or a withdrawal. At the end of the file there is a file trailer. A program is required to output the total value of deposits and withdrawals on file.

Step 1 Draw a data structure diagram of the transactions file (see Fig. 1.3).

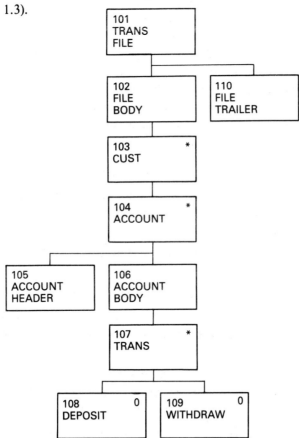

Figure 1.3

Note: a line linking an upper to a lower box denotes 'consists of'; left-to-right ordering of boxes indicates sequence; a circle denotes selection; an asterisk denotes iteration.

Step 2   Form a program structure diagram (see Fig. 1.4).

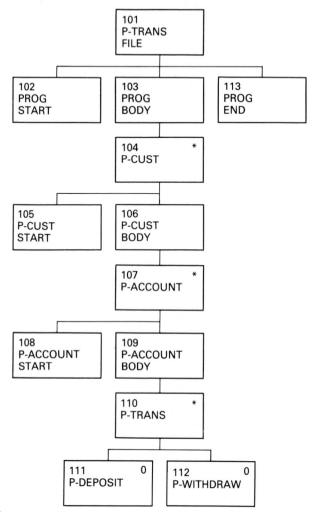

Figure 1.4
Note: P is an abbreviation of PROCESS.

Step 3.1   List and allocate operations (see Fig. 1.5).

    1   Open transactions file.
    2   Close transactions file.
    3   Read record from transactions file.
    4   Add transaction amount to deposit total.

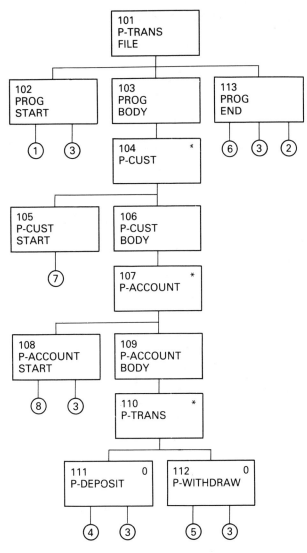

Figure 1.5

5 Add transaction amount to withdrawal total.
6 Output deposit total and withdrawal total.
7 Move customer number to current customer number.
8 Move account number to current account number.

Step 3.2   List and allocate conditions (see Fig. 1.6).

C1   File trailer.
C2   Customer number not=current customer number.
C3   Account number not=current account number.
C4   Deposit.

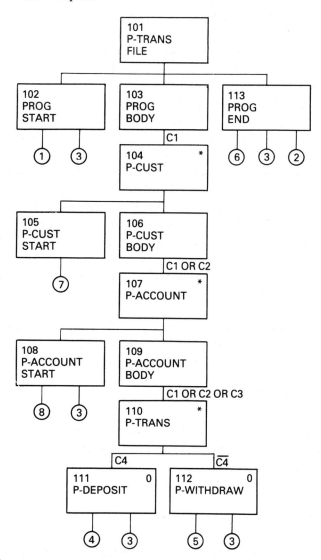

Figure 1.6

The three steps of the JSP procedure are explained in detail in the ensuing chapters of this book. Chapter 2 will show you how to draw data structure diagrams. Chapter 3 will show you how to construct program structure diagrams and list and allocate operations and conditions to them. Chapter 4 discusses the transformation of a designed program into source language code. Chapters 5 to 9 extend the design procedure to more complex programs. Chapter 10 introduces JSD.

Jackson Structured Programming is named after its originator, Michael A. Jackson, who studied classics at Oxford and mathematics at Cambridge before moving on to the computing industry and eventually into consultancy. During the late 1960s he began to formalize his ideas on program design and in 1971 he formed his own software company, Michael Jackson Systems Ltd (MJSL), to teach and support JSP. In 1975 his first book, *Principles of Program Design* [12], was published. He is now an independent consultant to Learmonth and Burchett Management Systems Ltd (LBMS), who in 1990 took over MJSL and now support JSP.

JSP is now the most commonly used formal method of program design in the UK and Europe; it has been taught to over 20 000 programmers world-wide and it is the UK government mandatory standard for all new projects [21].

James Martin, author of the Pulitzer Prize nomination, *The Wired Society*, has this to say about JSP:

In installations where it is used well, the Jackson methodology appears to give a better improvement than other forms of structured programming which are in common use. [14]

An IBM technical report concludes:

The techniques of Michael Jackson offer a constructive, teachable and repeatable method for the design of correct programs . . . Correctness is assured by the technique (JSP) itself, not by inspiration, insight or testing. [10]

An Infotech report refers to JSP as:

. . . a significant advance in the development of software engineering. [11]

Pressman's wide-ranging critical comparison of program design methods concludes:

> ...the Jackson methodology must be the recommended design technique. [19]

JSP has achieved this impressive set of credentials for some very good reasons:

Some advantages of using JSP

—JSP works. Do not underestimate the importance of this—traditional methods and top-down methods do not work or do not work very well.

—JSP is a prescriptive design method which can be taught and can be learned. It enables a trainee programmer to learn how to design programs without resort to trial and error or the 'sit by Fred' approach, in which he is asked to sit next to an experienced programmer until by some magical process he assimilates the latter's knowledge. Using JSP, different programmers will produce similar programs, which makes it easier for one programmer to understand and maintain another's.

—JSP improves reliability. Its insistence on the explicit diagramming of data relationships reveals omissions and resolves ambiguities in program specifications, and its step-by-step procedure provides a methodical route from specification to code. Because fewer bugs are put into the program many JSP users find that testing time is considerably reduced. Reported figures vary from around a 25% reduction in program testing time to almost 100%, where testing is judged to be no longer cost-effective in detecting errors.

—JSP reduces program development time because analysis, design and specification errors can be identified at an early design stage rather than during testing (if at all). Figures of 10 to 15% reduction in development time are common, although increases in the productivity of poor programmers of 100% have been reported.

—JSP improves technical communication and documentation. Structure diagrams are a useful communication aid between analysts, program- mers and other members of a systems development team, and they provide language-independent documentation as a by-product of the design process rather than as an extra add-on task.

—JSP aids project management by providing an early and reliable indication of the size and complexity of a program, and the distinct steps of the design procedure provide useful checkpoints by which progress can be assessed.

—JSP is capable of being automated to a large extent. Software packages exist which enable the interactive generation of structure diagrams on a VDU and the generation of code from diagrams (see Chapter 4).

—JSP increases confidence in the correctness of a program among both users and programmers, and increases a programmer's job satisfaction by improving his productivity and his image as a skilled professional.

—JSP facilitates maintenance and increases the life-span of a program because changes and enhancements are more easily incorporated. JSP programs are less likely to require structural change in order to incorporate changes in function—it is usually easy to identify those parts of a program requiring change, and to make changes without adversely affecting other parts of the program. Using JSP, reductions in resources required for maintenance of 50% plus have been reported.

It is perhaps worth considering this last point in greater detail, as an illustration of how JSP's data-driven approach to program design improves upon functional top-down design. Data structure is more stable than function. During its lifetime a program may undergo many functional changes and enhancements, but the structure of the data it processes (and hence its JSP program structure) remains relatively stable.

The program structure derived using JSP can be likened to a map on which many functional journeys can be made; the journeys may change without altering the nature and usefulness of the map. Changes made to a program structure derived from using functional decomposition, however, typically cause enormous maintenance problems. As an example, here is one of many top-down functional solutions to Example 1.2.1. The program is decomposed into the functional modules PROG-START (Open transactions file, Read first record), PROG-BODY and PROG-END (Output

Open transactions file
Read record from transactions file
Do while not file trailer
    If not account header
        Then if deposit
            Add transaction amount to deposit total
        Else
            Add transaction amount to withdrawal total
        Endif
    Endif
    Read record from transactions file
Enddo
Output deposit total and withdrawal total
Close transactions file
Figure 1.7

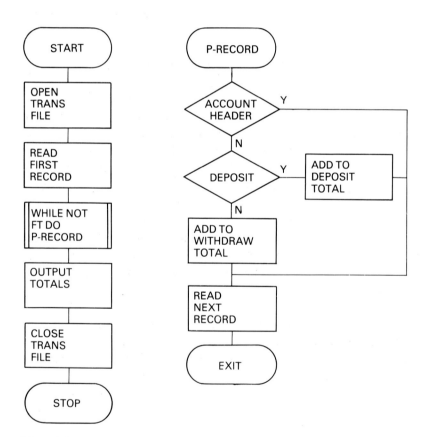

Figure 1.8

totals, Close transactions file). PROG-BODY is further decomposed into an iteration of ADD-TO-TOTALS and READ-NEXT-RECORD. The solution can be shown in the form of a tree diagram (see Fig. 1.2) or in more detail in the form of pseudocode (see Fig. 1.7) or a flowchart (see Fig. 1.8).

This program produces correct output in the same way as the JSP solution. It can even be proved mathematically correct, using formal proving techniques. Yet it is a totally inadequate DP program, and this can easily be seen if the following functional enhancements are considered:

1 Output the customer numbers of those customers who hold more than one account.

2 Output the account numbers of those accounts which have no transactions.

3 Output the average withdrawal amount for each account.

Incorporating these changes is not easy, even for such a trivial program. Typically they would be incorporated by the setting and unsetting of switches to indicate new customers and new accounts. Consider how you would code the program and how you would incorporate these changes. The basic flaw in the above program is that it is designed to handle a single function, and new functions cannot be incorporated into it easily (see also the discussion following Example 3.4.2).

The JSP solution, on the other hand, is based on the structure of the data and it already contains components for customer and account. Any of the above enhancements can be handled easily because no change to the program structure is required, all that needs to be done is to extend the operations list.

The merits of JSP are many and varied, but it is worth repeating that it is not a panacea for the software crisis, it is only one of a number of modern software tools and techniques. It also has limitations in the area of mathematical program design, as do all program methods, where the major design problem is algorithm construction. More importantly, a few DP professionals have resisted JSP and failed to realize its benefits, and it is instructive to understand why.

Do not expect JSP to provide instant miracles. If you are an inexperienced programmer used to rattling off quick programs in BASIC, the JSP design method may seem unwieldy and top heavy at first, but during this initial learning phase remember that the design procedure will remain valid and useful for programs whose size and complexity would outstrip your current design capabilities. You should even expect to take a step backward at first, because it is always more difficult to use a new method than one with which you are already familiar, even though that new method will eventually prove more productive. The message is simple: stick with it.

If you are an experienced programmer, used to modular programming, top-down design, or no design strategy at all, you should rightly maintain an initial scepticism towards a method which is so different and which claims so much. But do not let this cloud your judgment. Do not be tempted into trying out JSP on the hardest problem you know, just to see how it fares: it will fare miserably simply because you do not yet have enough experience in its use.

Scepticism is healthy, resistance to change is not. Resistance to change lies at the heart of the software crisis. The belief that programming is basically an art form requiring skills which are creative, intuitive, unteachable and incapable of being formalized into a method belongs in the museum alongside the flat earth theory. Programming can no longer afford to be an art form. A useful analogy can be made between software production today and book production in the fifteenth century, when there was a great leap forward from the hand written and unpredictable to the printed and predictable. A similar leap forward into standardisation and automation is now occurring in the field of software production. The future of computing lies with those who are prepared to accept this challenge.

Chapter 2

Drawing Data Structures

Step 1 of the JSP design procedure involves defining the structure of the data to be processed by a program in the form of data structure diagrams. A data structure diagram consists of four types of data component (elementary, sequence, selection and iteration) linked hierarchically in graphical form. This chapter introduces data structure diagrams and shows how to use them to describe the structure of data sets.

2.1 DATA COMPONENTS

Section 1.1 introduced the idea that a program is composed of two kinds of building block: operations, which form the functions of the program (the 'what' of the program), and control structures, which express the relationships among the operations (the 'how' of the program). In JSP a program structure is built from the control structures *sequence, selection* and *iteration,* and operations are 'hung' onto this structure.

The control structures of the program are based on the control structures of the data sets which the program processes; hence the sequences, selections and iterations of the program mirror the sequences, selections and iterations of the data. It follows that as there can be no GOTO in the description of a data set, in JSP there can be no GOTO in a program which processes that data set. A data set is any set of data which is input to or output from a program, e.g. a sequential input file, a direct access file, a stream of transactions from a terminal, a group of records on a database, a stream of interrupts from an operating system.

The first step of the JSP design procedure is to define a data set in terms of its control structures, and to represent that definition diagrammatically in the form of a data structure diagram. The data structure diagram will then form the basis of the program structure. In this chapter you will learn how to draw data structure diagrams such as that for the bank transactions file introduced in Example 1.2.1 in the preceding chapter (see Fig. 1.3). The diagram consists of rectangular boxes connected by lines. Each box represents a named data component. A data component may be a file (e.g. TRANS-FILE, which is a file of bank

25

transactions), a group of records (e.g. CUST, which consists of all the bank transactions for a single customer) or a record (e.g. ACCOUNT-HEADER record, DEPOSIT record). In some programs, discussed later, it may also be necessary to go below record level and define fields as data components.

The connecting lines between boxes represents the relationships among the data components, where a relationship is either a sequence, selection or iteration. A line can be read as meaning 'consists of'.

In Fig. 1.3 ACCOUNT has a sequence relationship with ACCOUNT-HEADER and ACCOUNT-BODY: i.e. ACCOUNT consists of an ACCOUNT-HEADER followed by an ACCOUNT-BODY. The order of ACCOUNT-HEADER and ACCOUNT-BODY is indicated by their left-to-right ordering beneath ACCOUNT.

TRANS has a selection relationship with DEPOSIT and WITHDRAW: i.e. TRANS consists of either a DEPOSIT or a WITHDRAW. The selection between DEPOSIT and WITHDRAW is indicated by the presence of a circle in the top right-hand corner of their boxes.

CUST has an iteration relationship with ACCOUNT: i.e. for each CUST there may be a number of ACCOUNTs. The iteration of ACCOUNT is indicated by the presence of an asterisk in the top right-hand corner of its box.

The whole diagram reads as follows. TRANS-FILE consists of a FILE-BODY followed by a FILE-TRAILER. FILE-BODY consists of a number of CUSTs. A CUST consists of a number of ACCOUNTs. An ACCOUNT consists of an ACCOUNT-HEADER followed by an ACCOUNT-BODY. An ACCOUNT-BODY consists of a number of TRANS, and each TRANS is either a DEPOSIT or a WITHDRAW.

The data components ACCOUNT-HEADER, DEPOSIT, WITHDRAW and FILE-TRAILER are neither sequence, selection nor iteration. They consist of nothing but themselves and are called elementary components.

The data structure diagram looks like an inverted tree. The top component is known as the root. The elementary components are known as leaves. A component and all the components of which it consists is known as a branch; e.g. the ACCOUNT-BODY branch consists of the components ACCOUNT-BODY, TRANS, DEPOSIT, WITHDRAW. All the components between the root and a leaf are known as a leg; e.g. the ACCOUNT-HEADER leg consists of the components TRANS-FILE, FILE-BODY, CUST, ACCOUNT, ACCOUNT-HEADER.

The terms tree, root, leaf, branch and leg will be used throughout this book, together with three other terms borrowed from family tree diagrams: parent, child and sibling. Parent and child describe the relationship between two connected components: the parent is the component at the upper end of the line, the child is the component at the lower end; e.g. FILE-BODY is the parent of CUST, CUST is the child of FILE-BODY and the parent of ACCOUNT (ACCOUNT is sometimes called the grandchild of FILE-BODY). ACCOUNT has two children—ACCOUNT-HEADER and ACCOUNT-BODY, which are called siblings.

Although a data structure diagram resembles an inverted tree, it is not arrived at through a process of top-down design, rather it emerges from a process of composition based on an analysis of the data set which it describes (see Section 2.6). Do no confuse the top-down description of a data set with the constructive process by which that description is obtained.

In this chapter you will learn how to draw a data structure diagram in order to describe data as a hierarchical structure of sequences, selections, iterations and elementary data components. Sections 2.2 to 2.5 will take each of these four component types in turn and show how to represent them on a data structure diagram. By the time you have completed the exercises at the end of the chapter, the data structure diagram will have become a simple yet powerful aid in helping you to describe the structure of data.

Note that in the following examples names of data components in data specifications are highlighted in capital letters for ease of data analysis.

2.2 ELEMENTARY COMPONENTS

An elementary component is one which has no lower-level consituent components and is represented in a data structure diagram simply by placing its name inside a rectangle, e.g. the components DEPOSIT and WITHDRAW in Fig. 1.3 (see Figs 2.1 and 2.2).

Figure 2.1   **Figure 2.2**

2.3 SEQUENCE COMPONENTS

A sequence component consists of two or more sub-components which occur, once each, in order. Here are four examples showing how sequence components are represented in a data structure diagram.

Example 2.3.1

In Fig. 2.3 the sequence component A consists of the elementary component B followed by the elementary component C. The lines connecting A to B and C are not equivalent to and should not be confused with the flow lines on a flowchart. In a data structure diagram a line connecting two components means that the component at the lower end of the line is a part of the component at the upper end. In this case, A consists of B and C, in that order; i.e. A is a sequence of B followed by C. The order of the components B and C within the sequence is indicated by their order of occurrence from left to right in the data structure diagram.

In Fig. 2.4 X is a sequence of C followed by B. The elementary components B and C in Figs. 2.3 and 2.4 are the same, but the sequence components A and X are entirely different. A is a sequence of B followed by C, X is a sequence of C followed by B.

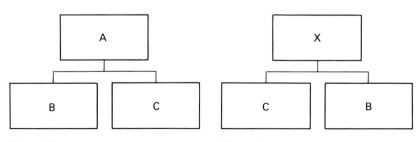

Figure 2.3   **Figure 2.4**

Example 2.3.2

A TRAIN consists of an ENGINE followed by a GUARDS-VAN (see Fig. 2.5).

The fact that ENGINE appears to the left of GUARDS-VAN in the diagram means that it comes in front of the GUARDS-VAN in the TRAIN. Fig. 2.6 would be an incorrect representation of this.

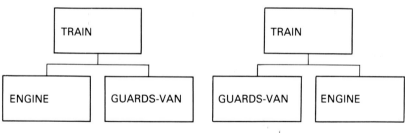

Figure 2.5   **Figure 2.6**

Example 2.3.3

A Customer File (CUST-FILE) consists of a FILE-HEADER, a single customer record (CUST-REC) and a FILE-TRAILER (see Fig. 2.7).

Again note that the three elementary components of the sequence component CUST-FILE must appear in the order shown. This order will have been determined during the design of the file, and any program written to process CUST-FILE will expect input in this order, i.e. the structure of the program will reflect the structure of the data.

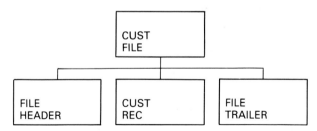

Figure 2.7

Example 2.3.4

SHIP-FILE consists of details about a ship, followed by a FILE-TRAILER. The ship details are held in the form of a SHIP-NAME record and a VOYAGE record (see Fig. 2.8).

This diagram introduces a *nested* sequence, and shows how components can begin to build into a hierarchical structure. SHIP-FILE is a sequence of SHIP-DETAILS followed by a FILE-TRAILER, and SHIP-DETAILS is itself a sequence of SHIP-NAME-REC and VOYAGE-REC. Note how the words 'and'

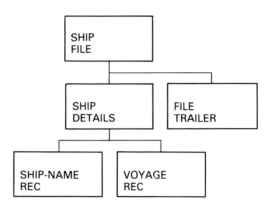

Figure 2.8

and 'followed by' in the data specification imply sequencing. A checklist of words commonly used to indicate sequencing is given in Section 2.6.

You should now attempt the sequence exercises at the end of this chapter before going on to the next section.

DO EXERCISES 1 TO 3 IN SECTION 2.7

2.4 SELECTION COMPONENTS

A selection component consists of two or more sub-components of which one, and only one, occurs once. Here are five examples showing how selection components are represented in a data structure diagram.

Example 2.4.1

In Fig. 2.9 the selection component A consists of either the elementary component B or the elementary component C, but not both. The fact that A is a selection rather than a sequence component is indicated diagrammatically by the presence of a circle in the top right-hand corner of each of its child components. As in the representation of a sequence, the lines connecting A to B and A to C mean that the component at the lower end of the line is a part of the component at the upper end. In a selection, however, only one of the components is present at any one time; i.e. B and C are mutually exclusive. It follows that Fig. 2.10 is equivalent to Fig. 2.9.

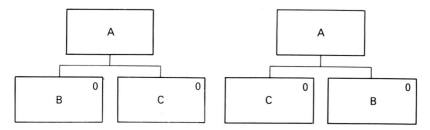

Figure 2.9   **Figure 2.10**

The left-to-right ordering of *B* and *C* has meaning in a sequence but not in a selection, because *B* and *C* cannot both be present at the same time. If it were required to show that either or both may be present, the data structure diagram in Fig. 2.11 would be required. All three elementary components in Fig. 2.11 are mutually exclusive: *A* consists of a *B* on its own, a *C* on its own, or a *B* and a *C* together.

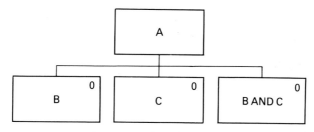

Figure 2.11

Example 2.4.2

A PERSON is either MALE or FEMALE (see Figs 2.12 and 2.13).

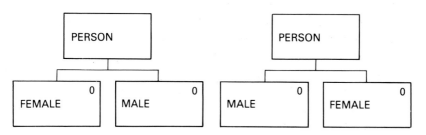

Figure 2.12   **Figure 2.13**
The two data structure diagrams are structurally equivalent.

Example 2.4.3

An online bank transaction (TRANS) is either a DEPOSIT, a WITHDRAW or a REQUEST. If it is a REQUEST, it is either a STATEMENT request or a CHEQUE BOOK request (see Fig. 2.14).

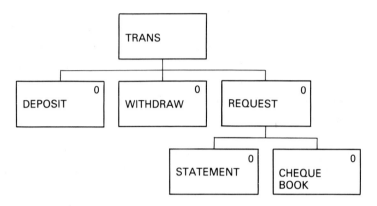

Figure 2.14

This is an example of a nested selection. TRANS is a selection between the elementary component DEPOSIT, the elementary component WITHDRAW and the selection component REQUEST, which in turn is a selection between the two elementary components STATEMENT and CHEQUE BOOK.

Example 2.4.4

This example contains both sequence and selection components, and requires a refinement to the drawing procedure.

A customer file (CUST-FILE) consists of a FILE-HEADER, followed by either a customer payment record (PAYMENT) or a customer receipt record (RECEIPT), followed by a FILE-TRAILER.

A first attempt at drawing the data structure diagram of CUST-FILE might produce the diagram in Fig. 2.15.

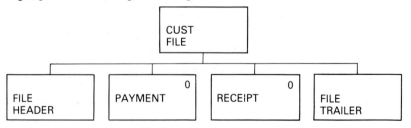

Figure 2.15

This appears to represent all the data components and the relationships between them, but it is incorrect. There is no doubt from the data specification that CUST-FILE is a sequence of three components, and this is not altered by the fact that one of these components is either a PAYMENT or a RECEIPT.

However, as shown on the data structure diagram, CUST-FILE is not a sequence, it is a mixed-type component—part sequence and part selection (two of its elementary components are annotated with circles, two are not). No such component exists in structured programming or in JSP. What is missing from the diagram is the selection component to which the elementary components PAYMENT and RECEIPT belong; let's call it CUST-REC.

Fig. 2.16 shows the correct data structure diagram of CUST-FILE. CUST-FILE is a sequence of a FILE-HEADER, a CUST-REC and a FILE-TRAILER, and CUST-REC is either a PAYMENT record or a RECEIPT record.

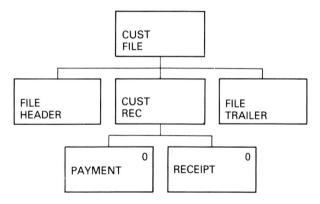

Figure 2.16

If you find that you have drawn components belonging to a selection (PAYMENT, RECEIPT) as siblings of components belonging to a sequence (FILE-HEADER, FILE-TRAILER), you must drop the components belonging to the selection down to a lower level and introduce in their place the missing selection component (CUST-REC). If you do not introduce this missing component then the diagram is no longer restricted to the control structures of structured programming and problems may occur in the future, e.g. the problem of amending a missing component and the problem of checking a diagram with mixed-type components such as CUST-FILE for correctness and consistency.

The problem stems from an inadequate data specification which does not describe all the components of CUST-FILE. This is common in English narrative descriptions, which are difficult to make thorough, concise and unambiguous. The author of the specification may well say that the existence of CUST-REC is implicit in the description of CUST-FILE, but this is exactly what is wrong with it. It is only by making all data components and their relationships explicit that obscure and difficult-to-maintain programs can be avoided. The explicit data structure diagrams of JSP are an extremely useful tool in overcoming the inadequacies of English language narrative specification.

Fig. 2.16 can be considered a refinement of Fig. 2.7 (assuming that both describe the same file). Whether such a refinement is necessary for program design depends upon whether the program which is to process CUST-FILE needs to distinguish between a customer record which is a payment and a customer record which is a receipt. Such data analysis considerations are discussed in relation to program design in Section 2.6.

Example 2.4.5

A stock file (STOCK-FILE) contains a single stock record (STOCK-REC). In addition there is a FILE-HEADER at the start of the file and possibly a FILE-TRAILER at the end (see Fig. 2.17).

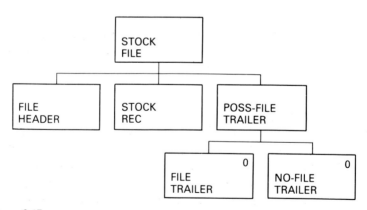

Figure 2.17

Note how the word 'possibly' in the data specification implies a selection component (moreover one that is not named) and how the selection

component POSS-FILE-TRAILER must be added to the diagram to prevent
STOCK-FILE becoming part sequence and part selection. The label POSS
(an abbreviation of POSSIBLE) is commonly used to name such a
selection.

Another way of labelling the two elementary components of POSS-
FILE-TRAILER would be to label one of them FILE-TRAILER-PRESENT and
the other FILE-TRAILER-ABSENT. When it comes to the naming of
components no steadfast rules can be set down: the aims are readability
and intelligibility, the means are meaningfulness and conciseness.

Note that the component NO-FILE-TRAILER is a null component, and
in such cases, when the selection is between the presence or absence of a
data component, the null component may be omitted from the diagram
(as in Fig. 2.23).

English narrative specifications do not always highlight selections
explicitly, as in this example, and the JSP designer must be constantly on
the lookout for implicit clues to data structure. A checklist of words
commonly used to indicate selection is given in Section 2.6.

You should now attempt the selection exercises at the end of this chapter
before going on to the next section.

DO EXERCISES 4 TO 8 IN SECTION 2.7

2.5 ITERATION COMPONENTS

An iteration component consists of a sub-component which occurs zero
or more times. Here are six examples showing how iteration components
are represented in a data structure diagram.

Example 2.5.1

In Fig. 2.18 A is an iteration of B; A is the iteration component, B is an
elementary component which is being iterated. The data structure
diagram does not indicate how many times B is being iterated, it merely
describes the components A and B and their structural relationship. As in
the representations of a sequence and a selection, the line connecting A to
B means that the component at the lower end of the line is a part of the
component at the upper end. The fact that A is an iteration component is
indicated diagrammatically by the presence of an asterisk in the top right-
hand corner of its child component.

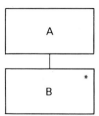

Figure 2.18

Example 2.5.2

A TABLE contains a number of ELEMENTS (see Fig. 2.19).

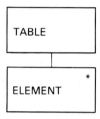

Figure 2.19

This diagram says nothing about how many ELEMENTs are in the TABLE. There may be none—remember that an iterated component occurs zero or more times. The diagram merely describes the components and their structural relationship.

Note that the label of the iterated component is specified in the singular: ELEMENT, not ELEMENTS; it is a single ELEMENT that is iterated.

Example 2.5.3

This example contains both sequence and iteration components, and requires the same refinement to the drawing procedure that was introduced in Example 2.4.4.

A PAGE consists of a HEADING followed by a number of LINEs.

A first attempt at drawing the data structure diagram of PAGE might produce the diagram in Fig. 2.20.

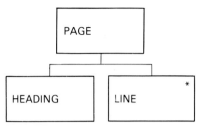

Figure 2.20

This appears to represent all the data components and the relationships between them, but it is incorrect. There is no doubt from the data specification that PAGE is a sequence of two components, and this is not altered by the fact that the second component is iterated.

However, as shown on the data structure diagram, PAGE is not a sequence, it is a mixed-type component—part sequence and part iteration (one of its elementary components is annotated with an asterisk, one is not). No such component exists in structured programming or in JSP. What is missing from the diagram is the iteration component to which the iterated component LINE belongs; let's call it REST-OF-PAGE.

Fig. 2.21 shows the correct data structure diagram of PAGE. PAGE is a sequence of HEADING followed by REST-OF-PAGE, and REST-OF-PAGE is an iteration of LINE.

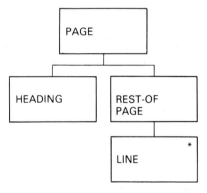

Figure 2.21

If you find that you have drawn a component belonging to an iteration (LINE) as a sibling of a component belonging to a sequence (HEADING), you must drop the iterated component down to a lower level and introduce in its place the missing iteration component, in a manner similar to the introduction of the missing selection component in Example 2.4.4.

Example 2.5.4

An employee file contains employee records in department number/employee number sequence (i.e. employee number within department number) (see Fig. 2.22).

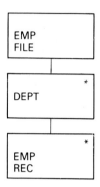

Figure 2.22

Note the introduction of the component DEPT. EMP-FILE is an iteration of DEPT, which is an iteration of EMP-REC. EMP-REC is therefore a nested iteration. The division of the employee file into departments, and departments into employees, is only implied in the data specification by the sequencing of employee records, but it must be shown explicitly on the data structure diagram. A checklist of common English narrative ways of indicating iteration is given in Section 2.6.

Example 2.5.5

A REPORT is divided into PAGEs, each of which consists of a possible HEADING followed by a number of LINEs (see Fig. 2.23).

This diagram contains a selected component (HEADING) and an iterated component (LINE) at the same diagrammatic level, but this is valid because they belong to different parent components. There are no mixed-type components in this program: REPORT is an iteration, PAGE is a sequence, POSS-HEADING is a selection, REST-OF-PAGE is an iteration, HEADING and LINE are elementary components.

Compare this correct diagram with the incorrect diagrams in Examples 2.4.4 and 2.5.3 and note the difference. Note also the omission of the null component NO-HEADING beneath the selection component POSS-HEADING, as suggested in Example 2.4.5.

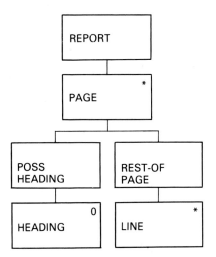

Figure 2.23

Example 2.5.6

SHIP-FILE consists of details about ships, followed by a FILE-TRAILER.
Each ship's details consist of a SHIP-NAME record and perhaps some

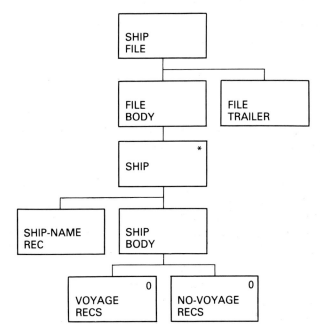

Figure 2.24

VOYAGE records. A first attempt at drawing the data structure diagram of SHIP-FILE might produce the diagram in Fig. 2.24.

Note the introduction of the components FILE-BODY and SHIP-BODY in order to avoid mixed-type components: FILE-BODY prevents SHIP-FILE from becoming the parent of both SHIP (iterated) and FILE-TRAILER (sequenced), and SHIP-BODY prevents SHIP from becoming the parent of both SHIP-NAME-REC (sequenced) and the selected components VOYAGE-RECS and NO-VOYAGE-RECS. The term BODY implies that a component with this name is the main child of its parent and is common usage.

But the diagram is still not correct. VOYAGE records are shown as an elementary component, whereas a VOYAGE record (singular) is in fact an iterated component. Morever, if a VOYAGE record is shown as an iterated component, then there is no need for the selection between VOYAGE-RECS and NO-VOYAGE-RECS, because an iteration includes the possibility of a null occurrence (remember that an iterated component occurs zero or more times). Fig. 2.25 shows the correct data structure diagram of SHIP-FILE.

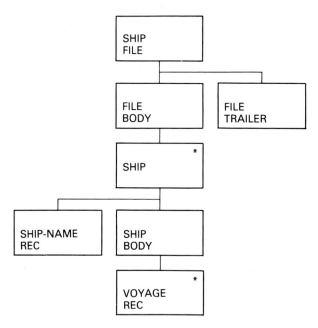

Figure 2.25

To reiterate: the component VOYAGE-REC, which appears to be a selected component in the data specification, is in fact an iterated component which occurs zero or more times. The word 'perhaps' in the data specification seems to indicate a selection, but it is misleading because the word 'some' indicates an iteration.

Section 2.6 expands upon this area of data analysis. After reading it you should be in a position to understand Fig. 1.3, introduced as a preliminary example of a data structure diagram in Section 1.2, and to tackle the iteration exercises at the end of this chapter.

2.6 DATA ANALYSIS

Step 1 of the JSP design procedure is a form of data analysis: an English narrative data specification is analysed in order to determine its underlying data structure. In installations which use JSP, program specifications normally include data specifications in the form of data structure diagrams, otherwise the programmer will have to work from narrative descriptions or even verbal descriptions, and data analysis in such cases requires practice to achieve competence.

If you experience problems with data analysis the pointers in this section may be of help. It is normally possibly to extract the structure of a data set from a narrative specification by examining the text for structural clues. These clues consist of certain words which are commonly used to describe sequence, selection and iteration. For example, in the data specification 'a table contains a number of elements', the word 'number' implies an iteration.

Here are checklists of words commonly implying sequence, selection and iteration:

Checklist of words implying sequence

and, start, beginning, end, after, before, next, then, first, last, following, preceding, header, trailer.

Checklist of words implying selection

either, or, sometimes, possible, perhaps, there may be, alternately, optional.

Checklist of words implying iteration

many, a number, some, a group, more, several.

These checklists are not exhaustive and must be applied with care; e.g. the presence of the phase 'perhaps some VOYAGE-records' in Example 2.5.6 implies an iteration despite the word 'perhaps'. The checklists do give some indication, however, of the alertness which must be shown by the program designer when analysing a data specification.

   If the structure of a data set still remains elusive after textual analysis, it may be useful to draw a sequential picture of it. In order to draw a data structure diagram you must have a clear picture in your head of what the real data looks like, and it may be helpful to write down a sample set of data. For example, Fig. 2.26 shows a sample Report which fits the data specification of Example 2.5.5, and Fig. 2.27 shows a sample Ship File which fits the data specification of Example 2.5.6.

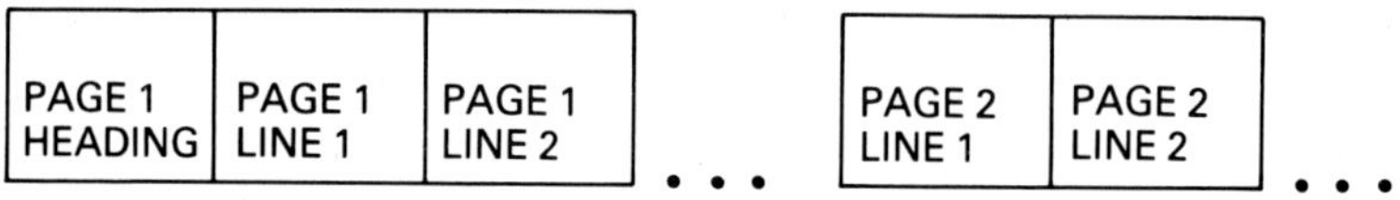

PAGE 1 HEADING	PAGE 1 LINE 1	PAGE 1 LINE 2		PAGE 2 LINE 1	PAGE 2 LINE 2	

. . .   . . .

Figure 2.26

SHIP 1 NAME REC	SHIP 1 VOYAGE REC	SHIP 2 VOYAGE REC	SHIP 2 NAME REC	SHIP 3 NAME REC	SHIP 3 VOYAGE REC	FILE TRAILER

Figure 2.27

Such sequential pictures can give a clearer idea of structure than a narrative description and can also be verified with the author of the data specification to ensure correctness before proceeding with JSP design.

   Sometimes the data specification contains omissions or ambiguities such that it is impossible to derive a data structure diagram or a sample data set from it, and it is necessary to demand clarification from the author. This should not be considered as a failing on the part of the JSP designer. In the past programs have been developed without a rigorous design procedure and ambiguities and misunderstandings have not been resolved until during or after testing. JSP enforces the resolution of design problems at an early stage of the development process and this is one of its merits.

As a final point it should be noted that the logical view taken of a data set may vary from program to program. For example, the data structure diagram in Example 2.3.3 (see Fig. 2.7) is logically sufficient for a program which processes the customer record. If the customer record is either a payment or a receipt, however, and the program wishes to process it only if it is a receipt, then the logical data structure diagram shown in Example 2.4.4 (see Fig. 2.16) is required.

If the logical diagram is insufficiently refined in this way it will prove impossible to allocate operations to it during Step 3.1 of the JSP design procedure. Without the refinement of a customer record into payment and receipt there would be nowhere to allocate a functional operation such as 'output receipt record'. This operation cannot be allocated to the component CUST-REC because that component includes the processing of both PAYMENT *and* RECEIPT. Step 3.1 therefore provides a useful verification that the correct logical data structure diagram has indeed been drawn. In essence the set of functions which can be supported by a program is dependent upon the logical view taken of its data sets (see also the discussion in Section 10.2).

Commonly, refinements below record level are necessary only to distinguish between record types. A refinement to describe the order of fields is usually unnecessary. For example, if an employee record contains name and address fields and it is required to output the name, it is unnecessary to refine the record component into name and address components on the data structure diagram. The operation 'Output employee name' may be allocated to the employee record component because it applies to *all* employee records.

The only occasions on which it is usually necessary to refine record components into fields are when the record contains a data structure other than a simple sequence of fields (see Chapter 6) or when fields are to be input one at a time from a terminal (see Section 3.2).

You should now turn to the iteration exercises at the end of this chapter.

DO EXERCISES 9 TO 14 IN SECTION 2.7

2.7 EXERCISES

Draw data structure diagrams from the following data specifications.

Sequence

1   A MEAL consists of three courses: SOUP, MAIN COURSE and DESSERT.

2   A customer transaction (CUST-TRANS) consists of a customer number (CUST-NO), a customer type (CUST-TYPE) and a quantity ordered (QTY).

3   A CAR HIRE transaction consists of a CUSTOMER NAME and CAR DETAILS, which consist of MODEL TYPE and DURATION OF HIRE.

Sequence and Selection

4   An AMOUNT consists of POUNDS or PENCE.

5   An EMPLOYEE RECORD consists of a NAME, an ADDRESS and a PAYCODE which is either *A, B* or *C*.

6   A TRAIN consists of an ENGINE and a CARRIAGE. Sometimes there is also a GUARDS-VAN on the end.

7   A MEAL consists of SOUP, perhaps an ENTREE, then a MAIN COURSE followed by either APPLE PIE or RICE PUDDING.

8   A small file contains a type $R1$ or a type $R2$ record, followed by type $R3$ or a type $R4$ record. If there is a type $R3$ record, it may also be followed by a type $R5$ record.

Sequence, Selection and Iteration

9   A COLLEGE has a number of FACULTYs and each faculty is made up a number of DEPARTMENTs.

10   An EXAMination PAPER consists of a FRONT PAGE and a number of QUESTIONs.

11   A TRAIN consists of an ENGINE which is perhaps followed by some CARRIAGEs. There may also be a GUARDS-VAN on the end.

12   Online input to an accounting program consists of a number of transactions, each of which is either an account payment or an account receipt. Input is terminated by an account number of all 9s.

13   A file of student records is held in faculty number/student matriculation number sequence. In addition to the student records the file also contains a trailer record for each faculty and one for the file as a whole.

14   A file of records containing information about when employees started work is held in chronological sequence, day (1–31) within month (1–12) within year. At the end of each month and year are trailer records containing monthly and annual totals respectively.

Chapter 3

Designing Simple Programs

This chapter introduces the basic 3-step JSP design procedure and applies it to the design of simple programs which process single sequential data sets:

Step 1   Draw a data structure diagram.
Step 2   Form a program structure diagram.
Step 3.1   List and allocate operations.
Step 3.2   List and allocate conditions.

An initial overview is followed by some elementary examples of the design of both interactive and batch programs, and the chapter ends with several further examples which extend the procedure.

3.1 DESIGN PROCEDURE

The 3-step design procedure of JSP was introduced in Section 1.2. Here it is again:

Step 1   Define the structure of the data to be processed by the program, by drawing a data structure diagram for each data set.

Step 2   Form a program structure diagram from the data structure diagram(s).

Step 3   List and allocate operations and conditions, i.e.

   Step 3.1   List the functional components (operations) of the program and allocate them to the program structure diagram.

   Step 3.2   List the conditions which determine each selection and the end of each iteration, and allocate them to the program structure diagram.

For certain kinds of program a refinement to the procedure is required (see Chapters 7 and 8) but this need not concern us at present.

In Chapter 2 you learned how to draw data structure diagrams in order to undertake Step 1. In this chapter you will learn how to turn a data structure diagram into a program structure diagram (Step 2) and add to it the operations and conditions which form the functions of the program (Step 3). All that remains to be done then to obtain a working program is to code and test it, which is discussed in Chapter 4.

The program examples in this chapter are simple in that they process only one data set, and at this level of simplicity it is likely that any design method other than JSP would produce a similar program. In Example 3.2.1, for instance, how many ways are there to design a trivial program which is a sequence of less than half a dozen instructions? Nevertheless, the principles introduced in this chapter will be equally applicable to more complex programs. It is the wide applicability of simple JSP design principles to all types of program which makes it such a rigorous and repeatable design method. It has been said that when using JSP there is no such thing as a complex program, there are merely some programs that are *larger* than others.

For a simple program which processes only one data set, Step 2 (the formation of a program structure diagram) is a trivial process, because the program structure diagram is the same as the data structure diagram. To turn the data structure diagram into a program structure diagram all that needs to be done is to change the names of the components to indicate that they have become program rather than data components, e.g. the data component name CUST-REC could be changed to the program component name P-CUST-REC (where P is an abbreviation of PROCESS). In this way every component in the data structure is represented by a component in the program structure which is responsible for processing it and to which can be allocated the operations necessary to undertake that processing.

Operations are identified, listed and allocated to program components in the next step of the JSP design procedure, Step 3.1. An operation is usually a single source language instruction. Here is a sample list of operations which contains all the instructions necessary to read a file of customer records. Count up how many customer records are on file, and output that total:

1　Open customer file.
2　Close customer file.
3　Read record from customer file.
4　Add 1 to customer total.
5　Output customer total.

This manual will adopt the practice of specifying operations in English narrative form in order to avoid programming language-specific statements wherever possible. For example, the operations Input and Output will be used to indicate terminal input and output, whereas the operations Read and Write will be used to indicate file input and output. A list of these operations, their meanings and their equivalent statements in COBOL and BASIC is given in Appendix A.

The operations are numbered so that the number can be allocated to the program structure diagram, but they are listed in no particular order, merely in the sequence in which the programmer deduces them from the functional requirements of the program specification. When dealing with file processing, Open, Close and Read operations spring immediately to mind, and these have been listed as the first three operations. A program which outputs a file total additionally requires an Add operation and an Output operation, and these have been listed as operations 4 and 5.

JSP does not address itself to the question of where these operations come from. JSP is a design method and no design method can tell you how to obtain the operations required to fulfil the function of the program. Nevertheless, using JSP you are less likely to omit necessary operations, because after Step 2 there already exists a program structure 'skeleton' which explicitly displays all the named program components. For example the existence of the program component P-CUST-REC will prompt consideration of exactly which operations are required to process a customer record.

You may find that you are less likely to omit operations if you list them in some standard sequence, e.g.

Input operations
    (e.g. operations 1, 2 and 3 in Example 1.2.1)
Calculation and data manipulation operations
    (e.g. operations 4 and 5 in Example 1.2.1)
Output operations
    (e.g. operation 6 in Example 1.2.1)
Preparation of condition operations
    (e.g. operations 7 and 8 in Example 1.2.1.)

In the author's experience, however, no such general list is foolproof and the best guide is a more detailed operations checklist. To help you draw up lists of operations during future program design exercises, an operations checklist has been included in Appendix B, comprising a list of the kinds of operation commonly found in DP programs.

Once an operation has been listed it can be allocated to the program structure diagram. This means that its number is placed in a circle and the circle is 'hung' on the program component to which it belongs. To determine to which component an operation is to be allocated ask the question: how often is this operation to be executed—once per...? Operation 4 (Add 1 to customer total), for example, is executed once per customer, because for every customer record the customer total must be incremented by one. It is therefore allocated to the program component which processes a customer record, say P-CUST-REC (see Fig. 3.1).

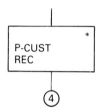

Figure 3.1

The allocation of operations is usually straightforward, e.g. an 'Open file' operation usually belongs at a start-of-program component, a 'Close file' operation at an end-of-program component, an 'Output file total' operation also at an end-of-program component. By the end of this chapter you will have become competent at devising and allocating operations in this way. When more than one operation is to be allocated to the same program component care must be taken with their sequencing, which is indicated by their left-to-right ordering.

Although operations are usually single source language instructions, this need not always be the case. It is permissible to use shorthand English-language macro operations which compound several instructions, e.g.

    5   Format and write printline.

This macro operation consists of several source language instructions which move data to a formatted printline and write it. Macro operations reduce paperwork while listing and allocating operations, but must be expanded into source language statements at the coding stage. An operation may also be an invocation of a subroutine of sub-diagram (see Appendix E).

It is also permissible to list operations which always occur together as a single operation, e.g.

    6   Input a number.
        Add 1 to total of numbers.

But do make sure that such operations always occur together; e.g. this operation adds one to the total of numbers even if the input operation detects an end-of-data condition.

The last step of the JSP design procedure, Step 3.2, involves the listing and allocating of conditions in a manner akin to operations. Every selected program component has an associated condition which determines whether it is to be executed or not, and every iterated component has an associated condition which determines when the iteration is to end. In the above program which processes customer records, the iteration of a customer record (P-CUST-REC) will stop when end-of-file is detected by operation 3. This is the only condition in the program, so the list of conditions consists solely of:

    C1   End of customer file.

The condition number is prefixed by a *C* to differentiate a condition from an operation. On the program structure diagram selection conditions are allocated to the lines connecting the selection component to its selected children. An iteration condition is allocated to the line connecting the iteration component to its iterated child (see Fig. 3.2).

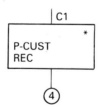

Figure 3.2

To help you draw up a list of conditions during future program design exercises, a conditions checklist has been included in Appendix B. The allocation of operations and conditions will become clearer when you study the worked-through program examples in the following three sections.

3.2 ELEMENTARY EXAMPLES

The three examples of JSP design in this section all concern the interactive processing of a simple data stream at a terminal. Example 3.2.1 processes a sequence of two inputs, Example 3.2.2 refines the processing of the same data stream to introduce a selection, and Example 3.2.3 refines processing still further to introduce an iteration. Batch programs are considered in Section 3.3. For purposes of simplification processing will be kept to a bare minimum and operations concerning validation of input and improving user-friendliness will be omitted for the time being.

Example 3.2.1

A retail shop sells products which cost ninety-nine pence each. A program is required to process a single customer transaction at a terminal; the transaction consists of customer number and quantity ordered, and the program is required to calculate the total cost of the order.

Step 1   Draw a data structure diagram of the input transaction (see Fig. 3.3).

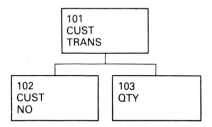

Figure 3.3

From Fig. 3.3 onwards components will be numbered beginning with a root number of 101 then proceeding in increments of 1 down each leg from left to right. These numbers will eventually become program labels when the program is coded. The benefits and a detailed explanation of the numbering system are given in Appendix C.

Step 2   Form a program structure diagram (see Fig. 3.4).

The program structure diagram is formed directly from the data structure diagram. All that is changed are the names of the components to indicate that they have become program rather than data components.

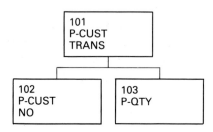

Figure 3.4

P is an abbreviation of PROCESS; P-CUST-TRANS, for example, is a program component which represents the processing of the data component CUST-TRANS.

Step 3.1   List and allocate operations (see Fig. 3.5).

Four operations are required to satisfy the function of this program:

     1 Input customer number.
     2 Input quantity.
     3 Calculate cost = quantity $\times$ 99.
     4 Output cost.

These operations are allocated to the program structure diagram by taking each one in turn, placing its number inside a circle and attaching it to an appropriate program component.

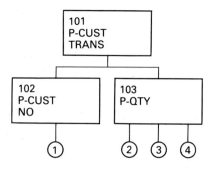

Figure 3.5

The operations are allocated by asking of each one the question: how often is it executed? Operation 1 is executed once per customer number and is therefore allocated to the program component which deals with the processing of a customer number (P-CUST-NO). Operation 2 is executed once per quantity ordered and is therefore allocated to the program component which deals with the processing of a quantity (P-QTY). Operations 3 and 4 are also executed once per quantity following the input of quantity and are therefore allocated to program component P-QTY following operation 2; the left-to-right ordering of operations beneath a component indicates their sequence.

Step 3.2   List and allocate conditions.

There are no selection or iteration components in this program, therefore there are no conditions to list and allocate.

The program design is now complete. The transformation of the diagram into source language code is a simple matter of writing down the operations in an appropriate programming language in box number sequence. Coding is discussed in detail in Chapter 4, and some sample codings of an expanded version of this program are given after Example 3.2.3.

Example 3.2.2

This example is a refinement of the previous example which includes a selection component in addition to sequence components. An amendment is required to the previous program such that if the quantity ordered is greater than ten a discount of 10% is to be applied to the cost before outputting it.

Step 1   Draw a data structure diagram of the input transaction (see Fig. 3.6).

The logical data structure diagram for this program is a refinement of Fig. 3.3 to distinguish a quantity greater than ten from a quantity not greater than ten.

Step 2   Form a program structure diagram (see Fig. 3.7).

The program structure diagram is structurally equivalent to the data structure diagram; only the component names have been changed to reflect the fact that they are now program rather than data components.

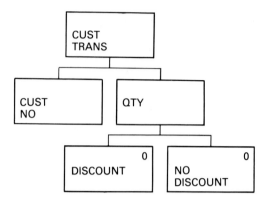

Figure 3.6

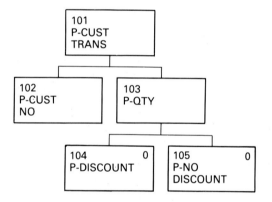

Figure 3.7

Step 3.1   List and allocate operations (see Figs 3.8 and 3.9).

The operations list required for this program is the same as that for the previous example with the addition of an operation which calculates discount:

1   Input customer number.
2   Input quantity.
3   Calculate cost = quantity × 99 × 0.9.
4   Calculate cost = quantity × 99.
5   Output cost.

Fig. 3.8 is a first attempt at allocating operations.

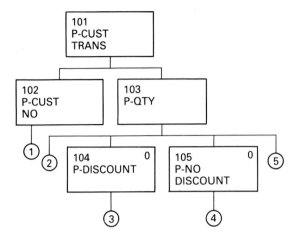

Figure 3.8

Note that the allocation of operations 2 and 5 has caused P-QTY to become a sequence of operation 2, followed by a selection between P-DISCOUNT and P-NO-DISCOUNT, followed by operation 5. In other words P-QTY has become part sequence and part selection, and no such component type exists in JSP. To rectify the diagram the selected components must be dropped down to a lower diagrammatic level, as in Example 2.4.4, and component P-QTY-BODY introduced in their place.

Moreover, in order to maintain program clarity and simplicity it is advisable not to mix program components and operations beneath the same parent: operations should be allocated to elementary components only. Operations 2 and 5 should therefore be dropped down to a lower diagrammatic level and components P-QTY-START and P-QTY-END introduced in their place (see Fig. 3.9).

The diagram is now correct. P-QTY is a sequence of P-QTY-START, P-QTY-BODY and P-QTY-END. P-QTY-START is an elementary component to which operations can be allocated, P-QTY-BODY is a selection between the elementary components P-DISCOUNT and P-NO-DISCOUNT, and P-QTY-END is a further elementary component.

Step 3.2 List and allocate conditions (see Fig. 3.10).

There are two selected components in this program, therefore there are two conditions.

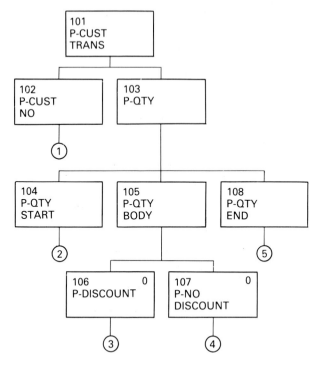

Figure 3.9

C1 Quantity > 10.
C2 Quantity not > 10.

These conditions are allocated to the lines connecting the selection component to its selected children.

Note that the condition for P-NO-DISCOUNT (C2) is the negation of the condition for P-DISCOUNT (C1). When this happens it is permissible to use the negation of C1, written as $\overline{C1}$, as the condition for P-NO-DISCOUNT rather than introduce a new condition C2. This notation is used in Example 3.2.3 (see Fig. 3.14).

The program design is now complete and can be transformed into code. Some sample codings of an expanded version of this program are given after Example 3.2.3.

Example 3.2.3

This example is a refinement of the previous example which includes an

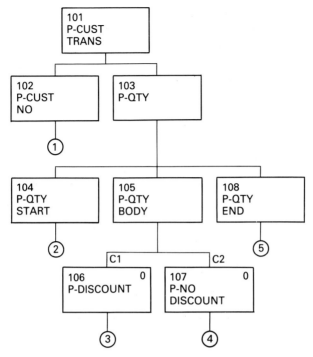

Figure 3.10

iteration component in addition to sequence and selection components.

An amendment is required to the previous program to process ten transactions rather than one.

Step 1   Draw a data structure diagram of the input transactions (see Fig. 3.11).

Step 2   Form a program structure diagram (see Fig. 3.12).

Step 3.1 List and allocate operations (see Fig. 3.13).

The operations list is the same as for Example 3.2.2 plus:

   6   Add 1 to COUNT.

Step 3.2 List and allocate conditions (see Fig. 3.14).

There are two selected components and one iterated component in this program, therefore there are three conditions. It is normal to list

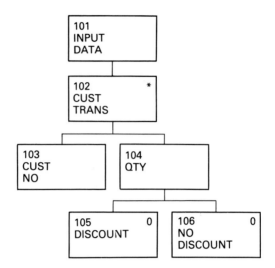

Figure 3.11

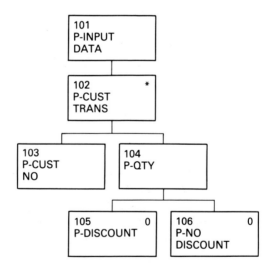

Figure 3.12

conditions as they appear on the diagram from left to right, leg by leg, with higher-level conditions before lower-level conditions.

C1　COUNT > 10.
C2　Quantity > 10.

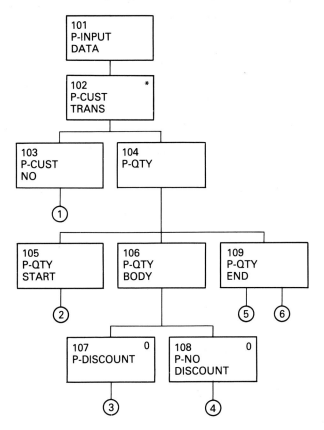

Figure 3.13

COUNT is a program-defined variable which is initialized to 1 during data declaration (if the source language permits this, otherwise by an additional operation), and is incremented by 1 after the processing of each transaction; the program terminates when COUNT is greater than 10. Some languages have constructs which handle the initialization, incrementing and testing of COUNT implicitly (e.g. BASIC's FOR ...NEXT... construct and COBOL's PERFORM...VARYING... construct; see sample coding below). Note that this manual adopts the convention of listing an iteration condition as that which ends the iteration (COUNT > 10) rather than that which ensures its continuation (COUNT NOT > 10), in order to prevent the proliferation of negatives. As suggested in Example 3.2.2, the negation of condition C2, written as $\overline{C2}$, may be used for selected component P-NO-DISCOUNT to save the introduction of a further condition C3.

Selection conditions are allocated to the lines connecting the selection component to its selected children. An iteration condition is allocated to the line connecting the iteration component to its iterated child.

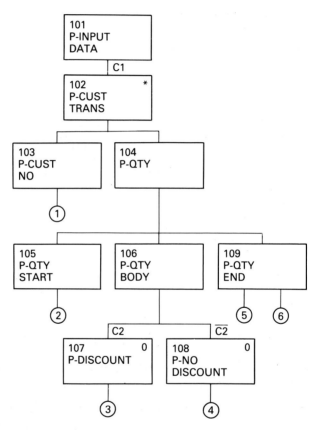

Figure 3.14

The program design is now complete. Coding is discussed in detail in Chapter 4, but here are some sample translations into program text obtained by coding operations and conditions in box number sequence.

BASIC:

```
10  FOR COUNT=1 TO 10
20  INPUT CUST.NO
30  INPUT QTY
40  IF QTY>10 THEN
        LET COST=QTY*99*0.9
    ELSE
        LET COST=QTY*99
50  PRINT COST
60  NEXT COUNT
70  END
```

COBOL:

```
PROCEDURE DIVISION.
P-INPUT-DATA-MAIN SECTION.
P-INPUT-DATA.
    PERFORM P-CUST-TRANS VARYING
        COUNT FROM 1 BY 1 UNTIL COUNT > 10.
    STOP RUN.
P-CUST-TRANS.
    ACCEPT CUST-NO.
    ACCEPT QTY.
    IF QTY > 10
        COMPUTE COST = QTY * 99 * 0.9
    ELSE
        COMPUTE COST = QTY * 99.
    DISPLAY COST.
```

In this section three elementary interactive programs have been designed, during the course of which you have:

1 Learned the three basic steps of the JSP design procedure.

2 Learned how to design programs processing hierarchical data structures.

3 Learned how the logical data structure diagram of a data set varies from program to program.

4 Learned how a program structure diagram may require refinement after allocation of operations to avoid mixing components and operations beneath the same parent.

The following section introduces the read-ahead principle, which is required for more complex interactive programs and for batch programs.

3.3 THE READ-AHEAD PRINCIPLE

In the following discussion the terms read and input are used interchangeably.

Operations which input data sometimes require a method of allocation different from all other operations. All other operations process known data, i.e. data which has already been input to the program and has been recognized, but an input operation may not know what data is about to be input.

In each program in the previous section the order of arrival of input is predetermined and known. The structure of the input data stream in Example 3.2.3, for example, is pre-set to ten iterations of customer number and quantity. The operation 'Input customer number' can therefore be allocated to the program component which processes a customer number (P-CUST-NO) because it is known that the result of the input statement will be the inputting of a customer number.

In many interactive programs and all batch programs, however, the order of arrival of input is not completely known, and the result of an input operation may be unpredictable. A 'file read' operation, for example, may result in the input of a record or the detection of an end-of-file condition. The decision as to whether to process a record or an end-of-file condition can therefore be taken only *after* the input operation. Compare this situation with the programs in the previous section, where the decision as to which input to process next can be taken *before* the input operation.

The operation 'Input customer number' can be allocated to program component P-CUST-NO only if it is known that the next input must be a customer number. If the next input cannot be determined in this way, input operations must be allocated according to the read-ahead principle, which consists of two rules:

The Read-ahead Principle

Rule 1   Allocate an input/read operation at start of program (immediately following the file open statement if the read is from a file).

Rule 2   Allocate a further input/read operation to each program component which processes a physical input data component, following all other operations allocated to that component.

If you are not sure when to allocate a read operation, because you are not sure which program components process physical input data components, it may help to create a sample data set, as suggested for data analysis in Section 2.6. The sample data set will clarify which data components require read operations. In the examples in Section 3.2 the physical input data components are customer number and quantity.

The requirement for the read-ahead principle will become apparent when you study the following examples. In the examples in the previous section a program structure diagram was shown during all stages of its development: at the end of Step 2, again at the end of Step 3.1 and again at the end of Step 3.2. To conserve space in future examples, a program structure diagram will be shown once only, in its completed form, after Step 3.2.

Example 3.3.1

This example consists of an amendment to Example 3.2.3 to process a variable number of transactions. The program ends when a customer number of 999999 is input.

Step 1   Draw a data structure diagram of the input transactions (see Fig. 3.15).

Step 2   Form a program structure diagram (see Fig. 3.16).

Note the changing of data component names INPUT-BODY and 999999 to program component names PROG-BODY and PROG-END, the addition of program component PROG-START in anticipation of the allocation of operation 1, and the addition of program components P-QTY-START, P-QTY-BODY and P-QTY-END as in Example 3.2.3. Such additional components may be added as required during Steps 3.1 and 3.2, but with practice the JSP designer will learn to anticipate their requirement and add them at Step 2.

Step 3.1   List and allocate operations (see Fig. 3.16).

The operations list is the same as for Example 3.2.2.

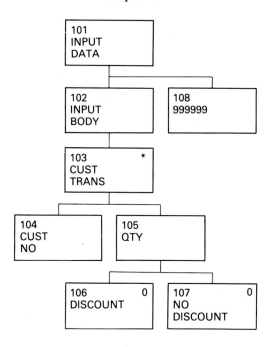

Figure 3.15

Step 3.2   List and allocate conditions (see Fig. 3.16).

C1   Customer number = 999999.
C2   Quantity > 10.

Input operations 1 and 2 must be allocated according to the two rules of the read-ahead principle. Because operation 1 may result in the input of either a customer number or the end-of-data marker (999999), each of which must be processed differently, the operation cannot be allocated solely to P-CUST-NO as in Example 3.2.3. If it was allocated to P-CUST-NO, and the end-of-data marker was input, the next program component to be executed would be (erroneously) P-QTY rather than PROG-END. Operation 1 can be allocated to P-CUST-NO only if it is known that a customer number is to be input at that point; in this program this is not the case, and therefore input operations must be allocated according to the read-ahead principle.

According to rule 1, an input operation is allocated to PROG-START. According to rule 2, input operations are allocated following the processing of each physical input data component, i.e. after processing of a

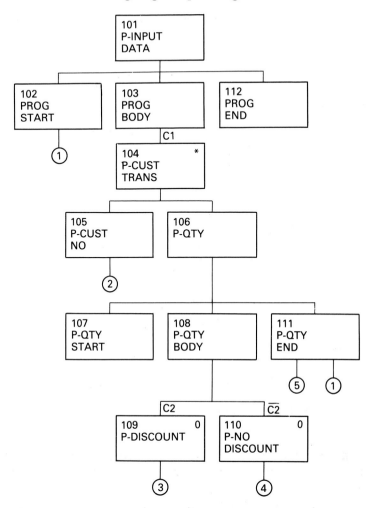

Figure 3.16

customer number (P-CUST-NO, to which operation 2 is allocated) and after processing of quantity ordered (P-QTY-END, to which operation 1 is allocated). If you remain unsure of this allocation, create a sample set of input transactions in order to clarify it, as suggested earlier, and desk-check the program structure diagram. For example:

000001 5 000002 17 000003 4 999999

If the operation 1 allocated to P-QTY-END results in a customer number being input, control passes once more into the iteration of P-CUST-TRANS;

if the end-of-data marker is input, condition C1 on P-CUST-TRANS causes control to pass to PROG-END.

In Example 3.2.3 the pattern of processing was:

   input, process ... input, process (end)

In this example the pattern of processing is:

   input ... process, input ... process, input (end)

It is this pattern, in which an input operation must be allocated ahead of the program components which are to process the result of that input operation, which gives rise to the term read-ahead. Note that program components P-QTY-START and PROG-END have no operations allocated to them and could be omitted from the program structure diagram.

As an exercise, consider what operations need to be added to the operations list, and to which program components they should be allocated, in order to output the total cost calculated by the program (see Appendix F for solution).

Example 3.3.2

A retail shop maintains a file of customer invoice records in invoice number sequence. A field on each record (PAID-SW) indicates whether the

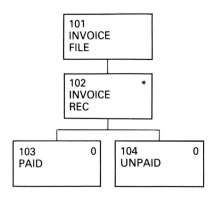

Figure 3.17

invoice has been paid (PAID-SW = '1') or not (PAID-SW = '0'). A program is required to output the total amount unpaid.

Step 1   Draw a data structure diagram of the invoice file (see Fig. 3.17).

Step 2   Form a program structure diagram (see Fig. 3.18).

Note the addition of the program components PROG-START, PROG-BODY and PROG-END in anticipation of the allocation of 'Open file' and 'Close file' operations.

Step 3.1 List and allocate operations (see Fig. 3.18).

1 Open invoice file.
2 Close invoice file.
3 Read record from invoice file.
4 Add invoice amount to unpaid total.
5 Output unpaid total.

Step 3.2 List and allocate conditions (see Fig. 3.18).

C1 End of invoice file.
C2 PAID-SW = '1'.

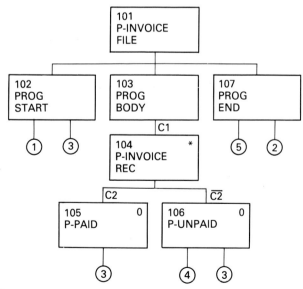

Figure 3.18

A note on the End-of-file Condition

In Microsoft BASIC and some other languages (e.g. PASCAL) condition C1 can be evaluated using the predefined variable EOF, which is set automatically at end-of-file and can be tested by any statement. In COBOL an end-of-file condition can be detected only by the AT END clause of a READ statement, and the condition is not made available for testing outside of the READ statement. Thus a paragraph cannot be PERFORMed UNTIL the end-of-file condition is detected. Instead the COBOL programmer must define his own end-of-file variable, e.g.

EOF-SW PIC × VALUE '0'.

and set it to '1' by a standard READ statement:

READ filename AT END MOVE '1' TO EOF-SW.

The condition end-of-file can then be tested outside the READ statement by the condition EOF-SW = '1'. A small number of additional COBOL statements also require the setting of a programmer-defined variable in order that a condition can be tested outside the statement, e.g. the direct-access READ statement (see Example 6.1.1) and the SEARCH statement (see Example 7.4.3).

The values '0' and '1' have been chosen because EOF-SW is in essence a binary switch, having one of two possible states. If you prefer you can initialize EOF-SW to '*N*' (for 'No'), and then either move '*Y*' (for 'Yes') to it at end-of-file, or initialize it to a space and then move '*E*' (for 'End-of-file') to it at end-of-file. The principle is the same. Conceptually, EOF-SW is an end-of-file record and is processed as such.

Without the additional components PROG-START, PROG-BODY and PROG-END, Open and Close operations would have to be allocated to component P-INVOICE-FILE before and after P-INVOICE-REC. Remember that it is not advisable to allocate operations alongside parts of a sequence, selection or iteration in this way: operations should be allocated to elementary components only. P-INVOICE-FILE must therefore become a sequence of PROG-START (an elementary component to which operations can be allocated), PROG-BODY (which iterates P-INVOICE-REC) and PROG-END (another elementary component to which operations can be allocated).

Operation 1 is executed once per invoice file at start of file; no other processing can be undertaken until the invoice file has been opened. Operation 1 is therefore allocated to PROG-START, which is the first child of the sequence P-INVOICE-FILE and represents all processing to be undertaken at the start of that sequence.

Operation 2 is executed once per invoice file at end of file; it is therefore allocated to PROG-END, which is the last child of the sequence P-INVOICE-FILE and represents all processing to be undertaken at the end of that sequence.

Operation 4 is executed once per unpaid invoice and must be allocated to P-UNPAID.

Operation 5 is executed once per invoice file at end of file—this is the only place at which totals can be output; it is allocated to PROG-END either before or after the invoice file is closed.

Operation 3 may return an invoice record or detect end-of-file, and must therefore be allocated according to the read-ahead principle. According to rule 1 it is allocated to PROG-START immediately following the file open operation. According to rule 2 it is allocated to P-PAID and P-UNPAID, both of which process physical input records, following all other operations allocated to those components. If you remain unsure of this allocation, create a sample invoice file and desk-check the program structure diagram, as suggested in the previous example.

As an exercise, consider what operations need to be added to the operations list, and to which program components they should be added, in order to output a warning message if the total of unpaid invoices is greater than the total of paid invoices (see Appendix F for solution).

3.4 FURTHER EXAMPLES

In this section you will find several further examples of the design of programs which process single sequential data sets, all requiring the read-ahead principle. Notes are appended to help you follow them, and by the time you have worked through them you should be in a position to attempt the exercises at the end of the chapter.

Example 3.4.1

A customer file consists of a file header record (with a customer number of zero), followed by a number of customer records, each of which is either a payment record or a receipt record, followed by a file trailer record (with a customer number of 999999). Whether a customer record is a payment or a receipt is indicated by the field REC-TYPE, which contains a '*P*' in a payment record and an '*R*' in a receipt record.

Each payment record contains a payment amount and the file trailer contains a total of all payment amounts. A program is required to output a warning message if the total is incorrect.

Step 1   Draw a data structure diagram of the customer file (see Fig. 3.19).

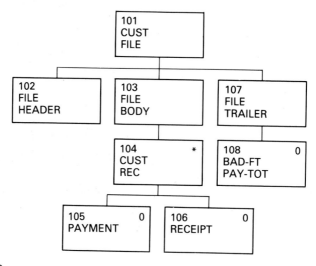

Figure 3.19

As the program is required to check the correctness of the file trailer total the logical data structure diagram must show the possibility of an incorrect total (BAD-FT-PAY-TOT).

Step 2   Form a program structure diagram (see Fig. 3.20).

Data components FILE-HEADER and FILE-TRAILER have been subsumed into program components PROG-START and PROG-END respectively. Other program components have been added in anticipation of the allocation of operations and should require no further explanation.

Step 3.1   List and allocate operations (see Fig. 3.20).

    1 Open customer file.
    2 Close customer file.

3 Read record from customer file.

4 Add payment amount to payment total.

5 Output 'PAY TOTAL INCORRECT'.

Operation 1 is allocated to PROG-START as per normal. Operation 2 is allocated to a child component of PROG-END following the processing of the file trailer. Operation 4 is executed once per payment record and is therefore allocated to P-PAYMENT. Operation 5 is executed once per file at end-of-file if the file trailer total is incorrect, and is therefore allocated to P-BAD-FT-PAY-TOT.

If data component FILE-TRAILER (and hence program component PROG-END) had not been refined into the constituent components required for this program, there would be nowhere to allocate operation 5. It could certainly not be allocated to PROG-END—PROG-END is always executed but operation 5 is not. The operations list therefore provides a useful verification check against the program structure diagram. If there is no component to which an operation can be allocated, the program structure diagram cannot be correct.

Operation 3 is allocated according to the read-ahead principle, once at PROG-START following operation 1, and once at the end of every program component which processes a physical input data component (i.e. a record). There are three record types in this program (file header, customer record and file trailer), and therefore three further allocations of operation 3.

A read is allocated to PROG-START following the processing of the file header record; as there is no file header processing to be undertaken, the read immediately follows the open and read operations already allocated. Any enhancement to the program to process the file header would require operations to be inserted between the two reads.

A further read is allocated to P-CUST-REC-END following all processing of a customer record. A final read is allocated to PROG-END following the processing of the file trailer record and before closing the file. This read is superfluous and could be omitted; its only function would be to detect end-of-file and ensure that there were no more records following. Rather than amend rule 2 of the read-ahead principle to cater for the optional omission of this final read, it is normal to continue to allocate it.

As a customer record consists of either a payment record or a receipt record, it is permissible to allocate operation 3 to both P-PAYMENT and P-RECEIPT instead of to P-CUST-REC-END. This was the solution adopted in

Example 3.3.2 (see Fig. 3.18), where the read operation was allocated to both P-PAID and P-UNPAID instead of to their parent component P-INVOICE-REC. Whether the operation is allocated to the parent or the children makes no difference from a program design or a program execution point of view.

Beware of allocating conditional operations, e.g.

> 5   If file trailer total not = payment total
>   Output 'PAY TOTAL INCORRECT'.

Operations should not be confused with conditions. Operations are unconditional verbs. It would be dangerous to include in an allocated operation the particular circumstances under which it is to be executed. Operations can be allocated to more than one component and should not be particularized by a condition. Moreover, the only way to ensure that all conditions for selection and iteration components have been defined is to list them in the conditions list.

Step 3.2   List and allocate conditions (see Fig. 3.20).

> C1   Customer number = 999999.
> C2   REC-TYPE = 'P'.
> C3   File trailer total not = payment total.

The graphical form in which the program is displayed makes it apparent that if the file trailer payment total is correct there will be no output from the program. In a live situation it would be prudent to query the systems analyst about this, but for the present you should merely note the usefulness of program structure diagrams in highlighting such a situation and assume that the program specification is correct.

Example 3.4.2

For this example refer back to Example 1.2.1, which was presented as an initial illustration of the JSP design procedure in Section 1.2. Re-read the example, which should now be completely comprehensible to you. Note especially the allocation of conditions and operations 7 and 8.

Care must be taken when allocating conditions to nested iterations. The iteration of P-CUST ends when the file trailer is read. The nested iteration of P-ACCOUNT ends when either the file trailer is read or a new customer is read. The nested iteration of P-TRANS ends when either the

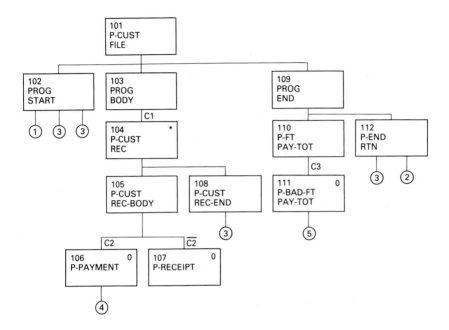

Figure 3.20

file trailer is read or a new customer is read or a new account is read. In such circumstances it is often necessary, as here, to carry conditions down from one iteration to another. The only occasions on which it is not necessary is when a nested iteration is performed a fixed number of times (e.g. condition C1 in Example 3.2.3) or is ended by a special input record (e.g. condition C2 in Example 3.4.3 following).

The detection of a new customer requires the maintenance of a store of the current customer number with which each new customer number read can be compared. Thus the condition 'new customer' becomes 'Customer number not=current customer number'. Current customer number (known as the reference criterion because it is the criterion with which the customer number, known as the identification criterion, is being compared) is a program-defined variable which is set to the current value of the customer number every time a new customer number is read; hence operation 7, allocated to P-CUT-START. Similarly, the variable current account number is used in the detection of end-of-account, and operation 8 is allocated to P-ACCOUNT-START to maintain it.

It is interesting to compare the JSP design of this program with a more traditional functional approach as shown in Figs 1.7 (pseudocode) and 1.8 (flowchart). The functional design is based on an iteration of a procedure (P-RECORD) which treats all record types as children of a selection, and this can be shown in terms of the program structure diagram in Fig. 3.21.

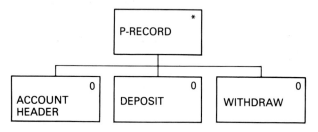

Figure 3.21

This would be coded as:

```
IF account header
   PROCESS account header
ELSE
   IF deposit
      PROCESS deposit
   ELSE
      PROCESS withdrawal.
Read record from transactions file.
```

Sometimes the file trailer is also included in the selection and the read-ahead principle is not used:

```
Read record from transactions file.
IF file trailer
   PROCESS file trailer
ELSE
   IF account header
      PROCESS account header
   ELSE
      IF deposit
         PROCESS deposit
      ELSE
         PROCESS withdrawal.
```

This version of the program contains only one READ statement (i.e. there is no initial READ following the opening of the transactions file) and is hopelessly unstructured. When the READ statement detects end-of-file a branch instruction to a PROG-END procedure must be generated in order to branch round the statement(s) following the READ. JSP does not use branches (i.e. GOTOs)—it gets the program structure correct to begin with.

Whichever way the program structure diagram in Fig. 3.21 is coded, using the read-ahead principle or not, the structure of the program is incorrect because it is based on a wholly inadequate data analysis in which the structural relationships among the records have been lost, making coding and future maintenance difficult. In this program a deposit could come before an account header.

These structural inadequacies are highlighted by 'control break' processing, which consists of operations to be undertaken at significant breakpoints in file processing. For example, if it is required to output the average withdrawal amount for each account (see enhancement 3 in Section 1.2), a control break occurs when account number changes in order that the average can be output.

The processing of a control break involves the processing of the end of one account (Calculate and output average) and the start of another (Set account totals to 0). This is true for all control breaks except the first (which consists of start of first account only) and the last (which consists of end of last account only). To overcome these exceptions switches are typically introduced, e.g. a first-time switch which prevents an average being output at start of first account. JSP does not use switches—it gets the program structure correct to begin with.

Any enhancement to the program concerning customers would require further switches to be introduced into the program. Consider how you would incorporate the enhancements noted in Section 1.2 into the JSP design and the functional design. Control break processing in JSP is possible without switches because all data components are present in the program structure and each component has a start and end to which the start and end elements of control break processing can be allocated.

Example 3.4.3

A file of student records is held in faculty number/student number sequence. At the beginning of each faculty is a faculty header, indicated by a student number of all zeroes, containing the faculty name. At the end of each faculty is a faculty trailer, indicated by a student number of all 9s.

At the end of the file is a file trailer, indicated by a faculty number of all 9s.

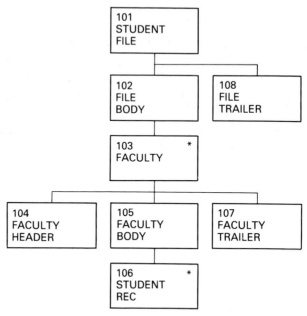

Figure 3.22

A program is required to output for each faculty the name of the faculty followed by the number of students within it, plus a total of all students on file.

Step 1   Draw a data structure diagram of the student file (see Fig. 3.22).

Step 2   Form a program structure diagram (see Fig. 3.23).

Step 3.1 List and allocate operations (see Fig. 3.23).

1 Open student file.
2 Close student file.
3 Read record from student file.
4 Set faculty total to 0.
5 Add 1 to faculty total.
6 Output faculty name store and faculty total.
7 Add 1 to file total.
8 Output file total.
9 Move faculty name to faculty name store.

Step 3.2   List and allocate conditions (see Fig. 3.23).

C1 Faculty number = all 9s.
C2 Student number = all 9s.

Operation 4 is allocated to P-FACULTY-START to zeroize the faculty total at the start of each faculty. No such operation is required for the file total, which can be initialized to zero by a VALUE clause in Working-Storage (COBOL) or is automatically initialized to zero at start of program (BASIC) and then never needs to be reset to zero. Note that some languages (e.g. Pascal) do not allow initialization during data declaration in this manner.

Some JSP beginners, having initialized the faculty total to zero at start of program, allocate operation 4 to P-FACULTY-END following operation 6. Although this works, it is not the logical allocation, and the care with which it has to be sequenced among the other operations of P-FACULTY-END is testament to this. The logical place to allocate an operation to zeroize the faculty total is at the start of the faculty: P-FACULTY-START.

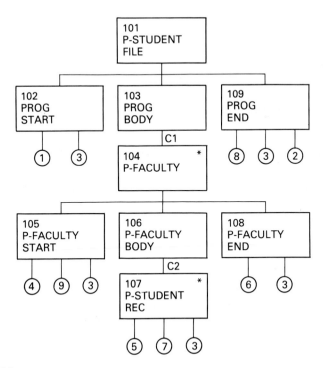

Figure 3.23

Note that operation 7 'Add 1 to file total' allocated to P-STUDENT-REC could equally be 'Add faculty total to file total' allocated to P-FACULTY-END.

Operation 9, which stores the faculty name on the faculty header into a work area, is required because the faculty header is no longer available at end of faculty when the name is to be output.

In this program the iteration of P-STUDENT-REC is nested within the iteration of P-FACULTY, but it is not necessary to carry down the condition which ends the higher-level iteration to the lower-level, because the iteration of P-STUDENT-REC is ended by a special input record—a faculty trailer. P-STUDENT-REC is iterated until student number=all 9s. It would be incorrect to iterate P-STUDENT-REC until faculty number=all 9s or student number=all 9s; the former condition can never be true because of the presence of a faculty trailer. Compare this with the nested iteration in the previous example, where a condition which ends a higher-level iteration can also be true at the lower level.

Example 3.4.4

A menu-driven currency conversion program is required. The menu is to consist of four options:

1 Input a sterling amount and convert it to US dollars.
2 Input a sterling amount and convert it to French francs.
3 Input a sterling amount and convert it to German marks.
9 Terminate program.

Step 1   Draw a data structure diagram of screen input (see Fig. 3.24).

Although the menu presents four options to the user, the data structure diagram shows MENU as a selection between three OPTIONs. Option 9 is a terminator which follows all other options, and it would be incorrect to show it as one of the options available at every iteration.

Step 2   Form a program structure diagram (see Fig. 3.25).

Step 3.1   List and allocate operations (see Fig. 3.25).

1 Output user instructions.
2 Output menu.
3 Input option.

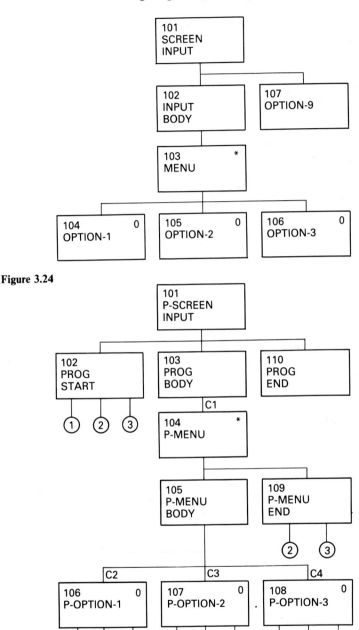

Figure 3.24

Figure 3.25

4 Input pounds.
5 Calculate dollars = pounds $\times$ dollar-rate.
6 Calculate francs = pounds $\times$ franc-rate.
7 Calculate marks = pounds $\times$ mark-rate.
8 Output dollars.
9 Output francs.
10 Output marks.

Note operations 1 and 2, which are macro operations consisting of several source-language statements which always occur together.

Step 3.2   List and allocate conditions (see Fig. 3.25).

C1 Option = 9.
C2 Option = 1.
C3 Option = 2.
C4 Option = 3.

3.5 EXERCISES

Design the following programs.

1   Examination results for thirty students are to be input via a VDU keyboard. Each result consists of seven digits, where the first four digits represent a student number, the next digit represents a subject code in the range 1 to 6, and the final two digits represent a percentage mark for that subject (N.B. no one ever gets 100%!). Each student has six examination results which are to be input in student number/subject code sequence.

A program is required to output each student's average examination result after the six results have been input.

2   Re-design Example 3.3.1 as a menu-driven program. The menu is to consist of the following options:

1   Apply discount to cost.
2   Do not apply discount to cost.
9   Terminate program.

3   An employee file contains employee records in department number/
employee number sequence. The field REC-TYPE on an employee record
indicates whether the employee is male (REC-TYPE='M') or female
(REC-TYPE='F').

A program is required to output departmental totals of male and
female employees.

4   A company maintains a file of its salespersons' monthly sales figures
in salesperson number/month number sequence. For each salesperson
there are twelve monthly sales records. At end of file there is a file
trailer.

A program is required to output the average monthly sales for each
salesperson together with the message 'BONUS' whenever an average is
greater than £1000. In addition the average monthly sales for the whole
file is to be output at end of file.

5   A library maintains a file of information on books in author
number/title number/copy number sequence. For each author there is
an author record containing the author's name, followed by a book
record for each copy of each of the author's titles held in the library.
There may be more than one copy of a title and so each book is
numbered copy one, copy two, etc. The field LOAN-INDIC on a book
record indicates whether the copy is out on loan

(LOAN-INDIC = '1')

or not

(LOAN-INDIC = '0').

A program is required to output for each author, the author's name,
how many copies of his books are held in the library and what
percentage are out on loan.

Chapter 4

Coding and Testing Programs

Following the three steps of the JSP design procedure all that remains to be done to obtain an executable program is to transform the program structure diagram with allocated operations and conditions into machine-readable form, e.g. a BASIC or COBOL program. This chapter discusses the variety of ways in which a designed program can be coded and examines some of the problems involved. It is suggested that the coding should be standardized and, wherever possible, automated, and to effect this a program design language is introduced as an intermediate step between a program structure diagram and its representation in source language code. In addition the testing of programs is discussed.

4.1 VARIETIES OF CODE

The development of programs and systems is a complex business requiring many and varied skills, as was noted in Chapter 1, and unless a systematic software engineering approach is adopted the individual's response to this complexity is likely to remain just that—individual.

In the absence of a systematic approach, any development task, be it analysis, design, coding, testing, documentation or whatever, is likely to be tackled in different ways by different individuals. For example, ask several programmers to design the same program by drawing a flowchart for it and they will draw several different flowcharts.

It is this variety of ways of doing things which is at the heart of the software crisis because one person's way may be incomprehensible to another. JSP tackles this problem by providing a formal, standard and repeatable design method. Ask several programmers to design the same program using JSP and they will produce similar program structure diagrams.

Such standardization is to be welcomed because it enables us to understand and easily maintain other people's programs, and it enables them to understand and easily maintain ours. Some programmers of the old spaghetti-bowl school object to a formal method such as JSP because they believe it de-skills the job, and there is an element of truth in this.

JSP reduces the amount of artistic skill traditionally involved in program design and replaces it by a craftsmanlike skill; in effect, JSP re-skills the job. Giving a craftsman a better toolkit will enable him to become a more effective craftsman, and giving a programmer a better design method will enable him to become a more effective programmer.

Rather than objecting to formal methods, the DP professional should be actively seeking them in all areas of systems and program development. In this chapter a more formal approach to coding and testing is advocated.

In the preceding chapter you learned how to design simple programs using the basic 3-step JSP design procedure. The starting point of this procedure is a program specification, and JSP can say very little about those stages of systems development which come before the program specification and result in its production (although the lessons learned from JSP have enabled JSD to apply itself to those stages—see Chapter 10). The end point of the design procedure is a program structure diagram with allocated operations and conditions, following which two further stages of program development are required before the program can go live: coding and testing.

There are a number of different ways in which a program designed using JSP can be coded and tested, just as there are with a program designed without the aid of JSP. However, it would be retrogressive to lose the benefits of a standard design method by adopting an individual and arbitrary approach to coding and testing.

In theory JSP can do no more to help us devise test data than it can do to help us devise operations, but just as the program structure diagram shows program components explicitly and so helps prevent the omission of necessary operations, it also shows selection and iteration conditions explicitly and so helps prevent the omission of important test cases. Testing is discussed in Section 4.5.

Also in theory JSP cannot tell us how to code a program, but in practice the implications of JSP for coding are immense, because the complete coding task can be automated. The program structure diagram with allocated operations and conditions is in fact directly executable, given a utility which can input it via a VDU screen (a JSP diagrammer), a utility which can transform it into source language code (a JSP code generator) and a source language compiler.

With such utilities all development and maintenance can be done graphically on a VDU screen via a program structure diagram—a very attractive, productive and rewarding way to develop programs. Such utilities do exist as of now, e.g. Program Design Facility and JSP-TOOL (marketed by LBMS) and PROBENCH (marketed by SCML; see page xi).

Without such utilities the program structure diagram must be transformed into code manually, but no intellectual effort should be necessary in order to accomplish the task. If coding can be automated in principle, the process of coding manually can and should be standardized. Coding is merely the process by which the program structure diagram is transformed into machine-readable form, and such a transformation should introduce no new elements of unpredictability. If any decision-making process involved in the coding process can be removed, it should be. The gains will be standardization, fewer errors and saving of time and effort.

A useful analogy can be drawn between the transformation of a program structure diagram into source code and the compilation of source code into Assembler and object code. There are many ways to transform source code into Assembler code; give several programmers a COBOL program to code in Assembler, and they will produce several different Assembler programs. But once the COBOL program is written it is complete and in principle directly executable; no further intellectual effort should be required to transform it into Assembler code. The transformation process could be automated and, of course, has been. No one hand compiles COBOL programs, there are utilities called COBOL compilers which do the job for us. The gains are standardization, an error-free transformation process and the saving of time and effort, among others.

Languages like COBOL are higher level than Assembler in that they are less machine-dependent, more problem-oriented and typically generate several Assembler instructions from a single source statement. Machine code is sometimes called a first-generation language, Assembler second-generation and COBOL third-generation.

The advantages of programming in a high-level third-generation language are several. From the programmer's point of view it means he is less of a one-machine specialist, he has fewer instructions to code and he can concentrate on interesting design problems rather than machine idiosyncrasies. From his employer's point of view it means he is more productive, because a high-level language is easier to code and the compilation process can be automated, and more generally useful, because he now works on user problems rather than machine problems.

Many Assembler programmers did not see the influx of third-generation languages in the same light. They displayed a resistance to change worthy of the dinosaur, and it took some years to consign Assembler to the same fate as that great beast. Assembler programming is still useful in certain circumstances, but not for the majority of DP applications. For most programmers today, weaned on third-generation languages, the intricacies of programming in Assembler seen unnecessary, uninteresting and best left to a compiler.

But now JSP throws down a new challenge to programmers. Just as the process of transformation from source code to Assembler and object code can be automated, so the process of transformation from program structure diagram to source code can be automated. Why waste time and effort on it? Let a JSP source code generator do it (see Fig. 4.1).

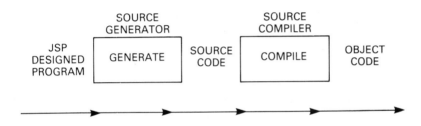

Figure 4.1

As an example, consider again the program structure diagram with allocated operations and conditions for Example 3.3.2 (see Fig. 3.18). The program is complete and in principle directly executable; all the required operations and how they fit together in sequences, selections and iterations have been specified. The transformation of the diagram into source code should require no further intellectual effort. Even if a JSP diagrammer and code generator are not available, and the program must be hand-coded and presented to the computer manually, it should be a simple, predictable exercise on the programmer's part.

But this turns out to be difficult to achieve in practice. The programmer will soon discover that there are a number of decisions to be made about how to code the program, and these are best illustrated by writing some sample program texts for Example 3.3.2. The samples will be given in BASIC and COBOL, but even if you have no knowledge of either language you should still be able to follow the discussion and supply relevant samples from a programming language with which you are familiar.

Code Example 1 Hierarchical Code

In this example the hierarchical structure of the program structure diagram is maintained by coding each program component except the root component as a subroutine of its parent.

BASIC:

```
110   REM P-INVOICE-FILE
120   GOSUB 200
130   GOSUB 300
140   GOSUB 700
199   END
200   REM PROG-START
210   OPEN "I", #1, "INV-FILE"
220   INPUT #1, . . .
299   RETURN
300   REM PROG-BODY
310   WHILE NOT EOF (1)
320   GOSUB 400
330   WEND
399   RETURN
400   REM P-INVOICE-REC
410   IF PAID.SW$ = "1" THEN
          GOSUB 500
      ELSE
          GOSUB 600
499   RETURN
500   REM P-PAID
510   INPUT #1, . . .
599   RETURN
600   REM P-UNPAID
610   LET UNPAID.TOT = UNPAID.TOT + INVOICE.AMOUNT
620   INPUT #1, . . .
699   RETURN
700   REM PROG-END
710   PRINT UNPAID.TOT
720   CLOSE #1
799   RETURN
```

COBOL:

```
PROCEDURE DIVISION.
P-INVOICE-FILE-MAIN SECTION.
P-INVOICE-FILE.
  PERFORM PROG-START.
  PERFORM PROG-BODY.
  PERFORM PROG-END.
  STOP RUN.
PROG-START.
  OPEN INPUT INVOICE-FILE.
  READ INVOICE-FILE AT END MOVE '1' TO EOF-SW.
PROG-BODY.
  PERFORM P-INVOICE-REC UNTIL EOF-SW = '1'.
P-INVOICE REC.
  IF PAID-SW = '1'
    PERFORM P-PAID
  ELSE
    PERFORM P-NOT-PAID.
P-PAID.
  READ INVOICE-FILE AT END MOVE '1' TO EOF-SW.
P-NOT-PAID.
  ADD INVOICE-AMOUNT TO UNPAID-TOT.
  READ INVOICE-FILE AT END MOVE '1' TO EOF-SW.
PROG-END.
  DISPLAY UNPAID-TOT.
  CLOSE INVOICE-FILE.
```

Note that in Pascal hierarchical code is possible, but subroutines must be listed in reverse sequence, i.e. with the root component last.

Code Example 2 Nested Code

In this example operations are coded in-line rather than as out-of-line subroutines, in order to maintain the nested structure of the program structure diagram.

BASIC:

```
010   OPEN "I", #1, "INV-FILE"
020   INPUT #1, ...
030   WHILE NOT EOF (1)
040     IF PAID.SW$ = "1" THEN
          INPUT #1, ...
        ELSE
          LET UNPAID.TOT = UNPAID.TOT + INVOICE.AMOUNT:
          INPUT #1, ...
050   WEND
060   PRINT UNPAID.TOT
070   CLOSE #1
080   END
```

COBOL:

In COBOL 68 and COBOL 74 it is possible to nest sequences and selections but not iterations, which must be coded out-of-line and invoked by the PERFORM...UNTIL...statement. COBOL 85 introduces an in-line PER-FORM, along with the selection delimiter END-IF (see coding constraint 1 in Section 4.2), and in the following example these are used to code the program in nested form.

```
PROCEDURE DIVISION.
P-INVOICE-FILE-MAIN SECTION.
P-INVOICE-FILE.
  OPEN INPUT INVOICE-FILE.
  READ INVOICE-FILE AT END MOVE '1' TO EOF-SW.
  PERFORM UNTIL EOF-SW = '1'
    IF PAID-SW = '1'
      READ INVOICE-FILE AT END MOVE '1' TO EOF-SW
    ELSE
      ADD INVOICE-AMOUNT TO UNPAID-TOT
      READ INVOICE-FILE AT END MOVE '1' TO EOF-SW
    END-IF
  END-PERFORM.
  DISPLAY UNPAID-TOT.
  CLOSE INVOICE-FILE.
  STOP RUN.
```

Note that the conditional READ statments in this program would cause a compilation error (see coding constraint 3 in Section 4.2).

Code Example 3 Mixed Code

If it is possible to code a program in either purely hierarchical or purely nested form, it is also possible to code it using a mixture of hierarchical and nested constructs. For example, the OPEN and READ statements at the beginning of the above nested COBOL program could be placed into a separate paragraph and PERFORMed, as in the hierarchical example. In the same way, the OPEN and INPUT statements at the beginning of the above nested BASIC program could be placed into a separate subroutine and invoked by a GOSUB, as in the hierarchical BASIC example.

Code Example 4 Linear Code

Linear code avoids subroutines and nesting by using GOTOs instead.

BASIC:

```
010   OPEN "I", #1, "INV-FILE"
020   INPUT #1,...
030   IF EOF (1) GOTO 100
040   IF PAID.SW$ <> "1" GOTO 70
050   INPUT #1,...
060   GOTO 30
070   LET UNPAID.TOT=UNPAID.TOT+INVOICE.AMOUNT
080   INPUT #1,...
090   GOTO 30
100   PRINT UNPAID.TOT
110   CLOSE #1
120   END
```

COBOL:

```
PROCEDURE DIVISION.
P-INVOICE-FILE-MAIN SECTION.
P-INVOICE-FILE.
  OPEN INPUT INVOICE-FILE.
  READ INVOICE-FILE AT END MOVE '1' TO EOF-SW.
P-INVOICE-REC.
  IF EOF-SW = '1'
    GO TO PROG-END.
P-PAID.
  IF PAID-SW NOT = '1'
    GO TO P-NOT-PAID.
  READ INVOICE-FILE AT END MOVE '1' TO EOF-SW.
  GO TO P-INVOICE-REC.
P-NOT-PAID.
  ADD INVOICE-AMOUNT TO UNPAID-TOT.
  READ INVOICE-FILE AT END MOVE '1' TO EOF-SW.
  GO TO P-INVOICE-REC.
PROG-END.
  DISPLAY UNPAID-TOT.
  CLOSE INVOICE-FILE.
  STOP RUN.
```

In languages lacking the necessary selection and iteration constructs (e.g. Assembler and some versions of BASIC), it is sometimes necessary to use linear code. Otherwise, with the lessons learned from structured programming (see Section 1.1), there is absolutely no justification for adopting linear code as a vehicle for the writing, understanding and maintaining of programs. As to whether hierarchical code, nested code or a combination of the two should be adopted, Section 4.2 following will discuss some of the problems associated with each and Section 4.3 will make some comparisons and suggestions for standardization.

4.2 CODING CONSTRAINTS

The ideal solution to the problem of transforming a program structure diagram into standard source code is to use an automated JSP diagrammer and code generator. Without such utilities current programming languages make a standardized approach to coding difficult to achieve in practice. Not only is there a variety of ways of coding any program, but programming languages often place constraints on what the programmer would like to code. This section outlines some of the constraints imposed by current programming languages, particularly COBOL. While reading it, consider the coding constraints imposed by any other language with which you are familiar.

Coding Constraint 1 The Nested Selection Constraint

In the previous section a sample program was coded in a variety of ways, including hierarchical and nested versions, but sometimes COBOL leaves the programmer with no choice as to whether to nest or not. Consider the following procedure.

A date record (DATE-REC) contains a date field (INDATE) which is to be validated. INDATE is in DDMMYY format, i.e. two characters day (INDD), two characters month (INMM), two characters year (INVY). Error messages are to be output for a non-numeric date or an out-of-range day or month.

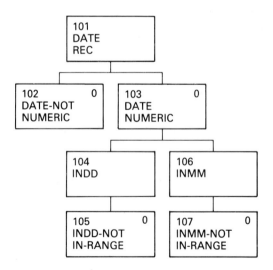

Figure 4.2

Step 1   Draw a data structure diagram of the date record (see Fig. 4.2).

Step 2   Form a program structure diagram (see Fig. 4.3).

Step 3.1   List and allocate operations (see Fig. 4.3).

For the purposes of this example, only operations pertaining to validation processing need be considered.

    1   Output 'DATE NOT NUMERIC'.
    2   Output 'DAY OUT OF RANGE'.
    3   Output 'MONTH OUT OF RANGE'.

Step 3.2   List and allocate conditions (see Fig. 4.3).

    C1   INDATE numeric.
    C2   INDD < 1 OR > 31.
    C3   INMM < 1 OR > 12.

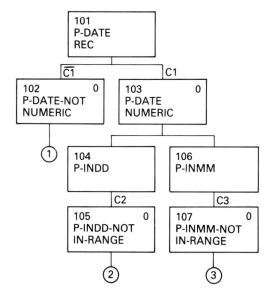

Figure 4.3

The program is now ready to code, but any attempt to reflect the nesting of selections in the diagram by nested COBOL code will prove impossible, e.g.

```
LINE 1    P-INDATE.
LINE 2      IF INDATE NOT NUMERIC
LINE 3        DISPLAY 'DATE NOT NUMERIC'
LINE 4      ELSE
LINE 5        IF INDD < 1 OR > 31
LINE 6          DISPLAY 'DAY OUT OF RANGE'
LINE 7        IF INMM < 1 OR > 12
LINE 8          DISPLAY 'MONTH OUT OF RANGE'
```

The IF statements on lines 5 and 7 should be dependent on the ELSE statement on line 4 and independent of each other, but this is not the case. The IF statement on line 7 will be executed only if the condition on line 5 is true. Just because line 7 has not been indented does not mean that it is not dependent upon line 5. Indentation may be an aid to programmer understanding, but it has no meaning to a COBOL compiler and in this case is misleading.

If a period is appended to line 6 in order to make line 7 independent of line 5, then line 7 will no longer be dependent on the ELSE statement in line 4. The fact that it is indented may imply dependency to the human reader, but not to the COBOL compiler.

In COBOL 68 and COBOL 74 there is no way to end a nested IF statement (line 5) without also ending any IF/ELSE statement (line 4) upon which it is dependent. COBOL 85 rectifies this deficiency by introducing the END-IF statement to delimit a condition, enabling the following to be coded.

```
P-IN-DATE.
  IF INDATE NOT NUMERIC
    DISPLAY 'DATE NOT NUMERIC'
  ELSE
    IF INDD < 1 OR > 31
      DISPLAY 'DAY OUT OF RANGE'
    END-IF
    IF INMM < 1 OR > 12
      DISPLAY 'MONTH OUT OF RANGE'
    END-IF
  END-IF.
```

Without COBOL 85 it is necessary to introduce elements of hierarchical or linear code to solve the problem. One hierarchical solution is to code Lines 5 to 9 as two independent IF statements in a separate paragraph, then PERFORM that paragraph from P-INDATE. One linear solution is to code Lines 5 to 9 as two independent IF statements within P-INDATE and replace the ELSE statement by a GOTO which branches round them to the end of P-INDATE paragraph.

Some versions of BASIC do not allow nested selection at all.

Coding Constraint 2 The Nested Iteration Constraint

If a selection can only *sometimes* be transformed into nested code in COBOL 68 and COBOL 74, an iteration can never be transformed into nested code. The iteration construct in COBOL is a hierarchical one—the PERFORM... UNTIL... statement, which involves the invocation of a lower-level subroutine/paragraph (see code example 1 in Section 4.1). COBOL 85 introduces an in-line iteration, using the construct PERFORM ... END-PERFORM (see code example 2 in Section 4.1), but without COBOL 85 iterations cannot be respresented by nested code.

Some versions of BASIC do not allow iterations to be coded in either nested or hierarchical form, only in linear form.

Coding Constraint 3 The COBOL Conditional Read Constraint

A conditional READ statement is a READ statement which occurs within an IF... ELSE... construct, as in code example 2 in Section 4.1. The COBOL compiler cannot handle a conditional READ statement because of the additional complication of dealing with the conditional AT END clause, and so the conditional READ would cause a syntax error. The solution is to use elements of hierarchical or linear code, as in code examples 1 and 3 in Section 4.1.

Another solution would be to allocate the READ operation to the end of the selection component P-INVOICE-REC rather than to the selected components P-PAID and P-UNPAID. This would require the introduction of additional components P-INVOICE-REC-BODY and P-INVOICE-REC-END, in a manner similar to the solution given for Example 3.4.1 (see Fig. 3.20). Such a solution avoids the conditional READ problem, but coding considerations should not be allowed to affect design in this way—program design should be based on data structure, not on source language constraints.

Coding Constraint 4 The Backtracking Constraint

Backtracking is a JSP technique which cannot be coded in any existing third-generation language in either hierarchical or nested form. The backtracking elements of a program structure diagram can be transformed only into linear code (see Chapter 7).

Coding Constraint 5 The Inversion Constraint

Inversion is a JSP technique which, like backtracking, can be coded only in a linear manner, unless the source language contains a suitable CASE-like statement, e.g. Pascal's CASE statement or COBOL 85's EVALUATE statement (see Chapter 8).

4.3 PROGRAM DESIGN LANGUAGES

Following on from the discussions in Sections 4.1 and 4.2 on the problems of transforming a program structure diagram into source code, a number of observations can be made.

1 The transformation process should be standardized and require no intellectual effort. If possible it should be automated.

2 In order to effect this a set of standardized transformation rules must be adopted. These rules will determine whether hierarchical code, nested code, linear code or mixed code is to be used. Of these, linear code can be dismissed immediately as an option, using all the arguments which structured programming has given us against the GOTO.

Mixed code can be similarly dismissed. If a mixture of code is to be used, then it requires time and effort to determine the specific mixture required for any one program; moreover, different programmers may mix hierarchical and nested code in different ways, making it more difficult to understand programs written by others. The results of mixed coding are variable, unpredictable and incapable of automation.

In order to effect standardization of coding the conclusion is inescapable: programs should be coded in *pure* hierarchical or *pure* nested form. Any other approach would be arbitrary, unsatisfactory and/or unpredictable.

3 The program text should mirror the structure and content of the program structure diagram. Only in this way will the program text be understandable and maintainable; good design work must not be ruined by poor coding. All program components and their structural relationships should be shown in the text, either by the way they are listed, named and numbered in hierarchical code, or by identation and comments in nested code. In the examples of nested BASIC and COBOL code in Section 4.1 comments could be inserted to name all program components. All

operations and conditions on the diagram must be shown in the text, directly related to an appropriate program component. The code should be no more and no less than a direct textual representation of the designed program.

Some programmers may object to the hierarchical examples as being over-modularized, but this objection arises from viewing the program as the product of a traditional flowcharted design. If the code is viewed simply as a textual representation of a program structure diagram, then the fact that every program component in the diagram has a corresponding label in the text enables the text to mirror the program structure diagram exactly and in practice aids comprehension of the program. The problem for the programmer is one of psychological set; he is used to seeing things in a certain way and may fall into the trap of rejecting anything which does not fit in with that way.

Some COBOL programmers may also object to the nested example because, among other things, they are used to seeing hierarchical PERFORMS and have been taught that modularizing code into paragraphs is a good thing. The problem is again one of psychological set. The tradition of hierarchical PERFORMs has arisen because of the lack of a nested PERFORM in the language. The code is in fact still modularized, but the modularization is shown by indentation rather than by out-of-line paragraphs.

4 When coding a program we should not be constrained by the idiosyncrasies of any programming language. Having decided on a standardized representation of a program structure diagram in either hierarchical or nested code, we must not be led astray by language difficulties. The language into which a correctly designed program is transformed (the 'target' language) must not be allowed to influence either the design of the program or the structure of the textual representation of that design. A language is the servant not the master of design; it is merely a means of transforming a design into machine-readable form. The correct, logical design of a program must not be altered by ensuing coding constraints.

But current programming languages do cause coding problems, as was noted in the preceding section, and to overcome these it is preferable to code programs not in a third-generation language at all but in a language which enables a direct textual representation of the

designed program to be made. Such a language is known as a Program
Design Language (PDL). The program structure diagram is coded in a
PDL, the PDL is transformed into source code, and then the source code
is compiled into object code. In other words, into the traditional
transformation process shown in Fig. 4.1 is inserted a further intermediate stage (see Fig. 4.4).

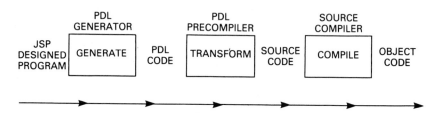

Figure 4.4

At first sight the use of a PDL may seem to be merely an extra
complication, but in reality it saves much time and effort. As an analogy,
compare the position of a COBOL programmer today with the position of
an Assembler programmer some twenty years ago, just after the new
language COBOL had appeared on the scene. The Assembler programmer
was suddenly faced with a language which could represent his program
design much more clearly and directly than the machine-oriented code
which he was accustomed to writing.

   To the objection that COBOL had to be compiled into Assembler code
anyway, making the introduction of COBOL merely an extra step between
program design and the production of object code, the COBOL programmer could reply that the transformation of COBOL code into Assembler
code required no intellectual effort and could be done automatically,
using a COBOL compiler.

   To the objection that the Assembler code produced by the COBOL
compiler was unreadable, unmaintainable and anathema to any self-
respecting Assembler programmer, the COBOL programmer could reply
that this was irrelevant as it was no longer necessary to look at the
Assembler code—all development and maintenance would be done in
COBOL. COBOL would take over from Assembler as the working language.
Today, of course, COBOL has become the most widely-used language in
DP and most modern COBOL compilers bypass the production of
Assembler code and produce object code directly.

To the objection that Assembler programming skills would be made obsolete, the COBOL programmer could reply that better tools and techniques must always be welcomed, no matter how reluctant we are to replace one set of skills by another.

Now consider the position of a COBOL programmer of today, faced with the introduction of a PDL. To the objection that the PDL has to be compiled into COBOL anyway, making the introduction of the PDL merely an extra step in the compilation process, the PDL programmer can reply that the transformation of PDL code into COBOL code can be standardized or done automatically, using a PDL precompiler.

To the objection that the COBOL code produced by the PDL compiler may be unreadable, unmaintainable and anathema to any self-respecting COBOL programmer, the PDL programmer can reply that this is irrelevant as it is no longer necessary to look at the COBOL code—the PDL will take over from COBOL as a higher-level working language.

To the objection that COBOL programming skills will be made obsolete, the PDL programmer can reply that better tools and techniques must always be welcomed. In any case, the PDL programmer must still code Identification, Environment and Data Divisions as per normal, and all Procedure Division operations and conditions as per normal. All that is different about the PDL is that it contains structural constructs which enable the coding constraints discussed in the preceding section to be ignored. It enables the programmer to structure the program text as he wishes to structure it and not as existing third-generation languages would force him to structure it because of their inadequate structural constructs.

The use of a PDL and a PDL precompiler is discussed further in Section 4.4 following the presentation of the PDL advocated in this manual.

4.4 HOST

If it is necessary to introduce a PDL in order to overcome the dificiencies of current programming languages, it must be decided whether the PDL is to have a nested structure of a hierarchical structure. Jackson uses a nested PDL which was called Schematic Logic in his book *Principles of Program Design* [12] and is now called Structure Text. This manual advocates a hierarchical PDL called HOST (Hierarchically Organized Structured Text), as used in PROBENCH.

The rules for converting a program structure diagram with allocated operations and conditions into HOST or Structure Text are listed in Appendix D (Section 1, rules 1.1 to 1.5), for ease of future reference. Read this section before continuing.

Briefly, a sequence is represented in HOST by a DO... statement, a selection by a DO... IF... statement and an iteration by a DO... UNTIL... statement. Applying these transformation rules to Example 3.3.2, for which several sample codings were presented in Section 4.1, produces the following HOST program:

```
101-P-INVOICE-FILE.
    Do 102-PROG-START.
    Do 103-PROG-BODY.
    Do 107-PROG-END.
102-PROG-START.
    Open invoice file.
    Read record from invoice file.
103-PROG-BODY ITER.
    Do 104-P-INVOICE-REC until (end of invoice file).
104-P-INVOICE-REC SEL.
    Do 105-P-PAID if (PAID-SW = '1').
    Do 106-P-NOT-PAID if (NOT PAID-SW = '1').
105-P-PAID.
    Read record from invoice file.
106-P-NOT-PAID.
    Add invoice amount to unpaid total.
    Read record from invoice file.
107-PROG-END.
    Output unpaid total.
    Close invoice file.
```

For comparison purposes, here is the Structure Text for the same program:

```
P-INVOICE-FILE seq
    PROG-START seq
        Open invoice file;
        Read record from invoice file;
    PROG-START end
    PROG-BODY itr while not end of invoice file
        P-INVOICE-REC select PAID-SW = '1'
            P-PAID seq
                Read record from invoice file;
            P-PAID end
        P-INVOICE-REC alt NOT PAID-SW = '1'
            P-UNPAID seq
                Add invoice amount to unpaid total;
                Read record from invoice file;
            P-UNPAID end
        P-INVOICE-REC end
```

```
PROG-BODY end
PROG-END seq
    Output unpaid total;
    Close invoice file;
PROG-END end
P-INVOICE-FILE end
```

Note that the source language instruction which terminates program execution (e.g. STOP RUN in COBOL, END in BASIC) can be taken as being implicit in the HOST and Structure Text. Among other advantages this facilitates flexibility of implementation when inversion is used (see Section 8.2).

It is suggested that a hierarchical PDL such as HOST has a number of advantages over a nested PDL such as Structure Text.

Advantages of a hierarchical PDL over a nested PDL

—COBOL is the main language used in DP programming, and a COBOL programmer's psychological set is towards discrete named paragraphs. HOST is in keeping with this psychological set and the COBOL programmer will find moving to it a trivial transition.

—The transformation of a program structure diagram into HOST is simpler than into Structure Text—it is not necessary to use indentation, to specify *end* constructs or to repeat component labels.

—HOST is less verbose than Structure Text because it does not use *end* constructs or repeat component labels.

—HOST more closely reflects the program structure diagram in that each program component name becomes a single paragraph name, always starting in the same column. In Structure Text program component names are less easily distinguished because of *end* constructs and indentation.

—Some program structure diagrams become too large to fit a single page (see Appendix E), and then they must be dismembered into a hierarchy of two or more parts. It would seem desirable to reflect this dismemberment in the PDL, which would require the introduction into nested Structure Text of a hierarchical component.

—Because a page has a finite width whereas levels of nesting (and hence indentation margins) are infinite, there may not be enough room at deeply indented levels of a nested PDL to specify operations on a single line. The solution is either to reduce indentation margins (which cannot be a universal solution) or more generally to split operations over two lines. Neither solution is desirable. HOST does not use indentation and presents no such problems.

—It is easier to number components meaningfully in hierarchical code and so tie them to boxes on a structure diagram.

—Experiments in software psychology [20] have cast doubts on the benefits of nesting and indentation. It has been found, for instance, that deeply nested conditional statements are difficult to follow and that indentation actively disrupts the visual scanning of program text.

For these reasons this manual advocates HOST as the recommended PDL for the transformation of program structure diagrams into source code. The structure of HOST code so exactly reflects the structure of a program structure diagram that with a minimum of practice it soon becomes easier to work with than a more arbitrarily structured third-generation language. As a further example, here is the HOST code for Example 1.2.1 (repeated as Example 3.4.2):

```
101-P-TRANS-FILE.
    Do 102-PROG-START.
    Do 103-PROG-BODY.
    Do 113-PROG-END.
102-PROG-START.
    Open transactions file.
    Read record from transactions file.
103-PROG-BODY ITER.
    Do 104-P-CUST until (file trailer).
104-P-CUST.
    Do 105-P-CUST-START.
    Do 106-P-CUST-BODY.
105-P-CUST-START.
    Move customer number to current customer number.
106-P-CUST-BODY-ITER.
    Do 107-P-ACCOUNT until ((file trailer)
        or (customer number not = current customer number)).
107-P-ACCOUNT.
    Do 108-P-ACCOUNT-START.
    Do 109-P-ACCOUNT-BODY.
```

108-P-ACCOUNT-START.
   Move account number to current account number.
   Read record from transactions file.
109-P-ACCOUNT-BODY ITER.
   Do 110-P-TRANS until ((file trailer)
      or (customer number not = current customer number)
      or (account number not = current account number)).
110-P-TRANS SEL.
   Do 111-P-DEPOSIT if (deposit).
   Do 112-P-WITHDRAW if (not deposit).
111-P-DEPOSIT.
   Add transaction amount to deposit total.
   Read record from transactions file.
112-P-WITHDRAW.
   Add transaction amount to withdrawal total.
   Read record from transactions file.
113-PROG-END.
   Output deposit total and withdrawal total.
   Close transactions file.

The coding of a HOST program from a program structure diagram is a facile exercise. Program components are listed in component number sequence; each component is represented by its name followed by the operations or invocations of sub-components (using the various Do constructs) which belong to it.

The transformation of HOST into linear source code is also straighforward even if it must be hand-coded. For ease of future reference rules for the (automated) transformation of HOST into BASIC and COBOL source code are listed in Appendix D (Section 2, rules 2.1 to 2.4). Read this section before continuing.

Applying these transformation rules to the HOST program for Example 3.3.2 will produce the following source programs:

BASIC:

```
100   REM P-TRANS-FILE
110   GOTO 200
120   GOTO 300
130   GOTO 700
140   END
200   REM PROG-START
210   OPEN "I", #1, "INV-FILE"
220   INPUT #1, . . .
230   GOTO 120
300   REM PROG-BODY
```

```
310   IF NOT EOF (1) GOTO 400
320   GOTO 130
400   REM P-INVOICE-REC
410   IF PAID.SW$ = "1" GOTO 500
420   IF NOT PAID.SW$ = "1" GOTO 600
430   GOTO 300
500   REM P-PAID
510   INPUT #1, . . .
520   GOTO 430
600   REM P-UNPAID
610   LET UNPAID.TOT = UNPAID.TOT + INVOICE.AMOUNT
620   INPUT #1, . . .
630   GOTO 430
700   REM PROG-END
710   PRINT UNPAID.TOT
720   CLOSE #1
730   GOTO 140
```

COBOL:

```
    PROCEDURE DIVISION.
    101-P-INVOICE-FILE-MAIN SECTION.
    101-P-INVOICE-FILE.
        GO TO 102-PROG-START.
    102-PROG-START-EXIT.
        GO TO 103-PROG-BODY.
    103-PROG-BODY-EXIT.
        GO TO 107-PROG-END.
    107-PROG-END-EXIT.
        STOP RUN.
    102-PROG-START.
        OPEN INPUT INVOICE-FILE.
        READ INVOICE-FILE AT END MOVE '1' TO EOF-SW.
        GO TO 102-PROG-START-EXIT.
    103-PROG-BODY.
    *ITER
    104-P-INVOICE-REC-EXIT.
        IF NOT (EOF-SW = '1')
           GO TO 104-P-INVOICE-REC.
        GO TO 103-PROG-BODY-EXIT.
    104-P-INVOICE-REC.
    *SELECT
      IF (PAID-SW = '1')
         GO TO 105-P-PAID.
      IF (NOT PAID-SW = '1')
         GO TO 106-P-NOT-PAID.
    105-P-PAID-EXIT.
    106-P-NOT-PAID-EXIT.
        GO TO 104-P-INVOICE-REC-EXIT.
    105-P-PAID.
        READ INVOICE-FILE AT END MOVE '1' TO EOF-SW.
        GO TO 105-P-PAID-EXIT.
```

```
106-P-NOT-PAID.
    ADD INVOICE-AMOUNT TO UNPAID-TOT.
    READ INVOICE-FILE AT END MOVE '1' TO EOF-SW.
    GO TO 106-P-NOT-PAID-EXIT.
107-PROG-END.
    DISPLAY UNPAID-TOT.
    CLOSE INVOICE-FILE.
    GO TO 107-PROG-END-EXIT.
```

Both source programs are verbose, full of GOTOs, inelegant and difficult to follow, but these issues are irrelevant. The one relevant issue is that their production from HOST is standard and capable of automation. The only time it is necessary to examine a source code listing is to clarify compiler error messages arising from language errors in the specification of operations and conditions. Otherwise HOST takes over from the source code as the working language; the fact that the source code produced from HOST contains GOTOs is as irrelevant as the fact that the Assembler produced from COBOL may contain GOTOs. If you remain unconvinced by this crucial point, reread the earlier sections of this chapter. Do not equate the use of GOTOs in generated BASIC, COBOL and Assembler with a lack of structure in the program design or the HOST code.

Note that although HOST becomes the working language, all debugging and maintenance in JSP is most easily done at the program structure level. First amend the diagram, then amend the HOST code, otherwise the diagram becomes out-of-date and loses its usefulness as a maintenance and documentation aid. An automated JSP diagrammer and code generator overcome these problems, making an intermediate PDL superfluous.

It could be argued that the program structure diagram for Example 3.3.2 could easily be transformed directly into hierarchical source code without going through the intermediate stage of HOST, or that the automated transformation rules listed in Appendix D could transform HOST into hierarchical source code by generating BASIC GOSUB and COBOL PERFORM statements. This is indeed the case, but it cannot be a general solution because the JSP techniques of backtracking and inversion can be coded only as *linear* code.

Note that in languages with a suitable CASE-like statement it is possible to code inversion in hierarchical or nested form, but backtracking still requires linear code—see Chapters 7 and 8. If backtracking and inversion are avoided, using techniques such as those presented in

Sections 7.1 and 5.5, then linear source code can also be avoided, but many of the benefits of JSP will be lost.

Coding in HOST is a universal solution enabling a standard transformation of program structure diagrams into source code. It is also language independent in that operations and conditions do not have to be specified in any particular language; all that would be required to compile the above HOST code into linear Pascal code, for example, would be a different set of transformation rules.

An objection sometimes raised is that it is all very well to work in a PDL if you have a PDL precompiler, but most JSP installations which would like to use JSP do not possess one. Therefore source code must be hand-compiled from the PDL, and that is one more stage where errors may creep in. Moreover, in such a situation it would be very tempting to use the source code for maintenance rather than the HOST code, and the source code is patently unmaintainable.

This is a serious objection, and it is certainly true that if the PDL must be hand-compiled then some of the benefits of the JSP design method will be lost. The programmer who does not have access to a PDL precompiler must adopt one of three strategies:

1 Learn to hand-compile HOST. This is a trivial task involving the application of very simple rules and is easily mastered. Refrain from maintaining the source code; amend the program structure diagram and the HOST code and re-compile into source code.

2 Despite what has been said above about the benefits of using a PDL, ignore HOST and hand-code the program structure diagram directly into linear source code, thereby omitting the intermediate step of hand-coding HOST. Refrain from maintaining the source code; amend the program structure diagram and recode it.

3 Ignore HOST and hand-code the program structure diagram directly into nested or hierarchical source code which is maintainable. In order to do this some non-JSP design will be required to replace backtracking (see Section 7.1) and inversion (see Section 5.5).

None of these strategies will reap all the benefits of JSP, but any is far better than not using JSP at all. There is no reason, however, why a PDL precompiler should not be used. There are a number of very good PDL precompilers available (e.g. MJSL's JSP-COBOL and SCML's PROBENCH), and it is in any case a simple matter to write a simple PDL precompiler. Compiler complexity arises from the variety of source statements which must be recognised and processed, but a basic PDL precompiler has to recognise only sequence, selection and iteration constructs and transform them into appropriate source language statements; all operations pass through untouched to the source language compiler.

The rules for the transformation of DO... , DO... IF... and DO... UNTIL... statements into linear BASIC and COBOL code are given in Appendix D, and the development of a HOST precompiler which applies them is a simple matter and a worthwhile investment. A HOST program provides a direct and obvious textual representation of a program structure diagram and is very easy to read, understand and maintain, especially for a programmer who is accustomed to coding using hierarchical constructs such as those in COBOL.

4.5 TESTING

The implications of JSP for coding practice are considerable, and the same is true of testing. It was noted in Chapter 1 that user experience of JSP shows that JSP-designed programs commonly require less testing because they are more likely to be correct. This fact should dispel once and for all the myth that it is better to ignore design and begin coding straightaway so that more time can be devoted to testing.

Moreover, data and program structure diagrams are very useful aids to the derivation of test cases and enable test data to be designed in a less haphazard fashion than is normal in DP. To many programmers the very idea that test data should be designed is a novel one, but it is precisely the lack of a methodical and standardized approach to testing that is a major reason why most bugs are not detected until after a program has gone live.

The problem of testing is basically one of sampling. If it were possible to test a program with every possible input stream then all bugs could be found, and every live run would be no more than a subset of the test run. But such 'all-input' testing is a physical impossibility. Beizer [2] has estimated that even a facile program which processes a ten-character input string would take four times the current estimated age of the universe to test, if all possible input strings were to be input.

The problem is therefore one of condensing test input into manageable amounts while losing as little of the total data coverage of the all-input test as possible. If this process is left to the imagination of the programmer then testing becomes subjective and piecemeal, with no guarantee that it is serving any useful purpose.

The situation is complicated by the very nature of testing. The aim of program design is constructive—to produce a correct program. The aim of program testing is destructive—to find errors; it is unrealistic to expect the programmer to approach this task with the same degree of motivation and thoroughness with which he approaches other tasks in the program development process. One solution to the motivational problem is to have another programmer test the program, but the only answer to the subjective nature of testing is to adopt a more objective approach to test data design, and this is where JSP has much to offer.

The methodical sampling of all-input test data in order to condense it into manageable amounts can be approached from two angles: black-box testing and white-box testing. Black-box testing approaches testing from the point of view of the program's function; it ignores the structural design of the program, treating it as a black-box, and bases test data on an examination of the program's functional specification. Black-box testing asks the question: what test data is required to verify that the program performs its required functions?

One entirely objective approach to black-box testing is to design test data using sampling theory: define the range of all possible input data then use a random number generator to obtain random samples. This approach has the advantage of being capable of automation, but it is limited by its very randomness, which means that important test cases may be omitted.

The fact that some test cases are more important than others is evident from any analysis of program errors: many errors occur just below, at or just above the boundary values of variables and iterated data components. For example, if the input variable Account Number has a range of values 1 to 999998, then 1 and 999998 are its boundary values. From a testing point of view values 2 to 999997 form what is known as an equivalence class—any single value in this range can be considered equivalent to any other, and one test case will suffice to test all of them.

The derivation of test cases for Account Number therefore proceeds by boundary value analysis (derive test cases to exercise boundaries) and equivalence partitioning (derive a test case to exercise the equivalence class). Boundary value analysis derives the test cases: 0 (just below lower boundary), 1 (at lower boundary), 999998 (at upper boundary) and 999999 (just above upper boundary). Test cases 0 and 999999 will be valid only if values outside the permitted range are allowable input to the program. Equivalence partitioning derives a test case for the equivalence class 2 to 999997, e.g. 123456. Ideally this test case will be derived using a random number generator.

If an input string is 1 to 10 characters long, boundary value analysis derives the test cases: 0 characters, 1 character, 10 characters and 11 characters. Equivalence partitioning derives a test case for the equivalence class 2 to 9 characters, e.g. 7 characters.

Boundary value analysis and equivalence partitioning should also be conducted on output variables as well as on input variables. For example, if the output variable Cost is the product of input variables Quantity and Price, then the boundaries of Cost should be exercised by a minimum Quantity and a minimum Price input together, and a maximum Quantity and a maximum Price input together.

Sometimes one derived test case will duplicate another, and then the duplicate can be ignored. For example, the equivalence class for Cost in the foregoing example will be exercised by the equivalence classes for Quantity and Price. If Cost is the product of an input Quantity and a Fixed Price, then all test cases for Cost will duplicate those for Quantity.

If a variable has no equivalence class, then every one of its possible values must be tested. For example, if Update Type has the value 'A', 'D' or 'I' (as in Example 5.4.2) then it will require three test cases; boundary value analysis and equivalence partitioning are applicable only to value ranges.

The boundaries of an iterated data component, i.e. the first iteration and the last iteration, should also be exercised by test data. Boundary value analysis derives the test cases: 0 times (just below the boundary), 1 time (at lower boundary) and last (of many) times (at upper boundary). Just above the upper boundary has no meaning for an iterated component. The upper boundary test case also normally duplicates the equivalence class for an iteration, which is any number of times other than 0 or 1.

As with variables, it is important to exercise output as well as input iterated data component boundaries. For example, if a paged report is to be output from a program (see Fig. 9.11), the iteration of output data component Page should be tested by 0 pages (i.e. a blank report, if possible), 1 page and many pages. The iteration of lines on a page should be tested by 0 lines (if possible), 1 line, maximum number of lines (upper boundary) and any number between 1 and the maximum (i.e. the equivalence class). Note that the maximum number and equivalence class test cases have meaning only if a component is iterated a fixed number of times (e.g. 20 lines per page).

Note that the test cases derived from boundary value analysis may require programmer interpretation to determine their validity, e.g. an out-of-range value for a variable may not be a valid test case, a 0 times value for an iteration will not be a valid test case if the component is iterated a fixed number of times. Complete objectivity in black-box testing is therefore difficult to achieve, but boundary value analysis and equivalence partitioning are far more objective, thorough and superior approaches to the design of test data than intuition and imagination.

As black-box testing derives test data from an examination of the program's functional specification, one would not expect a program design method to offer much help in this area. JSP, however, bases program design on data structure, and iterated data components whose boundaries are to be exercised are shown explicitly on data structure diagrams. JSP therefore aids the identification of iterations which may be only implicit in the program specification and thereby not tested (e.g. see the difference between the JSP and non-JSP designs for Example 1.2.1 in Section 1.2).

Black-box test cases for Examples 3.3.2, 3.4.1 and 3.4.3 are given below.

White-box testing approaches testing from the point of view of the program's structure; it ignores the functional specification of the program and bases test data on an examination of the logic flow. White-box testing asks the question: what test data is required to ensure that every logical path through the program is executed?

An ancillary question concerns the numer of times an iterated path should be executed in order to verify it. Is it sufficient to execute an iterated path once, or should it be executed two or more times, in order to ensure that it can be re-entered as well as entered? The simplest approach to white-box testing is minimal-path testing, in which each path is executed once only.

One could reasonably expect a program design method to have much to offer to aid white-box testing, and this is certainly true of JSP. If a program is composed of only the logical constructs sequence, selection and iteration, then the number of paths through the program is determined by the number of selections and iterations. Every time a two-way selection occurs the logic flow divides into two and two paths are created from one; every time an iteration occurs the logic flow also divides into two—it either goes into the iterated component or it does not. A JSP program structure diagram shows selections and iterations explicitly, and enables white-box testing to be undertaken easily in an objective and methodical manner.

In Example 3.3.2, for instance, the program structure diagram (see Fig. 3.18) contains one iteration and one two-way selection. There are therefore three paths through the program: the logic flow may go into P-INVOICE-REC or it may not, and if it does it goes into P-PAID or P-UNPAID. The algorithm for obtaining the number of paths is:

(2 × number of iterated components)
+(number of selected components)
−(number of iterated/selected components which have iterated/selected sub-components)

(Note that every one-way selection also has an additional null selected component—see Example 3.4.1 below).

Fig. 3.18 has one iterated component (2 paths) plus two selected components (2 paths) minus one iterated component which has selected sub-components (1 path). If the latter path was not removed there would be path duplication because the path which goes into the iterated component must of necessity go into one of the selected sub-components. The three paths are (using box numbers to represent the program components of Fig. 3.18):

1   101,102,103,107
2   101,102,103,104,105,107
3   101,102,103,104,106,107

The test data required to execute each path is obtained from an examination of the Input/Read operations allocated to the program components of each path, in conjuction with an examination of the input data structure(s) processed by the program. Here is the test data required to white-box test Example 3.3.2:

1 An empty file.
2 Paid record.
3 Unpaid record.

Test data for black-box testing:

Exercise iteration of P-INVOICE-REC:
  0 times (empty file).
  1 time (one invoice record).
  Many times (many invoice records).
Exercise field boundaries on invoice record.
Exercise output field boundaries:
  Unpaid total = 0 (all paid records).
  Unpaid total not = 0 (many unpaid records).

Duplication of derived test cases is discussed below.

In Example 3.4.1 the program structure diagram (see Fig. 3.20) contains one iterated component and four selected components (including the omitted null selected component beneath component 110); the iterated component has selected sub-components. There are therefore $(2 \times 1) + 4 - 1 = 5$ paths through the program:

1   101,102,103,109,110,112
2   101,102,103,109,110,111,112
3   101,102,103,109,110,null selected component,112
4   101,102,103,104,105,106,108,109,110,112
5   101,102,103,104,105,107,108,109,110,112

When one selection/iteration follows another, as in this example, it is possible to reduce the number of paths still further by combining them. Path 1, which does not enter component 104, is duplicated by and could be combined with path 3, which does not enter component 111. Or paths 2 and 3, which either enter selected component 111 or do not, could be combined with paths 4 and 5, which either enter component 106 or 107. The test data required to execute the five paths is:

1   File header, file trailer.
2   File header, bad file trailer.
3   File header, good file trailer.
4   File header, payment, file trailer.
5   File header, receipt, file trailer.

Test data for black-box testing:

Exercise iteration of P-CUST-REC:
   0 times (file header, file trailer).
   1 time (file header, one customer record, file trailer).
   Many times (file header, many customer records, file trailer).
Exercise field boundaries on input records.
Exercise output field:
   Warning message output (bad file trailer).
   Warning message not output (good file trailer).

In Example 3.4.3 the program structure diagram (see Fig. 3.23) contains two iterated components, one of which has an iterated sub-component. There are therefore $(2 \times 2) + 0 - 1 = 3$ paths through the program:

1   101,102,103,109
2   101,102,103,104,105,106,108,109
3   101,102,103,104,105,106,107,108,109

The test data required to execute these paths is:

1   File trailer.
2   Faculty header, faculty trailer, file trailer.
3   Faculty header, student record, faculty trailer, file trailer.

Test data for black-box testing;

Exercise iteration of P-FACULTY:
   0 times (file trailer).
   1 time (one faculty, file trailer).
   Many times (many faculties, file trailer).
Exercise iteration of P-STUDENT-REC:
   0 times (faculty header, faculty trailer).
   1 time (faculty header, one student record, faculty trailer).
   Many times (faculty header, many student records, faculty trailer).
Exercise field boundaries on input records.
Exercise output field boundaries:
   Faculty total = 0 (faculty header, faculty trailer).
   Faculty total not = 0 (faculty header, many student records, faculty trailer).
   File total = 0 (file trailer).
   File total not = 0 (many faculties, file trailer).

Additional Notes on White-box Testing

1 The path algorithm stated above is based on McCabe's measure of cyclomatic complexity [16], which ensures that every path through the program is tested at least once. Path testing is easily extended to test, for example, that an iterated component can be re-entered as well as entered correctly.

2 If the condition which determines entry to an iterated/selected component is a compound condition, path testing can be extended to generate a test case for each combination of conditions.

3 There are some iterations, called non-zero-based iterations, which must be performed a fixed number of times, and therefore non-entry to the iterated component is not a valid path. (Such iterations could be coded in BASIC using the FOR... NEXT... construct, and in COBOL using the PERFORM... *n* TIMES construct.)

4 In the above examples the number of paths could be derived from the input data structure diagram equally as well as from the program structure diagram, but this is not the case when the program processes two or more input data sets (see Chapter 5). Derive paths from the program structure diagram and examine Input/Read operations to derive test data.

5 When using backtracking (see Chapter 7) derive a path for every POSIT component plus a path for every QUIT condition.

6 When using inversion (see Chapter 8) make sure that path testing exercises every iterated/selected component in every procedure. The transformation of an inverted procedure into linear source code, if done correctly or automatically, does not generate any code which will not be tested by existing path testing.

When using JSP as an aid to test design there is much overlap between derived white-box and black-box test cases, because the testing of the boundaries of iterated data components (black-box) necessarily overlaps the testing of iterated progam paths (white-box). This follows from the fact that a JSP program structure is based on data structure, and only such a data-driven design method can aid the design of both black-box and white-box test data so greatly.

An ideal testing strategy must include both black-box and white-box testing as the overlap may not be complete; the former ensures that important data combinations are tested, the latter that every statement in a program is tested. White-box testing may not test the boundaries of a variable; black-box testing may treat as an equivalence class data which is processed in different ways (i.e. paths) or fail to test paths which result from the matching of data (see Section 5.4), among others. The only safe strategy is to derive both black-box and white-box test cases, optimize testing by dropping duplicate test cases and combining others where possible, then incorporate the remaining test cases into as few test runs as possible.

The methodical approach to testing advocated in this section is based on statistical and mathematical concepts such as sampling theory, boundary analysis and path analysis, and it is not possible to do more than skim the surface of such issues, suggest a simple application of black-box and white-box testing, and note the usefulness of JSP. As an exercise, consider the JSP and functional designs of Example 1.2.1 in section 1.2 and note how much more useful the JSP design is in the derivation of test data. Testing is an area of increasing research interest, and investigations into the automation of testing of JSP-designed programs (such as those at Napier Polytechnic, Edinburgh and Sunderland Polytechnic) promise much for the future. PROBENCH already contains a path generation module. For further reading interested readers should consult reference 2.

4.6 EXERCISES

Practise converting program structure diagrams into HOST and source code using any of the examples in Chapter 3.

Practise deriving test data using any of the examples in Chapter 3.

Chapter 5

Correspondence

Previous chapters have applied the JSP design procedure to simple programs which process single sequential data sets. This chapter extends the procedure to programs which process multiple sequential data sets. The program structure diagram for such programs must be formed from multiple data structure diagrams rather than a single one, and the correspondence technique is used to effect this. The special case of programs which match data sets is also discussed.

5.1 MULTIPLE DATA SETS

Chapter 3 introduced and illustrated the JSP design procedure with the design of programs which process a single sequential data set, whereas most DP programs process two or more data sets. The following programs, for example, all process two data sets:

A program which creates a copy of a file.
A program which sorts a file into a different sequence.
A program which produces a printed report of a file.
A program which validates a file and produces an error report.
A program which validates terminal input and produces an error report.
A program which updates a direct-access master file using update transactions input at a terminal.

The following programs all process three data sets:

A program which merges two files together to produce a third.
A program which produces a printed report of a file plus a managerial summary report.
A program which validates a file of input data, writes valid data to a valid file and reports invalid data on an error report.
A program which updates a sequential master file using a file of update transactions, producing an updated master file.
A program which validates terminal input, reports invalid data on an error report and uses valid data to update a direct-access master file.

Other programs process many more data sets, but in all cases the JSP design procedure remains the same. When a program processes a single data set, its program structure is formed from a single data structure. When a program processes multiple data sets its program structure must be formed from all their data structures; if it were not, there could be operations associated with a particular data set which could not be allocated to the program structure.

For example, if a program which merges INFILE1 with INFILE2 is based solely on the data structure of INFILE1 (ignoring the data structure of INFILE2), there will be no program component to which to allocate the operation 'Open INFILE2'. If a program which produces a report of INFILE1 is based solely on the data structure of INFILE1 (ignoring the data structure of the report), there will be no program component to which to allocate the operation 'Write printline'. To ensure that all operations can be allocated, all data structures processed by a program must be represented in the program structure.

There are two ways of forming a program structure from multiple data structures. One way is to keep the data structures separate, form a procedure structure for each and allocate operations and conditions to each in the normal manner, then link the procedures into a single program using the technique of *inversion*. Inversion is a very powerful technique with important ramifications, but it is a slightly heavy-handed solution to simple program design—judge for yourself once you have learned inversion (see Chapter 8).

The second way of forming a program structure from multiple data structures is to combine the data structures into a single program structure before allocating operations and conditions, using the *correspondence* technique. This involves searching for correspondences between the components of one data structure and the components of another; where a correspondence exists, the two data components can be subsumed into one program component. A correspondence exists between two data components when they occur:

1 The same number of times.
2 In the same order.
3 Under the same circumstances.

Corresponding data components are usually of the same component type, but this is not necessary (e.g. see Example 5.3.1).

The correspondence technique is only applicable if correspondences can be found; it is, therefore, a less general technique than inversion, but it is easier to learn and apply. Section 5.2 introduces correspondence using programs which process two sequential data sets, Section 5.3 considers programs which process three or more sequential data sets, and Section 5.4 programs which merge or match files. The limitations of the correspondence technique are discussed in Section 5.5. Direct access files and other data structures such as tables (arrays) and databases are discussed in Chapter 6.

The program design undertaken for all examples in this chapter will end at the production of a program structure diagram with allocated operations and conditions. The transformation of this into a program design language and source language code is a facile exercise requiring no additional rules to those presented in Chapter 4.

5.2 PROGRAMS WHICH PROCESS TWO DATA SETS

The simplest program which processes more than one data set is a program which creates a copy of a file. The correspondence technique is introduced using such a program in Example 5.2.1. Example 5.2.2 applies the technique to a program which produces a formatted report of a file.

Example 5.2.1

A program is required to create a copy of the file INFILE1; the copy is to be called INFILE2. INFILE1 contains only one record type (INREC1).

Step 1   Draw data structure diagrams of INFILE1 and INFILE2 (see Figs 5.1 and 5.2).

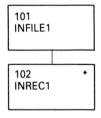

Figure 5.1

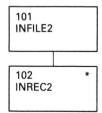

Figure 5.2

Step 2   Form a program structure diagram (see Fig. 5.5).

Using the correspondence technique a program structure is formed from a combination of the two data structure diagrams, by asking which data components in INFILE1 correspond with which data components in INFILE2.

In order for two data components to correspond they must meet each of the three rules of correspondence. They must occur the same number of times, in the same order and under the same circumstances. If any one of these three rules does not apply, there is no correspondence between the two data components. The data structures of INFILE1 and INFILE2 have two correspondences:

1 INFILE1 corresponds with INFILE2. Both are root components, and root components always correspond: they always occur the same number of times (i.e. once), in the same order and under the same circumstances (i.e. at the highest level of their respective data structure diagrams).

2 INREC1 corresponds with INREC2. INREC2s are formed from INREC1s, therefore they must occur the same number of times. INREC2s are not output in a different sequence, therefore they occur in the same order. And both are the children of parents which correspond, therefore they occur under the same circumstances.

To keep track of correspondence it may be of help to show them explicitly on data structure diagrams by using a correspondence number, and this manual will adopt the practice of annotating data components with a correspondence number to the right of the component number (see Figs 5.3 and 5.4).

To form a program structure diagram, data components which correspond are subsumed into the same program component. In the program structure diagram for this example (see Fig. 5.5) INFILE1 and INFILE2 are subsumed into program component COPY-INFILE1, and

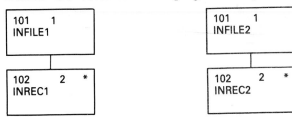

Figure 5.3   **Figure 5.4**

INREC1 and INREC2 are subsumed into program component COPY-INREC1. Note also the addition of components PROG-START, PROG-BODY and PROG-END, as usual, in anticipation of the allocation of operations.

The formation of the program structure diagram can be viewed as a superimposition of one data structure on another. If you can mentally raise one data structure from the page and overlay it on the other, the correspondences become obvious, and this is probably the strategy used by most experienced JSP programmers.

Step 3.1   List and allocate operations (see Fig. 5.5).

> 1 Open INFILE1.
> 2 Open INFILE2.
> 3 Close INFILE1.
> 4 Close INFILE2.
> 5 Read record from INFILE1.
> 6 Move INREC1 to INREC2.
> 7 Write INREC2 to INFILE2.

The operations list is straightforward, but make sure that you understand why each operation is required.

Step 3.2   List and allocate conditions (see Fig. 5.5).

> C1 End of INFILE1.

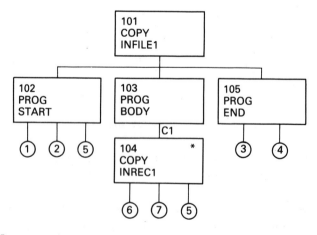

Figure 5.5

Example 5.2.2

An employee file contains employee records in department number/employee number sequence. A program is required to produce a report of employee records and provide at the end of each department a total of employees in the department. Report lines are allowed to flow over page perforations—no paging or heading is required.

Step 1   Draw data structure diagrams of the employee file and report (see Figs 5.6 and 5.7).

Note that from this example onwards correspondence numbers will be annotated at this step to avoid having to re-present them during Step 2.

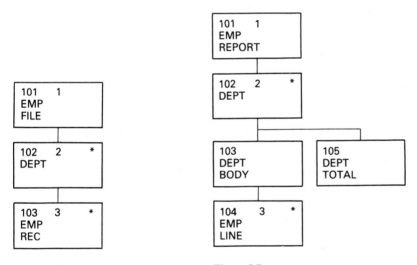

Figure 5.6   Figure 5.7

Step 2   Form a program structure diagram (see Fig. 5.8).

There are three correspondences between the two data structures.

1 EMP-FILE corresponds with EMP-REPORT. Both are root components of their respective data structures.

2 DEPT on EMP-FILE corresponds with DEPT on EMP-REPORT. Both occur the same number of times in the same order and both are children of parents which correspond.

3 EMP-REC corresponds with EMP-LINE. An EMP-LINE is formed from an EMP-REC, therefore they occur the same number of times in the same order, and both occur beneath components which correspond. The fact that on EMP-FILE an EMP-REC is the child of DEPT, whereas on EMP-REPORT an EMP-LINE is the grandchild of DEPT does not affect this correspondence. The presence of component DEPT-BODY on EMP-REPORT does not affect or determine the number of occurrences of EMP-LINE or its relative position in EMP-REPORT.

To form a program structure diagram, data components which correspond are subsumed into the same program component. In the program structure diagram for this example (see Fig. 5.8) EMP-FILE and EMP-REPORT are subsumed into program component P-EMP-PRINT, DEPT on EMP-FILE and DEPT on EMP-REPORT into program component P-DEPT, and EMP-REC and EMP-LINE into program component P-EMP-REC. The remaining data components DEPT-BODY and DEPT-TOTAL on EMP-REPORT are included in the program structure diagram in a position which maintains their structural relationship with the components of EMP-REPORT already included. They occur between DEPT and EMP-LINE on EMP-REPORT, therefore they are included between P-DEPT and P-EMP-REC on the program structure diagram, as program components P-DEPT-BODY and P-DEPT-END. In anticipation of allocation of operations, program component P-DEPT-START has been added along with PROG-START, PROG-BODY and PROG-END.

Try to picture how each data structure diagram is represented in this program structure diagram. The EMP-FILE data components EMP-FILE, DEPT and EMP-REC are represented by the program components P-EMP-PRINT, P-DEPT and P-EMP-REC. The presence of additional program components does not affect the fact that the EMP-FILE data structure diagram, with all its components and their structural relationships intact, is directly represented in the program structure diagram.

The EMP-REPORT data components EMP-REPORT, DEPT, DEPT-BODY, EMP-LINE and DEPT-TOTAL are represented by the program components P-EMP-PRINT, P-DEPT, P-DEPT-BODY, P-EMP-REC and P-DEPT-END. Again, the presence of additional program components does not affect the direct representation of the EMP-REPORT data structure diagram in the program structure diagram.

Try to obtain the program structure diagram by mentally superimposing one data structure diagram on the other. Mentally raise EMP-FILE from the page and lay it on top of EMP-REPORT, moving EMP-REC down over EMP-LINE to allow room for DEPT-BODY. Then add further components to allow the allocation of operations and the program structure diagram is complete.

Step 3.1   List and allocate operations (see Fig. 5.8).

1 Open employee file.
2 Open employee report.
3 Close employee file.
4 Close employee report.
5 Read record from employee file.
6 Format and write employee line.
7 Add 1 to department total.
8 Format and write department total line.
9 Set department total to 0.
10 Move department number to current department number.

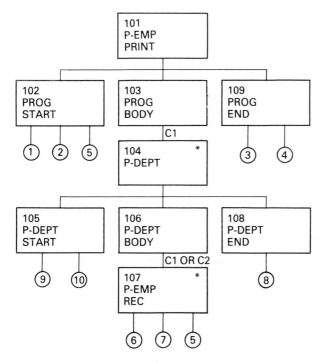

Figure 5.8

Step 3.1   List and allocate conditions (see Fig. 5.8).

       C1 End of employee file.

       C2 Department number not = current department number.

5.3 PROGRAMS WHICH PROCESS THREE DATA SETS

The correspondence technique is easily extended to cater for programs which process more than two data sets. This section presents one example of a program processing three data sets. It will be seen that the technique employed is the same as in the preceding section with one minor refinement, and one example will suffice to demonstrate this. The example also includes some elementary input validation and operations intended to improve the program's user-friendliness.

Example 5.3.1

A program is required to process bank transactions keyed in at a terminal. The program is to be menu-driven and the menu gives the user three options:

    1   Input a deposit.
    2   Input a withdrawal.
    9   Terminate program.

Deposits are to be written to a deposit file and withdrawals to a withdrawal file. Additionally, file trailers are to be appended to the deposit file and withdrawal file containing the total value of deposits and withdrawals respectively.

Step 1   Draw data structure diagrams of the input data stream and the deposit and withdrawal files (see Figs 5.9, 5.10 and 5.11).

Note the data component INVALID-OPTION which refers to all options other than 1, 2 and 9. Such a component is not specified in the data specification, which refers to valid data only, but enables the formation during Step 2 of a program component to which the outputting of an error message can be allocated.

Step 2   Form a program structure diagram (see Fig. 5.12).

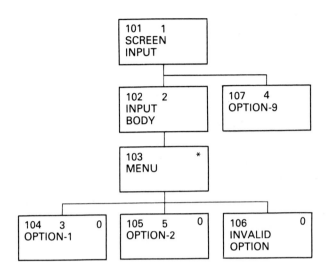

Figure 5.9

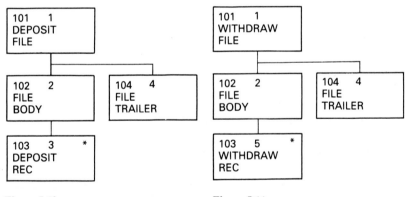

Figure 5.10   **Figure 5.11**

The correspondence technique for more than two data sets is as follows:

1 Note correspondence between any two data structures.

2 Note correspondences between a third data structure and the ones already examined. Repeat this step for fourth and remaining data structures.

3 Form a program structure from all the data structures using the correspondences noted.

To form a program structure for this example let us opt (arbitrarily) to examine the data structures SCREEN-INPUT and DEPOSIT-FILE first. There are four correspondences:

1 SCREEN-INPUT and DEPOSIT-FILE. Both are root components.
2 INPUT-BODY and FILE-BODY. Both are the major sub-components of root components which correspond.
3 OPTION-1 and DEPOSIT-REC. They are different types, but a DEPOSIT-REC is formed from OPTION-1 data and both occur the same number of times in the same order and under the same circumstances.
4 OPTION-9 and FILE-TRAILER. Both are the final sub-components of parents which correspond.

Next the third data structure WITHDRAW-FILE is examined, taking each component in turn and noting any correspondences between it and the other data structures.

1 WITHDRAW-FILE and SCREEN-INPUT and DEPOSIT-FILE.
2 FILE-BODY on WITHDRAW-FILE and INPUT-BODY and FILE-BODY on DEPOSIT-FILE.
4 FILE-TRAILER on WITHDRAW-FILE and OPTION-9 and FILE-TRAILER on DEPOSIT-FILE.
5 WITHDRAW-REC and OPTION-2.

None of these correspondences should require further explanation, but note the numbering. The re-use of numbers (1), (2) and (4) indicates a further component having the same correspondence, the non-use of (3) indicates no further component having that correspondence, the use of (5) indicates a new correspondence.

Note that it makes no difference which two data sets are chosen for initial correspondences; as the final program structure diagram includes all data structures, the result will always be the same.

Step 3.1   List and allocate operations (see Fig. 5.12).

      1 Open all files.
      2 Close all files.

  3 Output user instructions.
  4 Output menu.
  5 Input option.
  6 Output 'INVALID OPTION, PLEASE RE-ENTER'.
  7 Input deposit data.
  8 Input withdrawal data.
  9 Write deposit record from deposit data.
10 Write withdrawal record from withdrawal data.
11 Add 1 to deposit total.
12 Add 1 to withdrawal total.
13 Write deposit file trailer using deposit total.
14 Write withdrawal file trailer using withdrawal total.

Step 3.2   List and allocate conditions (see Fig. 5.12).

  C1 Option = 9.
  C2 Option = 1.
  C3 Option = 2.

More experience of programs which process multiple data sets will be gained in the following section, and you should then attempt the exercises at the end of the chapter.

5.4 MATCHING DATA SETS

The correspondence technique is easily extended to the design of programs processing any number of input and output data sets, but one class of programs requires more thought before the correspondence technique can be applied: programs which match/merge/collate data sets. The following programs all match two data sets:

A program which merges two files to produce a third.
A program which simultaneously processes two files held in the same sequence in order to produce a sequenced report of the data on both.
A program which updates a sequential master file using a file of update transactions, producing an updated master file.

This section considers examples of a simple merge program (Example 5.4.1), and a sequential update program (Example 5.4.2).

Example 5.4.1

A program is required to merge two accounts files, each of which contains

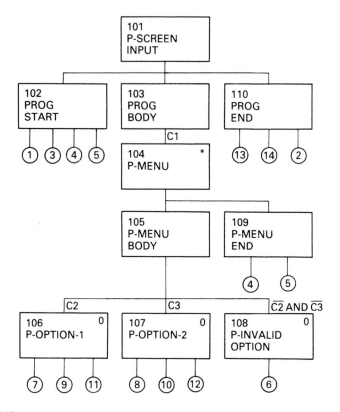

Figure 5.12

a number of account records in account number sequence. Matched records, i.e. records whose account number appears on both files, are to be written to a matched accounts file. Unmatched records, i.e. records whose account number appears on one file only, are to be reported on an unmatched accounts report, together with a message indicating their file of origin. (Headings, file trailers etc. will be ignored for purposes of simplification).

Sample data (account numbers only):

(input) ACC1-FILE	(input) ACC2-FILE	(output) MACC-FILE	(output) UNM-REPORT
1	1	1	2
3	2	7	3
7	4	8	4
8	7		9
9	8		

Step 1   Draw data structure diagrams of ACC1-FILE, ACC2-FILE, MACC-
          FILE and UNM-REPORT (see Figs 5.13 to 5.16).

Before moving on to Step 2 in detail let us briefly consider
correspondences between these four diagrams. When looking for correspondences there will be the usual correspondence between all four root
components, but that is all, no further correspondences exist. There is no
correspondence between an ACC1-REC and an ACC2-REC; there may be the
same number of each, but there may not. There is no correspondence
between a MACC-REC and either an ACC1-REC or an ACC2-REC; MACC-
RECs are formed from a subset of those ACC1-RECs and ACC2-RECs which
match. UNM-LINEs are similarly formed from a subset of those ACC1-RECs
and ACC2-RECs which do not match. And there is certainly no correspondence between a MACC-REC and an UNM-LINE; one is matched and one is
unmatched. If you try to superimpose mentally any one diagram on any
other, the two will simply not line up.

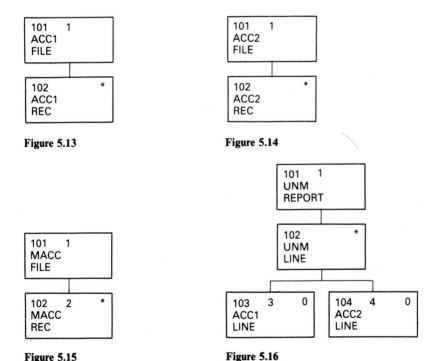

Figure 5.13   **Figure 5.14**

Figure 5.15   **Figure 5.16**

The problem arises because for a match program the logical data
structures of the two files being matched (ACC1-FILE and ACC2-FILE)

cannot be considered separately. If ACC1-FILE and ACC2-FILE are to be merged, their contents will logically overlap, as can be shown by a Venn diagram of the two files (see Fig. 5.17).

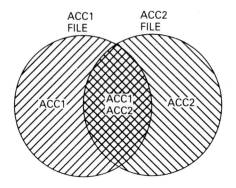

Figure 5.17

Some accounts are on ACC1-FILE only, some are on ACC2-FILE only, and some are on both files. This overlapping of contents must be reflected in the data structure diagrams of the two files, and so instead of drawing two separate data structure diagrams, a single composite data structure diagram must be drawn describing the two files together (see Fig. 5.18).

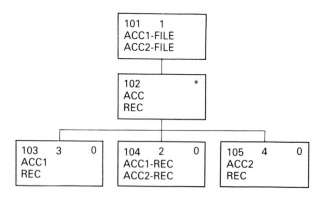

Figure 5.18

This composite diagram reflects the fact that when the two files are considered together for merge processing, an account will appear on either or both files. Once this concept has been grasped, match programs are no different from any other; correspondences will now appear and program design will continue as per normal.

Step 2   Form a program structure diagram (see Fig. 5.19).

There are three data structure diagrams from which to form a program structure diagram. Let us opt to note correspondences between ACC1-FILE/ACC2-FILE and MACC-FILE first, and then add any further correspondences with UNM-REPORT.

1 ACC1-FILE/ACC2-FILE and MACC-FILE. Both are root components.
2 ACC1-REC/ACC2-REC and MACC-REC. A MACC-REC is formed from a (matched) ACC1-REC/ACC2-REC.

Turning next to UNM-REPORT, we note the correspondences:

1 UNM-REPORT and the other two root components.
3 ACC1-LINE and ACC1-REC. ACC1-LINE is formed from an (unmatched) ACC1-REC.
4 ACC2-LINE and ACC2-REC. ACC2-LINE is formed from an (unmatched) ACC2-REC.

Step 3.1   List and allocate operations (see Fig. 5.19).

1 Open all files.
2 Close all files.
3 Read record from ACC1-FILE;
    at end-of-file move all 9s to ACC1-NO.
4 Read record from ACC2-FILE;
    at end-of-file move all 9s to ACC2-NO.
5 Write MACC-REC from ACC1-REC/ACC2-REC.
6 Write ACC1-LINE from ACC1-REC.
7 Write ACC2-LINE from ACC2-REC.

For simplification purposes many of these operations have been specified as macro operations. Operation 5, for example, concerns the writing of matched account records to the matched accounts file; in practice it would have to be decided whether to write both matched account records or drop one as a duplicate—it will be assumed that Operation 5 covers either requirement. The program processes two input files, and therefore two Read operations (operations 3 and 4) are required, which are discussed below.

   Step 3.2   List and allocate conditions (see Fig. 5.19).

        C1 ACC1-NO = all 9s.
        C2 ACC2-NO = all 9s.
        C3 ACC1-NO < ACC2-NO.
        C4 ACC1-NO = ACC2-NO.
        C5 ACC1-NO > ACC2-NO.

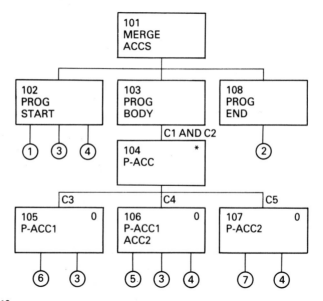

Figure 5.19

Note that ACC1-NO is assumed to refer to the account number on an ACC1-REC, ACC2-NO to the account number on an ACC2-REC. Conditions C1 and C2 are explained below.

   The merge process proceeds by comparing account records from each input file, one at a time, and processing the lower. If ACC1-NO is less than ACC2-NO, an ACC1-REC will be processed and another ACC1-REC read; if ACC1-NO is greater than ACC2-NO, an ACC2-REC will be processed and another ACC2-REC read; if ACC1-NO and ACC2-NO are equal, then both an ACC1-REC and an ACC2-REC will be processed and another one of each read. If you do not understand the merge process, desk-check this program using the sample data given at the beginning of the example.

The merge process (i.e. the iteration of P-ACC) cannot end until all account records on both files have been processed; the process cannot end when end-of-file is reached on either ACC1-FILE or ACC2-FILE alone. If ACC1-FILE reaches end-of-file first, the remaining (unmatched) records on ACC2-FILE must be written to the unmatched report. This is accomplished by program component P-ACC2, entered by condition C5, and to enforce condition C5 at end of ACC1-FILE, ACC1-NO is set to the highest possible value at end-of-file, i.e. all 9s. In COBOL this is accomplished by the READ statement:

READ ACC1-FILE AT END MOVE ALL '9' TO ACC1-NO.

In BASIC it is accomplished by the statements:

```
10   INPUT#1, ACC1.NO...
20   IF EOF(1)
30     THEN ACC1.NO=999999        (N.B. depending on field length)
```

If ACC2-FILE reaches end-of-file first, ACC2-NO must be similarly set to all 9s to enforce condition C3 and processing by program component P-ACC1. The merge process ends when end-of-file is reached on both files, i.e. conditions C1 and C2.

Note that if ACC1-FILE and ACC2-FILE contained file trailers with an ACC-NO of all 9s, end-of-file would be an error condition, because the iteration of P-ACC should be terminated by conditions C1 and C2 before end-of-file is detected.

Note also that although using a match-key of all 9s is the most common method of terminating a match program, there are other methods (see, for example, Jackson's *Principles of Program Design* [12]).

Example 5.4.2

A program is required to update a sequential-access Brought Forward (B/F) Employee File (BF-EMP-FILE) with a file of update transactions (UPD-FILE) so as to produce a Carried Forward (C/F) Employee File (CF-EMP-FILE). BF-EMP-FILE contains employee records (BF-EMP-REC) in employee number (BF-EMP-NO) sequence. UPD-FILE contains update records (UPD-REC) in employee number (UPD-EMP-NO) sequence. An update record is either an insertion (UPD-TYPE = 'I'), a deletion (UPD-TYPE = 'D') or an amendment (UPD-TYPE = 'A'). There is only one update record per employee record.

   In addition, an update report (UPD-REPORT) is to be produced containing updating details, i.e. details of records inserted, deleted and amended, of amendments and deletions for non-existent employees (NOT FOUND) and of insertions for already existing employees (FOUND).

   Step 1   Draw data structure diagrams of BF-EMP-FILE, UPD-FILE, CF-EMP-FILE and UPD-REPORT (see Figs 5.20 to 5.24).

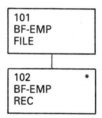

Figure 5.20

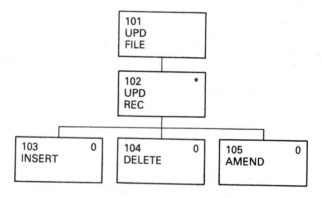

Figure 5.21

In order to apply update records to the B/F Employee File the two files must be matched, and when two files are matched, as in Example 5.4.1, there are always three match possibilities. There may be matched records (i.e. valid amendments or deletions, or invalid insertions), unmatched update records (i.e. valid insertions, or invalid amendments or deletions) and unmatched employee records (i.e. records which are not being updated). In order to obtain correspondences a composite data structure diagram must be formed from the two files to be matched (see Fig. 5.22).

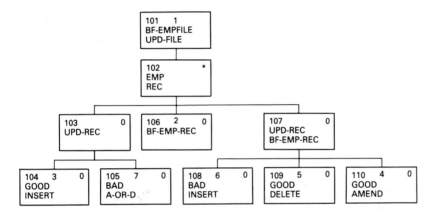

Figure 5.22

As UPD-REC occurs twice on the composite data structure diagram, its selected parts must also occur twice, but note the refinement of their names to reflect match processing.

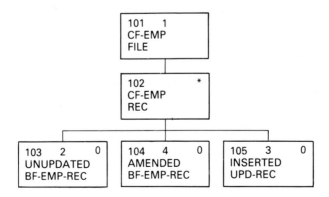

Figure 5.23

Note the refinement of CF-EMP-REC to indicate its source.

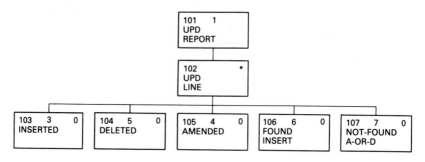

Figure 5.24

Step 2   Form a program structure diagram (see Fig. 5.25).

Let us opt to note correspondences between BF-EMP-FILE/UPD-FILE and CF-EMP-FILE first, and then add any further correspondences with UPD-REPORT.

Correspondences between BF-EMP-FILE/UPD-FILE and CF-EMP-FILE:

1 BF-EMP-FILE/UPD-FILE and CF-EMP-FILE. Both are root components.
2 BF-EMP-REC and UNUPDATED-BF-EMP-REC. The latter is formed from the former.
3 GOOD-INSERT and INSERTED-UPD-REC. The latter is formed from the former.
4 GOOD-AMEND and AMENDED-BF-EMP-REC. The latter is formed from the former.

Additional correspondences with UPD-REPORT:

1 The root component UPD-REPORT and the other two root components.
3 INSERTED and GOOD INSERT. The former is formed from the latter.
4 AMENDED and GOOD-AMEND. The former is formed from the latter.
5 DELETED and GOOD-DELETE. The former is formed from the latter.
6 FOUND-INSERT and BAD-INSERT. The former is formed from the latter.
7 NOTE-FOUND-A-OR-D and BAD-A-OR-D. The former is formed from the latter.

Note that the fact that one component is formed from another does not necessarily mean that there is a correspondence (see Section 5.5), but in all the above correspondences the two components occur the same number of times in the same order and under the same circumstances.

Step 3.1   List and allocate operations (see Fig. 5.25).

1 Open all files.
2 Close all files.
3 Read record from BF-EMP-FILE;
     at end-of-file move all 9s to BF-EMP-NO.
4 Read record from UPD-FILE;
     at end-of-file move all 9s to UPD-EMP-NO.
5 Amend BF-EMP-REC using UPD-REC fields.
6 Write CF-EMP-REC from BF-EMP-REC.
7 Write CF-EMP-REC from UPD-REC.
8 Format and write INSERTED UPDLINE.
9 Format and write DELETED UPDLINE.
10 Format and write AMENDED UPDLINE.
11 Format and write FOUND-INSERT-UPDLINE.
12 Format and write NOT-FOUND-A-OR-D UPDLINE.

Step 3.2   List and allocate operations (see Fig. 5.25).

C1   BF -EMP-NO = all 9s.
C2   UPD-EMP-NO = all 9s.
C3   BF-EMP-NO > U-EMP-NO.
C4   UPD-TYPE = 'I'.
C5   BF-EMP-NO < U-EMP-NO.
C6   BF-EMP-NO = U-EMP-NO.
C7   UPD-TYPE = 'D'.
C8   UPD-TYPE = 'A'.

Although this is a simple update program, the data structures are easily expanded to cater for file headers, file trailers, report headings and totals, multiple update transactions per employee record, etc. The resulting program structures would be larger, but the design process would not increase in complexity.

Similarly, if three files were to be matched rather than two, the resulting program structure would be larger but not more complex; there would simply be seven match combinations $(2^3 - 1)$ instead of three

(2^2-1). With four files to be matched there would be 15 (2^4-1) match combinations.

Match combinations, can be shown explicitly in the form of a truth table, with a column for each file and the presence or absence of a record denoted by a 0 or a 1. It can also be useful for program specification to list them in the form of a decision table, with a column for each match combination and a row for each operation to be undertaken for that combination. JSP forces the program designer to consider rigorously each possible match combination and the operations to be allocated to it, and often brings to light omissions in analysis and program specification.

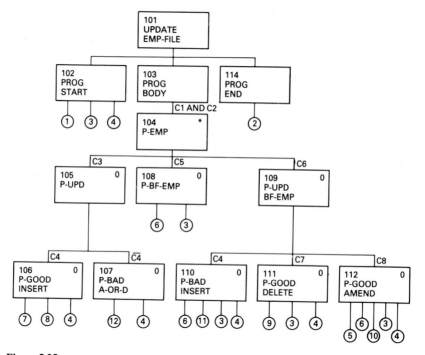

Figure 5.25

5.5 LIMITATIONS OF THE CORRESPONDENCE TECHNIQUE

In Section 5.1 it was stated that the correspondence technique is not universally applicable. This section presents two examples of programs in which it cannot be applied.

Suppose a file of customer records in ascending customer number sequence is to be sorted into descending customer number sequence. The data structure diagrams of the two files are shown in Figs 9.1 and 9.2. There is a correspondence between the two root components CUSTFILE and SORTED-CUSTFILE, but not between a CUSTREC and a SORTED-CUSTREC. Do not be misled into thinking that there is a correspondence between CUSTREC and SORTED-CUSTREC merely because the latter is formed from the former; they do not occur in the same order. If an attempt was made to combine the two components into a single program component, insurmountable problems would ensue, not the least of which would be the impossibility of reading a CUSTREC and writing a different SORTED-CUSTREC within the same program component (see Section 9.2).

This lack of correspondences is called a structure clash, and it is dealt with in depth in Chapter 9. It is introduced briefly here to demonstrate that the correspondence technique is not universally applicable, and care must be taken in applying it. Make sure that data components do correspond in more than name. Structure clashes are resolved by the technique of inversion explained in Chapters 8 and 9.

It is because of structure clashes that the problem of producing a paged report has so far been ignored. If a file is to be printed as a paged report, a structure clash often results. Consider what would have happened in Example 5.2.2 if EMP-REPORT had been a paged report, say ten lines per page, with a heading at the top of every page. The data structure diagram of this report is given as Fig. 9.11; compare it with the original EMP-REPORT diagram in Example 5.2.2 (see Fig. 5.7).

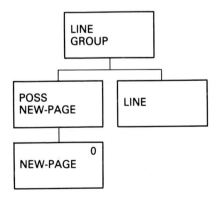

Figure 5.26

Although an EMP-LINE on the paged report is formed from an EMP-REC, there are a different number of EMP-RECs per DEPT than EMP-LINEs per PAGE, therefore they do not occur under the same circumstances. If an attempt was made to combine the two components into a single program component, it would be impossible to allocate a condition to end the iteration: an EMP-REC is iterated until end-of-DEPT, an EMP-LINE is part of the component LINE which is iterated ten times.

If you do not wish to wait for program inversion to resolve the paging problem two design options are open to you:

1 Omit consideration of the report structure when forming the program structure diagram and incorporate at every point a line to be written as the LINE-GROUP data structure shown in Fig. 5.26. The selection condition for the processing of NEWPAGE in the above example would be: LINE-COUNT > 9, where LINE-COUNT is a variable initialized to 0 beneath NEW-PAGE (along with the 'Write heading' operation) and incremented beneath LINE.

2 Instead of incorporating a LINE-GROUP component into the program structure diagram, change the 'Write printline' operation into a macro operation of the form:

　　If line count > 9
　　　　Write heading
　　　　Set line count to 0.
　　Format and write employee line.
　　Add 1 to line count.

It must be emphasized that neither solution is a strict JSP solution because the program structure diagrams into which they are incorporated will no longer represent faithfully the structure of the report. This makes it more difficult to incorporate report structure modifications (e.g. page footings) and requires that the selection for a new page (plus end-of-page, if page footings are required) be repeated at every point where a line occurs. Nevertheless these solutions are sometimes adopted by DP installations to resolve the structure clash caused by paging (see also Section 9.3).

5.6 EXERCISES

1 An enhancement to the program in Example 3.3.1 is required to write

records to a cost file instead of outputting cost information to a VDU screen. For each customer number and quantity input calculate cost and write to the cost file a record containing customer number, quantity and cost. At end of file append a file trailer containing the total cost on file.

2 A customer file contains a number of customers. Each customer has a header record followed by zero or more transaction records containing invoice amounts. A program is required to read the customer file and write a summary customer file. The summary customer file contains a summary record for each customer, containing information from the header record plus a total invoice amount from transaction records. In addition the summary customer file contains a file trailer containing a total invoice amount for all customers.

3 Three stock control files (STOCK-FILE1, STOCK-FILE2, STOCK-FILE3) each consist of a number of stock records. Design a program to match the three files and produce a match report containing, for each stock item, one of the following messages:

STOCK ITEM ON ALL THREE FILES
STOCK ITEM ON TWO FILES ONLY
STOCK ITEM ON ONE FILE ONLY

At end of report write a total line for each of the three categories of stock item.

4 A product file contains a number of product records in product number sequence. An orders file contains a number of order records in product number/order number sequence. A program is required to match the two files, output 'NO ORDERS' for a product which has no orders, output 'NO PRODUCT' for an order for a non-existent product, and output 'ORDER OK' for each order for an existing product.

5 An accounts file contains a number of accounts in account number sequence. For each account there is an account header followed by a number of transaction records. A program (see Fig. 5.27 for run chart) is

required to update the accounts file using a file of weekly transactions, which are in account number sequence. There may be zero, one or many weekly transactions for an account, and they are to be added to the end of the account to which they belong on the accounts file, following any existing transaction records for that account. Report any weekly transactions for which there is no account on the accounts file as an error.

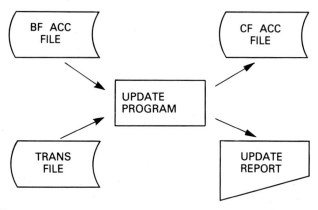

Figure 5.27

Chapter 6

Direct-Access Data Sets

This chapter considers the processing of non-sequential data sets, e.g. direct-access files, databases and tables (arrays). Examples are given of the interactive updating of an indexed-sequential file, the processing of internal and external tables, and the accessing of records on a database.

6.1 DIRECT-ACCESS FILES

In this chapter examples will be based on the use of COBOL, which is the language best suited to the processing of direct-access files. Users of other programming languages, however, should have little difficulty in translating the operations given into appropriate statements, and in addition notes on the use of BASIC will be given where appropriate.

All examples in previous chapters have concerned the processing of sequential data sets. The processing of direct-access files such as indexed-sequential and relative files (COBOL) or random files (BASIC) requires no additional design concepts and is easily incorporated into a program structure because the structure of a direct access file can be ignored. If a record on a file is accessed directly, then its relationship to records which come before and after it on that file is irrelevant, and therefore the structure of the file is irrelevant to the processing of that record.

Note that in previous examples the Output operation has been used to produce terminal output as though that output was direct-access and its structure irrelevant. In many cases this approach is justifiable, but if the structure of the output data stream is complex or the operations which produce it cannot clearly be allocated to input data stream components, then an output data structure diagram should be drawn and corresponded with the input data structure to clarify the situation.

When accessing a record on a direct-access file the only structural matter of concern to the accessing program is whether the record to be accessed exists or not. Direct accesses are therefore always of the form (in COBOL) shown in Fig. 6.1.

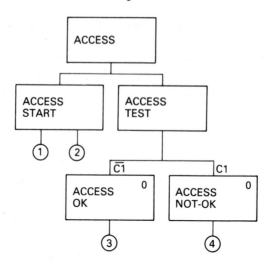

Figure 6.1

List of operations:

    1   Set INVAL-SW to '0'.
    2   Access record INVALID KEY MOVE 1 TO INVAL-SW.
    3   Process access-OK.
    4   Process access-not-OK.

List of conditions:

    C1   INVAL-SW = '1'.

Operation 2 may be a READ, WRITE, DELETE or REWRITE statement. Note the use of INVAL-SW to record the result of the operation for later testing, in a manner similar to EOF-SW in a sequential file Read operation (see discussion following Example 3.3.2). Just as COBOL does not provide an 'AT END' variable which can be tested outside the sequential READ statement, so it does not provide an 'INVALID KEY' variable which can be tested outside the direct-access READ statement.

Operations 3 and 4 will vary according to the nature of the direct-access operation. A direct-access READ, for instance, causes INVAL-SW to be set to '1' if the record to be read does not exist, and therefore operation 4 means 'Process record-not-found'. A direct-access WRITE, on the other hand, causes INVAL-SW to be set to '1' if the record to be written already exists, and therefore operation 4 means 'Process record-found'.

In Microsoft BASIC a direct-access GET or PUT statement does not have an INVALID KEY option to inform the program that a record is not present. Instead records must be initialized to a pre-determined value when the direct-access file is created, and the presence of that value in a record following a GET operation indicates the absence of a record.

Example 6.1.1

A program is required to process customer transactions at a bank's cash dispensing terminal. Each transaction consists of an account number, a personal identity number (PIN) and a withdrawal amount. The withdrawal amount is to be subtracted from the account balance, held on an indexed-sequential balance file accessed by account number.

Note that for purposes of simplification it will be assumed that the bank has only one cash dispensing terminal and that all input will be valid. Validation is best handled by backtracking (see Chapter 7; Example 7.4.1 is an expansion of this example which caters for validation). Multiple terminals, where input from one may be interleaved with input from another, is handled by parallel inversion (see Sections 9.4 and 9.5).

Step 1   Draw a data structure diagram of customer transactions (see Fig. 6.2).

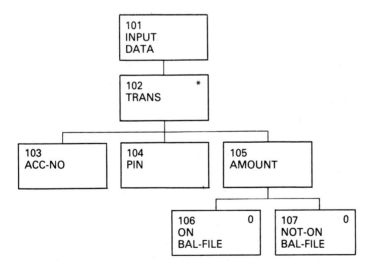

Figure 6.2

The balance file is accessed directly and its structure is irrelevant to the program. It is necessary only to refine component AMOUNT to indicate that an access will be made to the balance file.

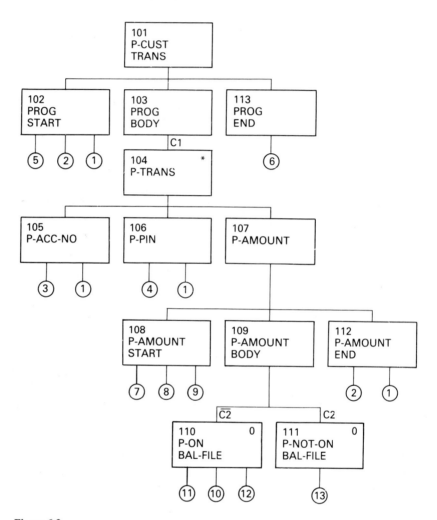

Figure 6.3

Step 2   Form a program structure diagram (see Fig. 6.3).

The program structure diagram is formed from a single data structure diagram.

Step 3.1   List and allocate operations (see Fig. 6.3).

    1   Input IN-FIELD.
    2   Output 'PLEASE ENTER ACCOUNT NUMBER'.
    3   Output 'PLEASE ENTER PIN'.
    4   Output 'PLEASE ENTER WITHDRAWAL AMOUNT'.
    5   Open balance file.
    6   Close balance file.
    7   Set INVAL-SW to '0'.
    8   Move account number to balance file key.
    9   Read balance file INVALID KEY MOVE '1' TO INVAL-SW.
   10 Subtract withdrawal amount from balance file amount.
   11 Pay out withdrawal amount.
   12 Output 'TRANSACTION COMPLETE. THANKYOU.'.
   13 Output 'TRANSACTION ERROR, CONSULT BANK MAN-
AGER'.

Step 3.2   List and allocate conditions (see Fig. 6.3).

   C1   Shutdown (e.g. account number = all 9s).
   C2   INVAL-SW = '1'.

Note that in COBOL all input data is ACCEPTed into IN-FIELD, which is REDEFINEd three ways as account number, PIN and amount. The appropriate definition is accessed according to which program component is being executed at the time. This is equivalent in batch processing programs to READing a record and processing it as, say, a file header, a transaction record or a file trailer according to which program component is being executed. In languages such as BASIC and Pascal which do not allow redefinition of data types, read-ahead is more difficult to program but not impossible. It is necessary to input data as a string of characters and then convert it to a different data type (e.g. integer or real) as appropriate (see also note following Example 7.4.1).

    Enhancements to this program, e.g. to check that an account balance is sufficient to cover the withdrawal, are easily incorporated.

6.2 TABLES

The structure of a data structure (e.g. a table) cannot always be so easily ignored as that of a direct-access file. Elements of a table may be accessed directly, using a subscript or an index, without any concern for the table's structure. But if the whole table is to be printed out from beginning to end, then the processing of the table is akin to the processing of a sequential data set, and the structure of the table must be taken into account.

For example, suppose a table contains ten totals (see Fig. 6.4).

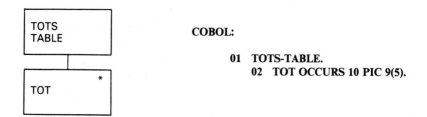

COBOL:

01   TOTS-TABLE.
02   TOT OCCURS 10 PIC 9(5).

Figure 6.4

Adding to any specific total merely requires the following operation to be allocated to an appropriate program component:

Add 1 to total (subscript).

To output the whole table, however, requires the program components shown in Fig. 6.5.

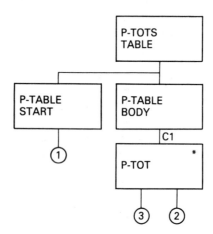

Figure 6.5

List of operations:

1   Set subscript to 1.
2   Add 1 to subscript.
3   Output total (subscript).

List of conditions:

C1   Subscript > 10.

In effect, the data structure diagram of the table must appear at every point on the program stucture diagram where the whole table is to be processed. If it does not, there will be operations (e.g. 'Set subscript to 1', 'Add 1 to subscript') which cannot be allocated. The principle is true whether the table is internal to the program or external (e.g. on a file). For example, if a record on a direct-access file contains six totals which are to be added to a grand total, the processing of a record would be of the form (in COBOL) shown in Fig. 6.6.

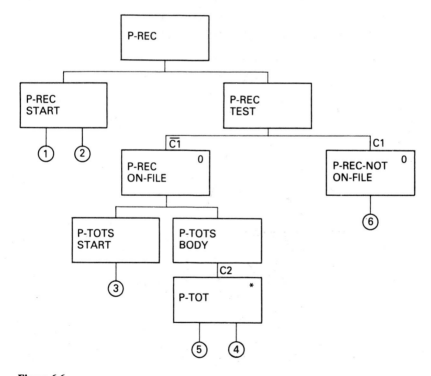

Figure 6.6

List of operations:

    1 Set INVAL-SW to '0'.
    2 Read file INVALID KEY MOVE '1' TO INVAL-SW.
    3 Set subscript to 1.
    4 Add 1 to subscript.
    5 Add total (subscript) to grand total.
    6 Process rec-not-found.

List of conditions:

    C1   INVAL-SW = '1'.
    C2   Subscript > 6.

Example 6.2.1

A series of student examination results is to be input via a VDU keyboard. Each result consists of seven digits, where the first four digits represent a student number, the next digit represents a subject code in the range 1 to 6, and the final two digits represent a percentage mark for that subject. Input is in no particular sequence and is terminated by a student number of all 9s.

Sample input:

    0001170
    0011240
    0010355
    0015563
    9999999

An indexed-sequential student file contains a record for each student, and as each result is input it is to be inserted into the appropriate student record. For this purpose each student record contains a field which holds up to six marks, i.e. one mark per subject (MARK OCCURS 6). In addition, results are to be displayed on the VDU screen in the form of a table, showing the number of marks for each subject in bands of 10, i.e.

	0–9	10–19	20–29	30–39	40–49	50–59	60–69	70–79	80–89	90–99
1	x	x	x	x	x	x	x	x	x	x
2	x	x	x	x	x	x	x	x	x	x
3	x	x	x	x	x	x	x	x	x	x
4	x	x	x	x	x	x	x	x	x	x
5	x	x	x	x	x	x	x	x	x	x
6	x	x	x	x	x	x	x	x	x	x

Step 1   Draw a data structure diagram of examination results (see Fig. 6.7).

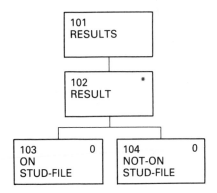

Figure 6.7

Note that in Example 6.1.1 the three fields of a customer transaction were input separately via three input operations, and therefore the three fields were shown on the data structure diagram, in order that an input operation could be allocated to each. In this example student number, subject and mark are to be input together via one 'Input exam-result' operation, and therefore it is unnecessary to refine data component RESULT into its constituent fields. It is necessary to refine it only to show that an access will be made to the student file.

Any data structures of relevance to the program should also be noted at this stage, i.e. a two-dimensional table which will be used to hold mark totals by subject and band for displaying at end of program (see Fig. 6.8).

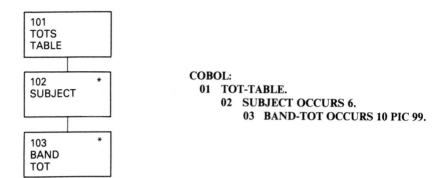

Figure 6.8

A data structure diagram of the table of marks held on each record of the student file is not required for this program as each mark will be accessed directly (see operation 6). A data structure diagram is required only when the whole data structure is to be processed sequentially from beginning to end.

Step 2   Form a program structure diagram (see Figs 6.9 and 6.10).

The program structure diagram is based on the data structure diagram of examination results, with the structure of the totals table incorporated at appropriate points (i.e. at PROG-END). As the diagram is too wide to fit on a single page of this book it has been dismembered into two smaller diagrams (see Appendix E).

Step 3.1 List and allocate operations (see Figs 6.9 and 6.10).

 1   Output 'PLEASE ENTER EXAM RESULT'.
 2   Input examination result.
 3   Open student file.
 4   Close student file.
 5   Set INVAL-SW to '0'.
 6   Move input student number to student record key.
 7   Read student file INVALID KEY MOVE '1' TO INVAL-SW.
 8   Move input mark to student record mark (input subject).
 9   Calculate band = (input mark/10) + 1.
10   Add 1 to band total (input subject, band).
11   Output 'STUDENT NOT ON STUDENT FILE'.
12   Output band heading.
13   Set subject subscript to 1.

14 Move subject subscript to output subject.
15 Add 1 to subject subscript.
16 Set band subscript to 1.
17 Add 1 to band subscript.
18 Move band total (subject subscript, band subscript) to output total (band subscript).
19 Output total line.

Step 3.2 List and allocate conditions (see Figs 6.9 and 6.10).

C1 Input student number = 9999.
C2 INVAL-SW = '1'.
C3 Subject subscript > 6.
C4 Band subscript > 10.

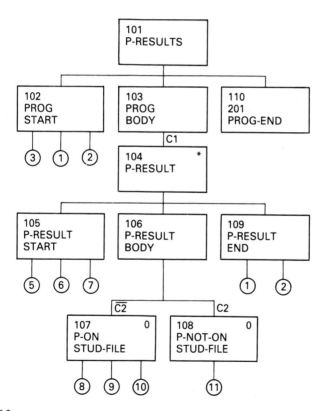

Figure 6.9

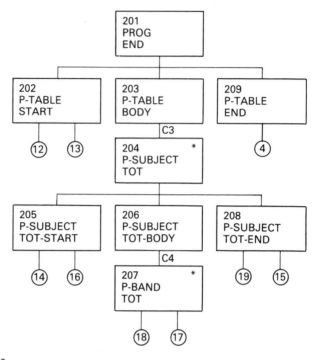

Figure 6.10

The table of band-totals is accessed sequentially from beginning to end at PROG-END and therefore its structure must be incorporated beneath that component. If the table were to be zeroized at PROG-START, then it would be necessary to show its structure here as well as at PROG-END, in order that all relevant operations could be allocated. In BASIC, initialization is automatic, however, and in COBOL it can often be accomplished by means of REDEFINES and VALUE clauses in Working-Storage; such initialization will be assumed in this example.

Alternatively, initialization in COBOL could be accomplished by the following macro operation:

```
PERFORM ZEROIZE VARYING SUBJECT-SUB FROM 1 BY 1
    UNTIL SUBJECT-SUB > 6
AFTER BAND-SUB FROM 1 BY 1
    UNTIL BAND-SUB > 10.
GO TO ZEROISE-EXIT.
```

ZEROIZE.
    MOVE 0 to BAND-TOT (SUBJECT-SUB, BAND-SUB).
ZEROIZE-EXIT.

The printing of the table at PROG-END could be handled in a similar manner, with a PERFORM... VARYING... macro operation allocated to P-TABLE-BODY and the sub-components and operations of P-TABLE-BODY omitted.

    PERFORM... VARYING... is an example of a powerful COBOL macro operation whose use enables the removal of operations and parts of a program structure diagram. Other similar macro operations in COBOL are the SEARCH verb (see Example 7.4.3) and the SORT verb (see Section 9.2).

6.3 DATABASE

Like the table of marks held on each student record on the student file in Example 6.2.1, a database is also a data structure external to the program. The structure of a database determines the way in which its records can be accessed, and it may be necessary, as with tables, to incorporate that structure into the program. It is not necessary, however, to incorporate the structure of the whole database into the program, only that part of the structure relevant to the accessing of a specific record, i.e. the record's access path.

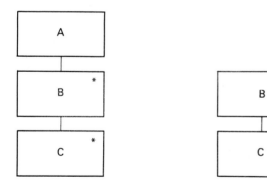

Figure 6.11   **Figure 6.12**

    The access path of a record in a database, whatever the structure of the database, is always hierarchical. For example, suppose an *A* record owns a number of *B* records, and each *B* record owns a number of *C* records.

If a *C* record can be accessed only via an access to an *A* record, it is necessary to incorporate into a program at each point a *C* record is to be accessed, the access path structure shown in Fig. 6.11. If, on the other hand, a *C* record can be accessed via an access to a *B* record, then the access path structure shown in Fig. 6.12 is required.

A direct access to *C*, as with all direct accesses, would require no access path structure. Note also that database accesses, like direct accesses, will almost certainly need to be followed by found/not found selections.

Example 6.3.1

A retail shop maintains a database on the activities of its customers. The database contains four types of record: a record for each customer, a record for each order placed by a customer, a record for each item on an order and a record for each invoice sent to a customer.

Record relationships:

A customer places a number of orders and has a number of invoices.
An invoice contains a number of orders.
An order contains a number of items.

Fig. 6.13 shows the relationships among the four types of record.

Record access paths:

A customer record is accessed by customer number and contains pointers to the first invoice record and the first order record which it owns.

An invoice record is accessed by invoice number or via a customer record, and contains pointers to the customer record which owns it and to any subsequent invoice records for the same customer.

An order record is accessed by order number or via a customer record or an invoice record, and contains pointers to the customer record which owns it, the invoice record which owns it and to the first item record which it owns.

An item record can be accessed only via an order record and contains pointers to the order record which owns it and to subsequent items for the same order record.

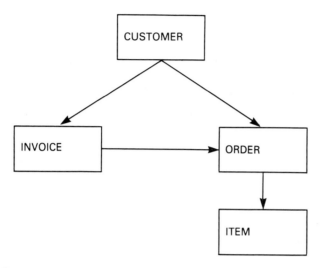

Figure 6.13

A menu-driven program is required to access the database and provide the following information to the user on request:

1 Details of all items ordered by a customer.
2 Total invoice amount owed by a customer.
3 Information on a particular item on an order.

These three options are presented to the user in the form of a screen menu, from which he can choose one. A fourth option (option number 9) is used to terminate the program.

  Step 1   Draw a data structure diagram of screen input (see Figs 6.14 to 6.17).

Database access paths of relevance to this program are:

  For option 1: access path to items ordered by a customer (see Fig. 6.18).
  For option 2: access path to a customer's invoices (see Fig. 6.19).
  For option 3: access path to an item on an order (see Fig. 6.20).

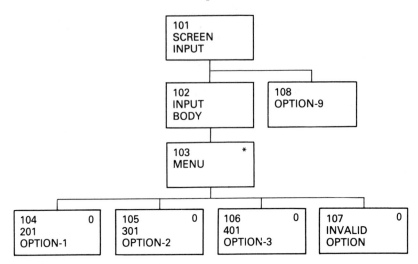

Figure 6.14

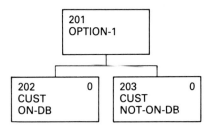

Figure 6.15

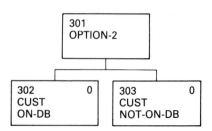

Figure 6.16

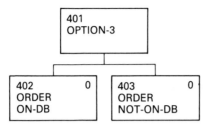

Figure 6.17

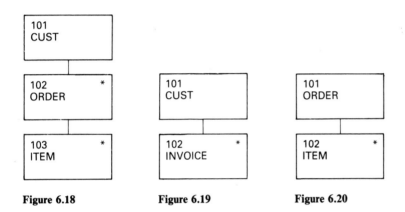

Figure 6.18   **Figure 6.19**   **Figure 6.20**

Step 2   Form a program structure diagram (see Figs 6.21 to 6.24). Note the inclusion of database access paths at appropriate points, together with Start, Body and End components where necessary.

Step 3.1 List and allocate operations (see Figs 6.21 to 6.24).

1   Output user instructions.
2   Output menu.
3   Input option.
4   Invoke database.
5   Exit from database.
6   Set customer record key.
7   Fetch customer record on error MOVE '1' TO INVAL-SW.
8   Set invoice record key.
9   Fetch invoice record on error MOVE '1' TO INVAL-SW.
10   Set order record key.

11 Fetch order record on error MOVE '1' TO INVAL-SW.
12 Set item record key.
13 Fetch item record on error MOVE '1' TO INVAL-SW.
14 Set INVAL-SW to '0'..
15 Output 'CUSTOMER NOT FOUND'.
16 Output item information.
17 Add invoice total to customer total.
18 Output customer total.
19 Output 'ORDER NOT FOUND'.
20 Output 'INVALID OPTION, PLEASE RE-ENTER'.
21 Set customer total to 0.

Step 3.2   List and allocate conditions (see Figs 6.21 to 6.24).

C1 Option = 9.
C2 Option = 1.
C3 Option = 2.
C4 Option = 3.
C5 INVAL-SW = '1'.
C6 No more orders.
C7 No more items.
C8 No more invoices.
C9 Item found.

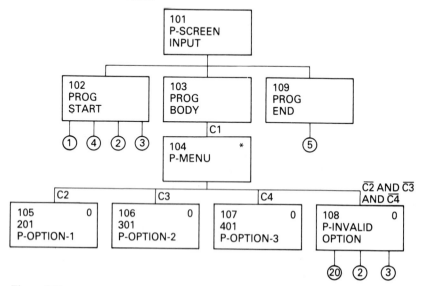

Figure 6.21

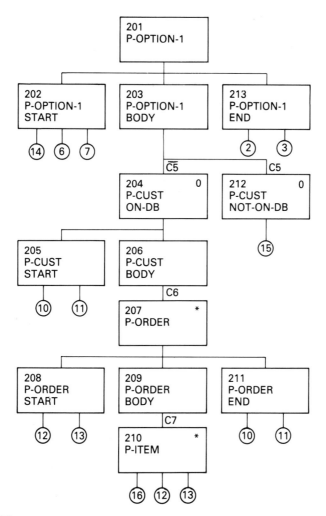

Figure 6.22

The program has been simplified as much as possible in order not to confuse program design issues with operational details. The observant reader will note, among other simplifications, the following assumptions:

1 Option 1 assumes that a customer must have orders.
2 Option 2 assumes that a customer must have invoices.
3 Option 2 assumes that all invoices are unpaid.
4 Option 3 assumes that the item on which information has been requested is in the database.

5   All options assume that once the first record on the access path has
been read, all further accesses will be valid.

If assumptions 1, 2 and 3 are incorrect, the program must be enhanced to
cater for this by the addition of selection components at appropriate points.

If assumption 4 is incorrect (i.e. the requested item may not be in the
database), the program must be enhanced to search for the item.

Assumption 5 is probably a correct assumption; it is not the function
of a database accessing program to check the integrity of the database.
However, if such checking is required this is again easily catered for by
the addition of selection components at appropriate points.

Note also that because of the possibility of a lockout situation it may
be necessary to make several attempts at a 'fetch' operation, in which case
the data structure diagram of the record access path must show a number
of possible failed attempts followed by a successful attempt (which may

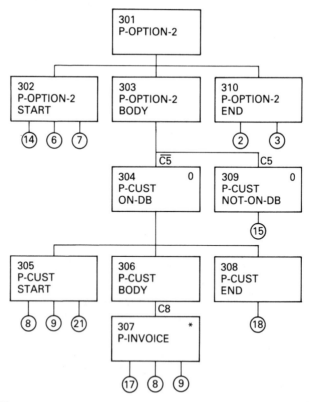

Figure 6.23

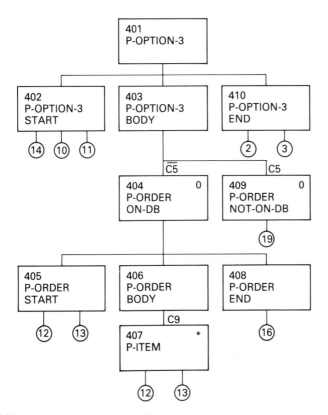

Figure 6.24

be 'found' or 'not found'). Alternatively, it is possible to develop a macro operation to cater for this.

The processing of data structures other than tables, e.g. a tree structure, is handled in the same way as the processing of a database: the access path used to process the data structure must be included in the program structure diagram at appropriate points. If such processing involves a recursive procedure, this can be shown diagrammatically on the program structure diagram by drawing a curved line from the procedure's exit point (i.e. the component containing the recursive call) to its entry point (i.e. the root component).

Whether to code a recursive procedure using recursion or an equivalent iteration is not a JSP design issue but a programming language issue. COBOL and Microsoft BASIC, for example, do not implement recursion.

6.4 EXERCISES

1 Amend the program in Example 6.3.1 to cater for the situation in which assumptions 1, 2 and 3 (discussed following Fig. 6.24) are incorrect.

2 An online file enquiries program is required to interrogate an indexed-sequential file of salesperson records. Each salesperson record contains a salesperson code (the record key) followed by twelve monthly sales figures.

A file enquiry from a terminal consists of the keying in of a saleperson code, and the program's response is to display the salesperson's twelve sales figures. Input is terminated by a salesperson code of 999999. It can be assumed that input will be valid, but it cannot be assumed that the required salesperson record will be on file.

Note that the twelve sales figures on a salesperson record should be handled as a table.

3 A car dealer requires a menu-driven program to update a direct-access file of cars in stock. The menu is to consist of four options:

1   Delete a car record from thc filc.
2   Insert a car record onto the file.
3   Amend a car record.
9   Terminate program.

It can be assumed that input will be valid, but it cannot be assumed that records to be amended/deleted are on file or that records to be inserted are not on file. The result of each update is to be output to the screen.

4 Train departure times from Central Station are held on a direct-access file in departure time sequence (based on the 24-hour clock). Each record consists of a (unique) departure time (2 digits hours, 2 digits minutes) and destination.

A program is required to output to a screen at every minute of the day, until midnight, the next ten departure times and destinations, starting from the user-input time (2 digits hours, 2 digits minutes).

Assume that the program can accesss the computer's internal clock (2 digits hours, 2 digits minutes) by an input operation.

Clue: the program structure is based on an iteration of screens; at end of screen is an iteration of accesses of the internal clock until a minute has passed.

Chapter 7

Backtracking

This chapter considers problems connected with the evaluation of conditions. In the examples in previous chapters it has always been possible to allocate conditions to selection and iteration components, but this is not always the case. Sometimes it is impossible to evaluate the conditions under which each selected or iterated sub-component occurs. When this happens it is necessary to adopt the technique of backtracking, which involves a new step in the JSP design procedure:

Step 3.3   List and allocate quits and backtracking operations.

7.1   CONDITION EVALUATION PROBLEMS

The benefits of JSP accrue from the use of a formal design procedure which is based on an analysis of the data to be processed by a program. In JSP the structure of a program does not arise phoenix-like from the programmer's imagination as in top-down design; it is already implicit in the structure of the data, and the structure of the data exists in the real world.

Any sequence, selection or iteration which exists in the program but not in the data is a programmer invention, and it is such artistry that is a root cause of the software crisis. Nowhere is this more true than in the invention of program switches, and selections which test their settings. Consider the following problem.

A college maintains a file of student records, which is updated by a transactions file. A program is required to validate the transactions file, write valid transactions to a valid transactions file and invalid transactions to an error report.

It is apparent from this program specification that a transaction record is either valid or invalid (depending on validation checks which have not been specified). There is an obvious selection here, which can be shown explicitly on the data structure diagram of the transactions file (see components VAL-TRANS and INVAL-TRANS in Fig. 7.4).

164

This diagram is perfectly correct, and later in the design process when it becomes a program structure diagram it will be possible to allocate the operation which writes a valid record to P-VAL-TRANS, and the operation which writes an error line to P-INVAL-TRANS.

However, when it comes to allocating conditions to P-VAL-TRANS and P-INVAL-TRANS a problem arises. The condition for the processing of P-VAL-TRANS is (in English): 'Transaction record valid'. But this condition cannot be evaluated until after a transaction record has been processed and its validity determined. There is a chicken-and-egg situation: once a record has been read it is to be processed by P-VAL-TRANS or P-INVAL-TRANS, but until some of that processing has been undertaken it cannot be determined which branch of the selection is to be entered.

The traditional solution of this problem is to use a validation switch, which can be shown in the form of the program structure diagram shown in Fig. 7.1.

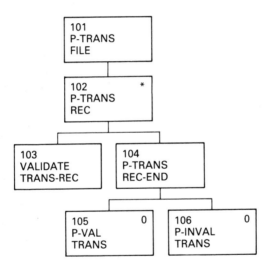

Figure 7.1

For each transaction record the program undertakes a number of validation checks (VALIDATE-TRANS-REC), and if any invalidity is detected a validation switch is set on. After all validation checks have been made (P-TRANS-REC-END) the switch is tested and the record processed as valid or invalid accordingly. In this program, therefore, the condition for the processing of P-VAL-TRANS *can* be evaluated: 'Validation switch on'.

The program structure, however, is incorrect. It is not based on data structure at all, and the use of a program switch testifies to this. The program structure includes a selection based on the setting of a switch, but there is no such switch in the data and no such selection in the data structure. A switch is a programmer invention, and therein lies its danger.

If a programmer can invent one switch, in order to overcome a logic problem as he sees it, then he can invent many. Every time he uses a binary switch (i.e. a switch which has two settings—on or off, implemented as a Boolean variable in some languages), the number of internal states of the program doubles. If one switch is used the program has twice as many logic paths through it, if two switches four times as many, if three switches eight times as many, etc. Of course, not all combinations of switch settings may be possible—one switch may be set on in a part of the program which is only entered if another switch is on. But switch dependencies increase rather than diminish the problem: they may be accidentally altered after an amendment, and they increase the complexity of the logic flow, the common result of which is the detection of untested and erroneous paths through the program during live running.

Just as important from a design point of view, who is to say that the switches invented by a programmer are the best ones? The switches he invents are just that—an invention, conjured out of his own head to solve the problem as he sees it. Might there be a better solution? Would a different programmer use different switches?

Switches destroy program structure; they are programmer-dependent and can play no part in a structured design method. Data is structured (and hence a program should be structured) in sequences, selections and iterations. In such an approach there can be no such concept as a GOTO and no such concept as a program switch. GOTOs and switches derive from flowcharts but cannot exist in JSP design.

N.B. Do not confuse program switches with data switches such as PAID-SW in Example 3.3.2. A data switch is a valid way of recording alternatives of data which exist in the real world; a data switch can be input to and output from a program. A program switch is a programmer invention which is not used outside the program. In a few cases the inadequacies of COBOL force the COBOL programmer into a restricted invention of switches (e.g. EOF-SW), but this does not invalidate the general case against programmer-invented switches. This point is discussed further following Example 7.4.3.

The JSP design of the above program forms Example 7.3.1. The data structure diagram will explicitly show the selection between a valid transaction record and an invalid transaction record, just as that selection is explicitly stated in the program specification. The fact that the condition for that selection cannot be evaluated does not invalidate the data structure diagram and must not be allowed to affect program structure, any more than coding constraints should be allowed to cause changes in program structure. The design is sacrosanct, and a solution to the condition evaluation problem which does not involve GOTOs or switches is required.

The JSP solution is called backtracking and involves the constructs posit, quit and admit. Faced with the impossibility in the above example of evaluating the condition which distinguishes between a valid and an invalid transaction, the program posits (i.e. postulates, assumes) that a record is valid and begins to execute P-VAL-TRANS. If at any point during this processing an invalidity is detected, the program quits P-VAL-TRANS and admits that P-INVAL-TRANS should be executed in its stead. P-VAL-TRANS is known as the posit branch of the selection, P-INVAL-TRANS as the admit branch; the quit conditions are in effect the validity checks.

Other common examples of backtracking occur in online transaction processing (see Example 7.4.1), table searching (see Example 7.4.3), syntax processing (see Exercise 7.6.4) and premature program termination (see Example 8.2.3). If an online transaction may be cancelled after part of it has been input (e.g. because of keying errors), it is necessary to posit a complete transaction and admit an incomplete one if cancellation occurs. If a table is to be searched for a particular item, it is necessary to posit that the table does not contain the item, and admit that it does if the item is found ('item found' would be the quit condition). If a line of text is to be checked for correct syntax, it is necessary to posit that the line is correct and admit that it is incorrect if an element which does not conform to the syntax rules is detected. If a program may terminate prematurely owing to the detection of a processing error, it is necessary to posit a complete execution and admit an incomplete execution if an error is detected.

Backtracking is not supported by any existing programming language but is easily incorporated into a PDL such as HOST and converted into linear source code. The lack of adequate constructs in current programming languages should not be used as an excuse to use switches rather than backtracking; the correct program structures obtained using JSP should not be changed to suit the vagaries of any language, otherwise implementation and maintenance problems will ensue. A detailed exposition of backtracking is presented in the following sections of this chapter, beginning with an analogy of condition evaluation problems.

7.2 HAMISH GOES FOR A WALK

Let us forsake the problems of DP programming for a while and join Hamish, who, after a harrowing week in the office debugging a particularly intransigent program full of GOTOs and switches (written long ago by the now DP manager), takes off to the Highlands for a breath of fresh air. With his rucksack on his back he sets out on foot to climb the Ben. He has always had a yearning to climb the Ben, but until now the long approach march through a wild and remote glen has always seemed beyond his capabilities. Now, however, his friend Angus has told him that at the end of the glen is a bothy, not marked on the map, where he can spend the night. In addition, he has agreed to secrete a food cache in the area for Angus who is planning a future cross-country backpacking expedition.

After a gruelling walk through the glen Hamish arrives at the foot of the Ben, and with the light beginning to fade he re-reads the instructions written down by Angus concerning the situation of the bothy:

Follow the main glen North until you reach a fork in the river at the foot of the Ben. The bothy lies about a mile along the river from there. You'll pass a large boulder with room underneath it to shelter—leave the food cache there. Then you'll come to a lone pine tree, and the bothy's just beyond that.

Unfortunately Angus has omitted to tell Hamish which branch of the river to follow when he comes to the fork! Fig. 7.2 shows a sketch-map of the area.

As an experienced walker Hamish naturally has a map with him, but on his map neither the boulder, the tree nor the bothy are marked. He must follow one branch of the river or the other, but cannot determine which is the correct one until after he has set off walking. After a few minutes deliberation at the fork he decides there is only one course of action open to him: try one branch or the other, it doesn't matter which. Arbitrarily he opts for the left branch and sets off at a good pace in order to reach the bothy before nightfall.

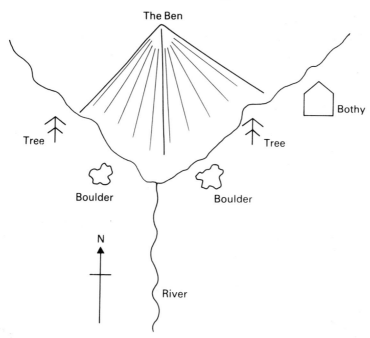

Figure 7.2

Soon he comes to a large boulder with a large space beneath it where it rests against the hillside, and believing he is on the correct track he deposits the food cache there. A little further along he comes to a boulder-strewn part of the river which would make a good crossing point for his attempt on the Ben the following day, and he builds a small cairn beside the track to mark the spot. A little further along he notices some driftwood washed high and dry by a winter spate, and gathers it for a bothy fire.

After a mile he comes to a lone pine tree, but when he looks for the expected bothy it is nowhere to be seen. It dawns on him that he must have taken the wrong branch after all, and in gathering darkness he rushes to retrace his steps. As he passes the boulder he removes the food cache. At the fork he takes the right branch, and before long he comes to another large boulder, beneath which he again leaves the food cache. Further along is a lone pine tree, and there beyond it lies the bothy. He arrives just as the light fades and before long has a lovely fire burning in the hearth, using the driftwood he has collected during his unexpected detour.

If only all programmers behaved as logically as Hamish! Then, perhaps, the DP department would be as peaceful and welcoming as that bothy at the foot of the Ben. Let us analyse Hamish's activities. When he reached the fork he made an arbitrary decision about which branch to take, and then, having taken the wrong branch, he retraced his footsteps and took the other (correct) branch. He adopted a backtracking solution to the problem—he tried one branch and as soon as he was able to detect that it was the wrong branch he backtracked.

In order to distinguish between the two branches and describe the backtracking procedure without ambiguity, the constructs posit, admit and quit are used.

The posit branch is the first branch chosen. When Hamish came to the fork he posited (i.e. postulated, assumed) that the left branch was the correct branch. The admit branch is the other branch. When Hamish discovered that there was no bothy on the left branch, he admitted to himself that he was on the wrong branch; the right branch was the admit branch. In order to get from the posit branch to the admit branch he quit the posit branch by retracing his footsteps. To sum up the backtracking procedure: posit one branch is correct and quit to the admit branch if you are wrong.

The backtracking solution is not the only solution to Hamish's problem. A less experienced programmer, on reaching the tree on the left branch of the river and finding no bothy beyond it, might have been tempted to take a short cut across the country round the foot of the Ben to the right branch. This is a GOTO solution. It may save time, but it may not. It may involve a difficult river crossing and detours round rock faces, and it would risk being overtaken by darkness in difficult country. Backtracking is the only safe, logical solution, and it is the one adopted by JSP for the resolution of condition evaluation problems.

Because Hamish took the wrong branch initially, a number of interesting things happened: he deposited the food cache under the wrong boulder, he built a cairn which would serve no purpose and he found some driftwood which did serve a useful purpose. In backtracking terminology such events are called side-effects, and it can be seen that there are three kinds of side-effect: favourable, neutral and intolerable.

Finding the driftwood was a favourable side-effect of taking the wrong branch—there may have been no driftwood on the correct branch, and that would have meant no fire. Building the cairn was a neutral side-effect—it would no longer serve any useful purpose as Hamish would no longer have to cross the left branch of the river in order to climb the Ben, but it did no harm to leave it there. Leaving the food cache under the wrong boulder, however, was an intolerable side-effect—it had to be retrieved and stored under the correct boulder if Hamish was not to incur the wrath of Angus.

Backtracking does not necessarily cause side-effects, but when they occur they must be considered and dealt with.

7.3 BACKTRACKING WITH NO SIDE-EFFECTS

Incorporating backtracking into program design involves the following steps:

1 When drawing data and program structure diagrams, indicate selection conditions which cannot be evaluated by drawing a '?' preceding the '0' in selected components. The left branch becomes the posit branch, the right branch becomes the admit branch. In Fig. 7.3, for example, *A* is a selection component, *B* is a posit component/branch, *C* is an admit component/branch.

Multi-way selections must be split into nested two-way selections. A null admit branch which contains no operations cannot be omitted; unlike a null selected component it must be present in order that quits can be generated correctly in the source code.

2 Insert quit conditions into the posit branch at points where its correctness can be disproven. This forms a new step of the JSP design procedure: Step 3.3. A quit condition is specified in the form:

    Quit posit-component-name if (condition).

3 Handle side-effects.

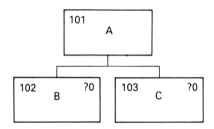

Figure 7.3

The examples in this section illustrate the basic backtracking procedure; side-effects are discussed in Sections 7.4 and 7.5.

The transformation of posit, quit and admit constructs into HOST and COBOL is undertaken for Example 7.3.1 only; it is a trivial exercise which does not bear repeating.

Example 7.3.1

A college maintains a file of student records, which is updated by a transactions file. A student record consists of the fields: student matriculation number, student name and address, and course code. A transaction record consists of these same fields plus transaction type (*A, D* or *I,* indicating amend, delete or insert). A program is required to validate the transactions file, write valid transactions to a valid transactions file and invalid transactions to an error report.

 Validation checks required:
  Student number : in range 1–999998
  Transaction type: *A, D* or *I*
  Course code : in range 1–50

 Step 1 Draw data structure diagrams of the transactions file, the valid
     transactions file and the error report (see Figs 7.4, 7.5 and 7.6).

Note how the presence of a selection condition which cannot be evaluated is indicated on selected components by a '?' preceding the '0'. VAL-TRANS is the posit branch of the selection, INVAL-TRANS is the admit branch.

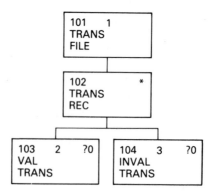

Figure 7.4

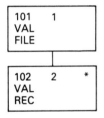

Figure 7.5

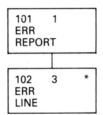

Figure 7.6

Step 2   Form a program structure diagram (see Fig. 7.7), (using the correspondences indicated above, which should need no explanation).

Step 3.1   List and allocate operations (see Fig. 7.7).

1   Open all files.
2   Close all files.
3   Read record from transactions file.
4   Format and write valid record.
5   Format and write error line.

For the purposes of this example error line will be considered to contain the details of an invalid transaction record together with the message 'INVALID TRANSACTION', irrespective of the cause of invalidity. Example 7.4.2 illustrates the case where different messages are required for different causes of invalidity.

Step 3.2   List and allocate conditions (see Fig. 7.7).

C1   End of transactions file.

No conditions can be allocated to P-VAL-TRANS and P-INVAL-TRANS.

To complete the program design it is necessary to insert quit conditions into the posit branch at points where its correctness can be disproved. This forms a new step of the JSP design procedure: Step 3.3.

Step 3.3   List and allocate quits and backtracking operations (see Fig. 7.7).

Note: backtracking operations concerned with side-effects are discussed in Section 7.4.

Conditions cannot be allocated to P-VAL-TRANS and P-INVAL-TRANS, but quit conditions can be allocated to the posit branch (P-VAL-TRANS) at points where its correctness can be disproved (i.e. at points where the record's validity can be disproved). There are three such points: following examination of student number, following examination of transaction type and following examination of course code. Therefore there are three quits to be allocated.

!1 Quit P-VAL-TRANS if (student number < 1 OR > 999998).

!2 Quit P-VAL-TRANS if (transaction type not=('A' OR 'D' OR 'T')).

!3 Quit P-VAL-TRANS if (course code < 1 OR > 50).

The '!' before the quit condition number differentiates quit conditions from normal conditions and operations on a program structure diagram. Note that in a practical COBOL program the above conditions should be replaced by condition names.

Note that quit conditions are allocated in the same way as operations in order to indicate sequencing.

The program design is now complete, and all that remains to be done is to transform the program structure diagram with allocated operations

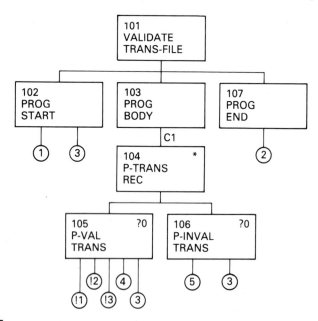

Figure 7.7

and conditions into HOST and source language code. HOST uses the backtracking constructs posit, quit and admit directly as statements, coded according to the transformation rules given in Appendix D (Section 1, rule 1.6).

Applying these transformation rules to Example 7.3.1 will produce the following HOST program:

```
101-VALIDATE-TRANS-FILE.
    Do 102-PROG-START.
    Do 103-PROG-BODY.
    Do 107-PROG-END.
102-PROG-START.
    Open all files.
    Read record from transactions file.
103-PROG-BODY ITER.
    Do 104-P-TRANS-REC until (end of transactions file).
104-P-TRANS-REC POSIT.
    Do 105-P-VAL-TRANS POSIT.
    Do 106-P-INVAL-TRANS ADMIT.
105-P-VAL-TRANS.
    Quit P-VAL-TRANS if (student number < 1 or > 999998).
    Quit P-VAL-TRANS if (transaction type not = ('A' or 'D' or
    'T')).
    Quit P-VAL-TRANS if (course code < 1 or > 50).
    Format and write valid record.
    Read record from transactions file.
106-P-INVAL-TRANS.
    Format and write error line.
    Read record from transactions file.
107-PROG-END.
    Close all files.
```

Ideally this program will be compiled into source code using a HOST precompiler, in which case all operations must be specified as source language instructions rather than as macro operations. If hand-compiling into source code it is permissible to use macro operations in HOST to avoid writing detailed operations in both HOST and the source language.

The HOST statements posit, quit and admit are easily compiled into linear BASIC and COBOL code using the transformation rules given in Appendix D (Section 2, rule 2.5). Applying these transformation rules to the above HOST program will produce the following BASIC and COBOL programs. Note that macro operations have been retained in the source code for purposes of simplification.

BASIC:

```
100   REM VALIDATE-TRANS-FILE
110   GOTO 200
120   GOTO 300
130   GOTO 700
140   END
200   REM PROG-START
210   Open all files
220   INPUT #1,...
230   GOTO 120
300   REM PROG-BODY
310   IF NOT EOF (1) GOTO 400
320   GOTO 130
400   REM P-TRANS-REC
410   GOTO 500
420   GOTO 300
500   REM-P-VAL-TRANS
510   IF STUD.NO <1 OR STUD.NO >999998 GOTO 600
520   IF NOT (TRANS.TYPE$='A' OR TRANS.TYPE$='D'
          OR TRANS.TYPE$='T') GOTO 600
530   IF COURSE.CODE <1 OR COURSE.CODE >50 GOTO 600
540   Format and write valid record.
550   INPUT #1,...
560   GOTO 420
600   REM P-INVAL-TRANS
610   Format and write error line.
620   INPUT #1,...
630   GOTO 420
700   REM PROG-END
710   Close all files
720   GOTO 140
```

COBOL:

```
PROCEDURE DIVISION.
101-VALIDATE-TRANS-FILE-MAIN SECTION.
101-VALIDATE-TRANS-FILE.
    GO TO 102-PROG-START.
102-PROG-START-EXIT.
    GO TO 103-PROG-BODY.
103-PROG-BODY-EXIT.
    GO TO 107-PROG-END.
107-PROG-END-EXIT.
    STOP RUN.
```

```
102-PROG-START.
    Open all files.
    READ TRANS-FILE AT END MOVE '1' TO EOF-SW.
    GO TO 102-PROG-START-EXIT.
103-PROG-BODY.
104-P-TRANS-REC-EXIT.
    IF NOT (EOF-SW = '1')
        GO TO 104-P-TRANS-REC.
    GO TO 103-PROG-BODY-EXIT.
104-P-TRANS-REC.
    GO TO 105-P-VAL-TRANS.
105-P-VAL-TRANS-EXIT.
106-P-INVAL-TRANS-EXIT.
    GO TO 104-P-TRANS-REC-EXIT.
105-P-VAL-TRANS.
    IF (STUD-NO NOT NUMERIC) OR (STUD-NO < 1 OR > 999998)
        GO TO 106-P-INVAL-TRANS.
    IF TRANS-TYPE NOT = 'A' AND NOT = 'I' AND NOT = 'D'
        GO TO 106-P-INVAL-TRANS.
    IF (COURSE-CODE NOT NUMERIC) OR (COURSE-CODE < 1 OR
    > 50)
        GO TO 106-P-INVAL-TRANS.
    Format and write VAL-REC.
    READ TRANS-FILE AT END MOVE '1' TO EOF-INDIC.
    GO TO 105-P-INVAL-TRANS-EXIT.
106-P-INVAL-TRANS.
    Format and write ERR-LINE.
    READ TRANS-FILE AT END MOVE '1' TO EOF-INDIC.
    GO TO 106-P-INVAL-TRANS-EXIT.
107-PROG-END.
    Close all files.
    GO TO 107-P-PROG-EXIT.
```

As with sequence, selection and iteration, the backtracking constructs posit, quit and admit are transformed into source code using the GOTO statement. It is worth repeating that the program design and the HOST program are wholly GOTO-less, and the fact that the source code contains GOTOs is irrelevant. The quit statement in particular is transformed directly into a GOTO and is the first JSP construct you have come across which can only be represented in current programming languages as a GOTO.

Programmers not familiar with the JSP design method often mistake the quit for a GOTO, but this merely underlines their misunderstanding of JSP. The quit is not a GOTO, it is a statement used to exit from a posited program component. The destination of a GOTO is completely without constraint, the destination of a quit can only be the admit component.

The fact that a quit must be coded as a GOTO does not mean that it is a GOTO; one might as well say that a COBOL PERFORM is a GOTO because this is one way of coding it in Assembler.

At the risk of repeating part of the discussion presented in Chapter 4: current programming languages are inadequate for the coding of constructs used in the JSP design method. This does not mean that the method is incorrect, merely that the languages are outdated and inadequate. Hence the use of a PDL such as HOST in which programs can be coded and maintained, with the aid of a HOST precompiler to transform the program automatically into source code if at all possible. Note that there are some current languages which do have quit-like statements (e.g. Pascal's BREAK statement which jumps out of an iteration), but these are very restricted in their use and should not be confused with the JSP quit construct which can only be implemented using a GOTO.

7.4   USING FAVOURABLE SIDE-EFFECTS

Example 7.4.1

This example is an expansion of Example 6.1.1.

A program is required to process customer transactions at a bank's cash dispensing terminal. Each transaction consists of three inputs: an account number, a PIN and a withdrawal amount. The following validation checks are required:

Account number   : a five-figure number in range 1–10000
PIN   : a four-figure number
Withdrawal amount: a three-figure number in range 1–100

A customer is allowed three attempts at each stage of the transaction to get an input correct, else the transaction is terminated with the message 'TRANSACTION ERROR'.

Step 1   Draw a data structure diagram of customer transactions (see Figs 7.8 to 7.11).

A complete transaction consists of some possible invalid account numbers (there may be none) before the customer gets it right, then some possible invalid PINs before the customer gets it right, then some possible invalid withdrawal amounts before the customer gets it right. A transaction is incomplete if it is cancelled because the customer requires more than three shots at getting any one input correct. It cannot be determined at the start of a transaction whether the customer will complete it or not, so it is necessary to posit a complete transaction and quit to an incomplete transaction if the customer makes three failed attempts at any input.

An incomplete transaction has a very complex data structure; it will contain at least a number of invalid customer numbers, but it may or may not contain any other data, depending on when the transaction is cancelled. As a result of the favourable side-effects of backtracking, however, the structure of an incomplete transaction is irrelevant. On entry to the admit branch all necessary processing of a transaction has already been undertaken by the posit branch; all that remains to be done is to output the message 'TRANSACTION ERROR'. As a favourable side-effect, therefore, the whole data structure of an incomplete transaction can be omitted.

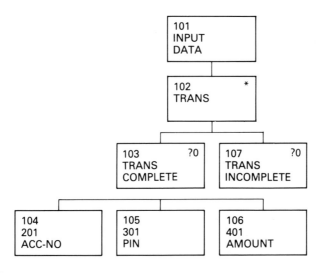

Figure 7.8

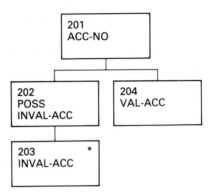

Figure 7.9

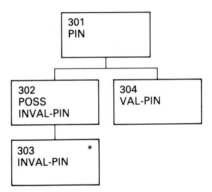

Figure 7.10

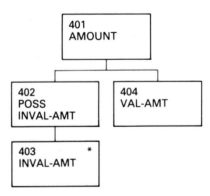

Figure 7.11

Step 2   Form a program structure diagram (see Figs 7.12 to 7.15).

Step 3.1   List and allocate operations (see Figs 7.12 to 7.15).

    1   Input IN-FIELD..
    2   Output 'PLEASE ENTER ACCOUNT NUMBER'.
    3   Output 'PLEASE ENTER PIN'.
    4   Output 'PLEASE ENTER WITHDRAWAL AMOUNT'.
    5   Output 'INVALID ACCOUNT NUMBER, PLEASE RE-EN-
       TER'.
    6   Output 'INVALID PIN, PLEASE RE-ENTER'.
    7   Output 'INVALID AMOUNT, PLEASE RE-ENTER'.
    8   Pay out withdrawal amount.
    9   Output 'TRANSACTION COMPLETE. THANKYOU.'.
   10   Output 'TRANSACTION ERROR. CONSULT BANK MAN-
       AGER.'.

Step 3.2   List and allocate conditions (see Figs 7.12 to 7.15).

    C1   Shutdown (e.g. account number=all 9s).
    C2   Account number valid.
    C3   PIN valid.
    C4   Withdrawal amount valid.

Step 3.3   List and allocate quits and backtracking operations (see Figs
       7.12 to 7.15).

    !1   Quit P-TRANS-COMPLETE if (three invalid inputs).

In real terms quit condition !1 requires some counting mechanism in the list of operations, but these will be ignored for purposes of simplicity.

Extensions to this type of problem are common and easily handled. One necessary extension, as in Example 6.1.1, would be to access an account balance file in order that the account balance could be updated following the withdrawal transaction. Another common extension would be to allow the customer to cancel a transaction at any point, which would require further quit conditions within the posit branch. Another common extension would be to output different error messages depending upon the cause of cancellation. This is akin to a validation program where different error messages are required depending upon the cause of invalidity, and an example of this is given next (see Example 7.4.2).

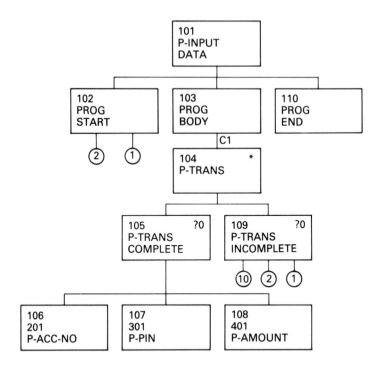

Figure 7.12

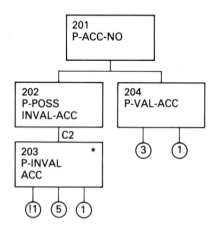

Figure 7.13

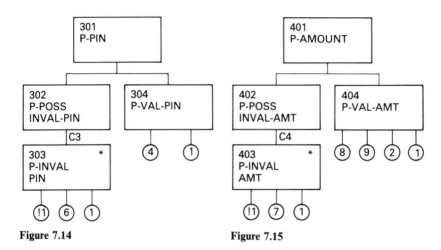

Figure 7.14   **Figure 7.15**

Note

There is an alternative method of designing this program which does not use the read-ahead principle. The processing of a transaction could be written as (ignoring any possible invalidity, as in Example 6.1.1):

> Input account number.
> Process account number.
> Input PIN.
> Process PIN.
> Input withdrawal amount.
> Process withdrawal amount.

This transaction processing can be regarded as continuing indefinitely (i.e. posit that P-TRANS is iterated forever), and a quit taken to PROG-END when shutdown is detected. Quits to an incomplete transaction component in cases of invalidity or cancellation can be incorporated as usual. In this approach there is no condition to end the iteration of P-TRANS, which is called a positer construct. P-TRANS-COMPLETE becomes a posit component nested within the positer component P-TRANS forever. You must be careful when specifying quits in a nested posit; the component name specified in the quit statement will determine whether the quit is from the nested posit or the higher-level posit (see Example 7.4.4). It is left to the reader to decide whether he wishes to use the positer construct in this way.

Example 7.4.2

Example 7.3.1 considered the validation of a file of transaction records to a Student File (see Fig. 7.7). Invalid records were printed on an error report together with the message 'INVALID TRANSACTION'. Commonly an indication of the cause of invalidity would also be required, e.g. one of the error messages 'INVALID STUD-NO', 'INVALID TRANS-TYPE' or 'INVALID COURSE-CODE'.

One way to program this requirement would be to include a selection between the three possible causes of invalidity in the P-INVAL-TRANS branch, i.e. P-INVAL-TRANS would become a selection between P-INVAL-STUD-NO, P-INVAL-TRANS-TYPE and P-INVAL-COURSE-CODE. Then an operation which outputs the appropriate error message could be allocated to each of the three selected components.

The only problem with this approach is its long-windedness—the validation checks which form the quit statements in the posit branch would have to be repeated as selection conditions in the admit branch.

A second solution makes use of the favourable side-effects that at the point where the posit branch is quit, the cause of invalidity is known, and therefore the appropriate error message can be set up in the error line at the time of the quit. The program structure diagram remains as in Fig. 7.7; all that changes are the quit statements:

List of new quits and backtracking operations:

!1   Quit P-VAL-TRANS if (student number < 1 or > 999998
     Move 'INVALID STUD-NO' to error message).
!2   Quit P-VAL-TRANS if (transaction type not $= $ ('*A*' or '*D*' or '*T*')
     Move 'INVALID TRANS-TYPE' to error message).
!3   Quit P-VAL-TRANS if (course code < 1 or > 50
     Move 'INVALID COURSE-CODE' to error message).

In BASIC !1 would be coded as:

```
IF STUD.NO < 1 OR STUD.NO > 999998 THEN
   LET ERRMESS$ = "INVALID STUD-NO":
   GOTO nnn
```

In COBOL !1 would be coded as:

```
IF (STUD-NO NOT NUMERIC) OR (STUD-NO < 1 OR > 999998)
   MOVE 'INVALID STUD-NO' TO ERR-MESS
   GO TO 106-P-INVAL-TRANS.
```

In this example all the quit conditions occur together, but it is quite possible for them to be separated by operations. Consider an amendment to the program to check that a student number, in addition to being numeric and in range, also exists on a Student Number File, accessed directly (see Fig. 7.16).

Additional operations (in COBOL):

6 Set INVAL-SW to '0'.
7 Read Student Number File INVALID KEY MOVE '1' TO INVAL-SW.

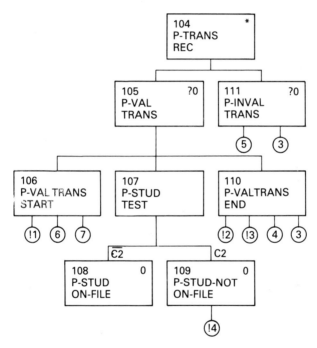

Figure 7.16

Additional condition:

    C2   INVAL-SW = '1'.

Additional quit:

    !4   Quit P-VAL-TRANS if (INVAL-SW = '1'
        Move 'NON-EXISTENT STUD-NO' to error message).

Note that as there are no operations allocated to components P-STUD-ON-FILE and P-STUD-NOT-ON-FILE in this program, they could be omitted and quit statement !4 allocated directly to component P-STUD-TEST. In fact all sub-components of P-VAL-TRANS could be omitted and all operations and quit conditions allocated directly to P-VAL-TRANS, although care would have to be taken with their ordering.

There is a further common extension to a validation program such as Example 7.3.1. The original specification required that all invalid transactions be reported in the same way. In the above example it was required to distinguish the cause of invalidity, with validation processing being terminated on detection of the first invalidity. Often, however, it is required to continue processing beyond the first invalid field detected, in order to report all invalid fields.

Consider the design of a program which prints for each invalid transaction an error line containing the three input fields, followed by a star line containing asterisks (stars) beneath each invalid field. The solution given for Example 7.3.1, which posits a valid transaction record and quits to the invalid branch if an invalid field is detected, is no longer a good solution for this new program specification, because further validation would be required within the admit branch to determine whether any other fields were also invalid. A better solution is to posit an invalid transaction (see Fig. 7.17).

A valid transaction record consists of valid fields only, but an invalid record may have an invalid student number and/or an invalid transaction type and/or an invalid course code.

Additional operations:

  6   Move all '*' to star line student number.
  7   Move all '*' to star line update type.
  8   Move all '*' to star line course code.
  9   Write star line.
 10   Set star line to spaces.

New list of quits:

  !1   Quit P-INVAL-TRANS if (star line = spaces).

This is the only quit required.

The moral of this example is: make sure that you choose the correct logical structure diagram for the program. Incorporating validation

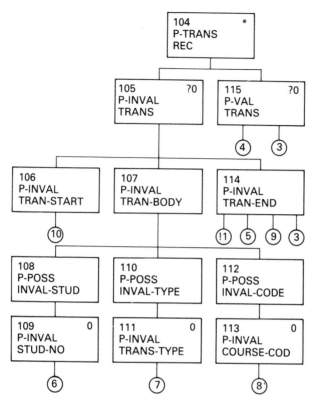

Figure 7.17

processing into a program structure is never easy, no matter what design method is used, because the set of invalid data is always so much greater and more intricately structured than the set of valid data. Nevertheless, if you get into difficulties with validation programs (or any programs containing condition evaluation problems), re-ordering the posit and admit branches will normally resolve any problems concerning the allocation of quits. As a general rule of thumb, choose as the posit branch the one whose entry hypothesis is most easily disproved.

Example 7.4.3

A table contains 100 items. A program is required to search the table using a key input at a terminal, and output the message 'FOUND' or 'NOT FOUND' depending upon whether a matching item is found.

The traditional, flowcharted solution to this problem would use a 'found switch', initialized to '0', set to '1' if a match was found and then tested following the search. JSP does not use switches. The program specification explicitly mentions a selection between 'found' and 'not found' states, and this is a clue to the correct logical data structure diagram of the table—the table either contains a matched item or it does not.

Step 1   Draw a data structure diagram of the table (see Fig. 7.18).

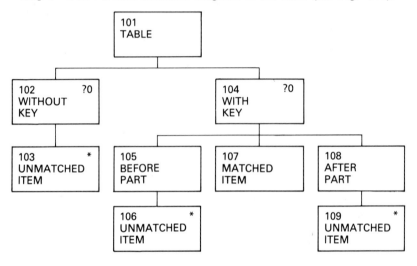

Figure 7.18

If the table does not contain an item which matches the key, it consists only of unmatched items; if it does contain a matched item, it consists of a number of unmatched items occurring before the matched item, followed by the matched item, followed by a number of other unmatched items. Backtracking is required because the condition which determines whether the table contains a matched item cannot be evaluated until after the table has been processed. The backtracking solution is to posit that there is no matched item (WITHOUT-KEY) and quit to the admit branch (WITH-KEY) if there is. This results in the favourable side-effect that when the admit branch is entered the matched item has already been found, and therefore the data structure of the component WITH-KEY is superfluous. It is a common result of a favourable side-effect, as in Examples 7.4.1 and 7.4.2, that parts of the structure of the admit branch can be removed.

Step 2   Form a program structure diagram (see Fig. 7.19).

Step 3.1   List and allocate operations (see Fig. 7.19).

    1   Input key.
    2   Set subscript to 1.
    3   Add 1 to subscript.
    4   Output 'FOUND'.
    5   Output 'NOT FOUND'.

Step 3.2   List and allocate conditions (see Fig. 7.19).

    C1   Subscript > 100.

Step 3.3   List and allocate quits and backtracking operations (see Fig. 7.19).

    !1   Quit P-WITHOUT-KEY if (key = item (subscript)).

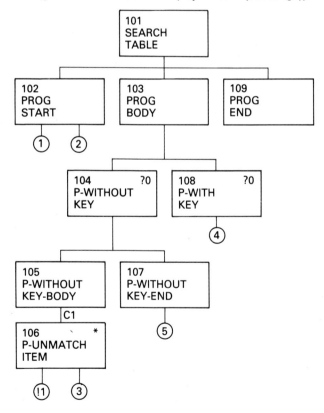

Figure 7.19

Another way to write this program in COBOL would be to use the SEARCH verb. SEARCH is a COBOL macro operation which handles the incrementing of the subscript (in the form of an index) automatically. The purpose of such macro operations is to save design and coding work by providing high-level operations, enabling simple operations and parts of a program structure diagram to be removed. When using the SEARCH verb, for instance, the logical structure used in Fig. 7.19 is redundant.

The SEARCH operation is akin to a Read operation on a direct-access file. A direct-access Read results in a 'found' or 'not found' condition, and as COBOL does not provide a predefined field to test this condition, the programmer must invent his own—INVAL-SW (see Section 6.1). A COBOL SEARCH operation also results in a 'found' or 'not found' condition, and again the programmer must invent his own field to test the condition—FOUND-SW.

```
SET INDEX1 TO 1.
SEARCH ITEM
    AT END
        MOVE '0' TO FOUND-SW
    WHEN INPUT-KEY = ITEM (INDEX1)
        MOVE '1' TO FOUND-SW.
```

Fig. 7.20 shows the program structure diagram with allocated operations and conditions.

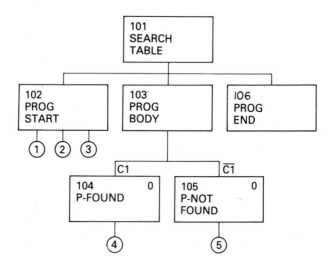

Figure 7.20

List of operations:

    1   Input key.
    2   Set INDEX1 to 1.
    3   SEARCH ITEM
         AT END
            MOVE '0' TO FOUND-SW
         WHEN INPUT-KEY = ITEM (INDEX1)
            MOVE '1' TO FOUND-SW.
    4   Output 'FOUND'.
    5   Output 'NOT FOUND'.

List of conditions:

    C1   FOUND-SW = '1'.

It is probably worth repeating here that JSP does not condone the use of programmer-invented switches, but that switches such as EOF-SW (on a sequential file READ), INVAL-SW (on a direct-access file READ) and FOUND-SW (on a SEARCH) are required on certain COBOL operations because COBOL does not provide any means of testing the result of those operations outside the statement in question. This restricted use of switches is forced upon the programmer, and does not invalidate the general case against programmer-invented switches.

Example 7.4.4

A program is required to undertake an interactive test of a student's knowledge. Questions are displayed one at a time on a VDU screen and the student has three attempts to get the answer correct. In addition, the student may cancel the test at any time. The program is required to output the number of correct answers.

Step 1   Draw a data structure diagram of the test (see Fig. 7.21)

This is an example of nested backtracking. Posit a complete test and quit to an incomplete test if the student cancels; a favourable side-effect of this is that the structure of an incomplete test is irrelevant. A complete test consists of a number of answers. The student is allowed three shots at getting an answer correct, so posit a correct answer and quit if his three attempts fail; a favourable side-efect of this is that the structure of an incorrect answer is irrelevant. A cancel terminates the whole test, but three incorrect answers to a question merely terminates the question, hence the nested backtracking.

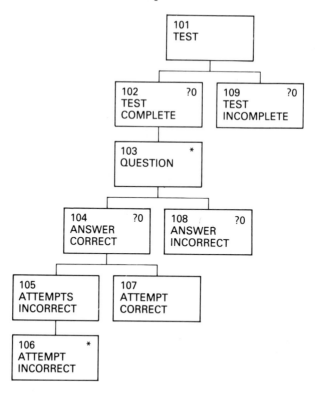

Figure 7.21

Step 2   Form a program structure diagram (see Fig. 7.22).

Step 3.1   List and allocate operations (see Fig. 7.22).

     1   Output next question.
     2   Input answer.
     3   Output 'ANSWER CORRECT'.
     4   Output 'ANSWER INCORRECT – TRY AGAIN'.
     5   Output 'ANSWER INCORRECT – TRY NEXT QUESTION'.
     6   Add 1 to answer total.
     7   Output answer total.
     8   Output instructions.

Step 3.2   List and allocate conditions (see Fig. 7.22).

     C1   No more questions.
     C2   Answer is correct.

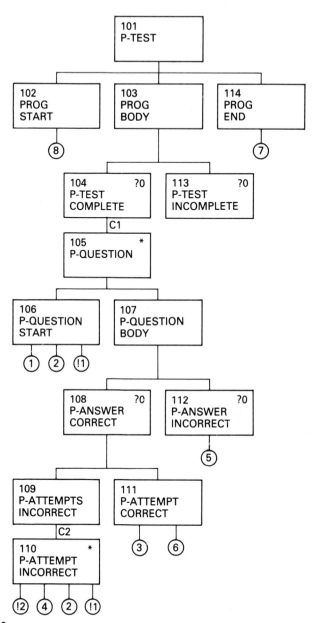

Figure 7.22

Step 3.3   List and allocate quits and backtracking operations (see Fig. 7.22).

!1 Quit P-TEST-COMPLETE if (cancel).

!2 Quit P-ANSWER-CORRECT if (three incorrect answers).

Note the allocation of quits. Quit conditions !1 and !2 are allocated to the same program component P-ATTEMPT-INCORRECT but apply to different posit components. !1 quits from P-TEST-COMPLETE (to P-TEST-INCOM-PLETE); !2 quits from P-ANSWER-CORRECT (to P-ANSWER-INCORRECT).

Note also that it is not strictly necessary to use the read-ahead principle for operation 2 in this program, because the order of arrival of input is known. If there are ten questions, P-QUESTION will be iterated ten times; therefore (unless the student cancels) there will be ten iterations of question and answer.

7.5 HANDLING INTOLERABLE SIDE-EFFECTS

Favourable side-effects are, by their very nature, useful, but intolerable side-effects must be cancelled out. Consider a validation program which posits a valid record and admits an invalid record. Any processing dependent upon the validity of the record which is undertaken before a quit may cause intolerable side-effects for the admit invalid branch, e.g.

1 An operation to add 1 to a total of valid records. If this total is incremented and then a quit taken to the invalid branch, the total will be incorrect.

2 An operation to move a record key to a current valid record key, in order that a sequence check can be undertaken. If the record turns out to be invalid following this operation, the current valid record key will be incorrect.

3 An operation to write a valid record to a valid file. If the record turns out to be invalid following this operation, the valid file will contain invalid records.

Of course, none of these operations should be undertaken until the complete validity of a record has been established, but they serve as simple examples of intolerable side-effects for purposes of exposition.

There are three strategies which can be adopted to cancel out intolerable side-effects:

Store ... Restore ...

Before doing an operation which may cause an intolerable side-effect, *store* the value of the variable upon which it is operating, then *restore* the value in the event of a quit. In 1 above, before adding 1 to a total of valid records, store the total (Move valid-total to valid-total-store), then restore it in the event of a quit (Move valid-total-store to valid-total). In 2, before moving the record key to the current valid record key, store the current valid record key (Move current-key to current-key-store), then restore it in the event of a quit (Move current-key-store to current-key). The store ... restore ... strategy will not work for the Write operation in 3 because once a record has been written to a file the situation which existed before the Write operation cannot then be restored.

Do ... Undo ...

After *doing* an operation which may cause an intolerable side-effect, *undo* it in the event of a quit. This was the strategy adopted by Hamish to recover the food cache which he had deposited beneath the wrong boulder. In 1, after adding 1 to a total of valid records, subtract 1 in the event of a quit. The DO ... UNDO ... strategy will not work for the Move and Write operations in 2 and 3 because they cannot be undone.

Pretend ... Really ...

Instead of doing an operation which may cause an intolerable side-effect, only *pretend* to do it, then *really* do it only when you are sure that there will be no quit following. In 1, instead of adding 1 to a valid total, add 1 to a temporary total then add that temporary total to the valid total only when there can be no more quits. In 2, instead of moving the record key to the current key, move it to a store, then move the store to the current key only when there can be no more quits. In 3, instead of writing a valid record to the valid file, 'write' it to a store (Move record to record-store), then really write it only when there can be no more quits (Write valid record from record-store).

Different strategies are best in different circumstances, and it would be difficult to present hard and fast rules about which to use in which situation. Sometimes, as indicated in the foregoing, more than one strategy is possible, and the choice is largely one of programmer preference.

Example 7.5.1

This example contains neutral and favourable side-effects as well as intolerable˙ side-effects. An accounts file contains details of customer accounts. For each account there is an account header followed by a number of transaction records and an account trailer. An account header contains customer name, a field which contains the value '*S*' if the account is designated as a special account, and other information. A transaction record contains a transaction amount field. An account trailer contains a total of all transaction amounts for that account.

A program is required to check that the account trailer totals are correct. If an account trailer total is correct it is to be printed on a report, along with the customer name from the account header and the legend 'SPECIAL' if the account is a special account. In addition, a total of transaction amounts for all printed accounts is required.

Step 1   Draw data structure diagrams of the accounts file and report (see Figs 7.23 to 7.26).

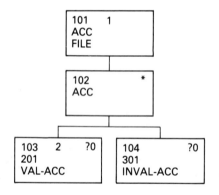

Figure 7.23

An account is either valid or invalid depending on the correctness of its account trailer total, but until its transaction records have been processed and the account trailer examined its validity cannot be established, hence the need for the posit and admit components VAL-ACC and INVAL-ACC.

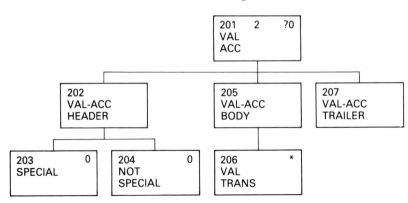

Figure 7.24

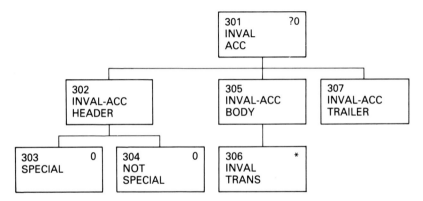

Figure 7.25

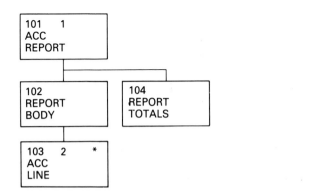

Figure 7.26

Step 2   Form a program structure diagram (see Fig. 7.27)

The program posits a valid account and quits if the account trailer total is incorrect. This has the favourable side-effect that the admit branch is entered with an invalid account trailer, and therefore the structure of an invalid account is redundant and can be omitted.

Step 3.1   List and allocate operations (see Fig. 7.27).

  1   Open all files.
  2   Close all files.
  3   Read record from accounts file.
  4   Move customer name from account header to printline.
  5   Move 'SPECIAL' to 'special' field on printline.
  6   Move spaces to 'special' field on printline.
  7   Write printline using account total.
  8   Add transaction amount to account total.
  9   Add transaction amount to report total.
10   Set account total to 0.
11   Write report total line.

Step 3.2   List and allocate conditions (see Fig. 7.27).

C1   End of accounts file.
C2   Special account.
C3   Account trailer.

Step 3.3   List and allocate quits and backtracking operations (see Fig. 7.27).

!1   Quit P-VAL-ACC if (account trailer not = account total).
!2   Move report total to report total store.
!3   Move report total store to report total.

The allocation of quit condition !1 should be obvious. Backtracking operations !2 and !3 are discussed below.

Information from the account header must be processed before transaction records and the account trailer are read, and hence before it can be ascertained whether the account is a valid one. Moving the customer name to the printline (operation 4) causes a neutral side-effect: if the account is invalid it does not matter that an invalid customer name has been moved to the printline, because it will be overwritten by the name of the next customer. The same considerations apply to moving the legend 'SPECIAL' to the printline (operation 5).

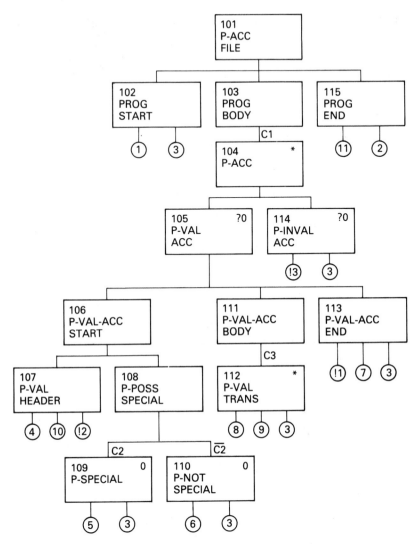

Figure 7.27

Adding the transaction amount to the report total (operation 9), however, is an intolerable side-effect if the account turns out to be invalid. It is not possible to undo this operation in the admit branch because it is not known at that point what amount has been added. It is possible to use the pretend ... really ... strategy and add amounts to a temporary total (pretend), then add the temporary total to the report total once the account trailer has been validated (really). But the designer of this program has opted for a store ... restore .. strategy. Operation !2 stores the report total before any amount is added to it and operation !3 restores if it the account turns out to be invalid.

There is another solution to this example which avoids intolerable side-effects altogether. Operation 9 allocated to P-VAL-TRANS could be specified as 'Add account total to report total', allocated to P-VAL-ACC-END following quit condition !1, in which case no intolerable side-effects would ensue.

There is also another solution to this example which does not involve backtracking. Backtracking is required because it cannot be determined whether an account is valid until after the account trailer has been read. So another solution would be to expand the read-ahead principle to read all the records for a single account into a store, then process the account trailer alongside the stored transaction records. This is known as multiple read-ahead.

P-ACC would become a sequence of P-ACC-START and P-ACC-BODY. All records for the account would be read into an internal table at P-ACC-START, and P-ACC-BODY would become a selection (which could now be evaluated) between P-VAL-ACC and P-INVAL-ACC.

However, multiple read-ahead becomes unwieldy if more than two or three records are required, because of the problem of storing records and processing those stores. Backtracking is a more general solution.

Example 7.5.2

The file INFILE consists of a number of batches. Each batch consists of a number of records followed by a batch trailer which contains a count of the number of records in the batch. If the batch trailer count is correct the whole batch is to be written to a valid file, else it is to be written to an invalid file.

    Step 1   Draw data structure diagrams of INFILE, the valid file and the invalid file (see Figs 7.28 to 7.30).

A batch is either valid or invalid, but until its records have been processed and the batch trailer examined its validity cannot be established, hence the need for the posit and admit components VAL-BATCH and INVAL-BATCH on the data structure diagram of INFILE.

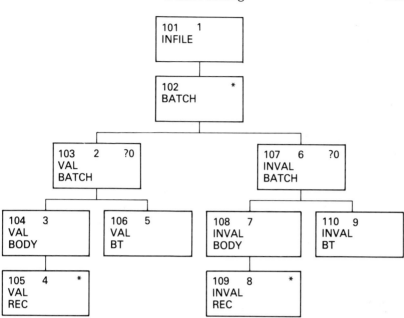

Figure 7.28

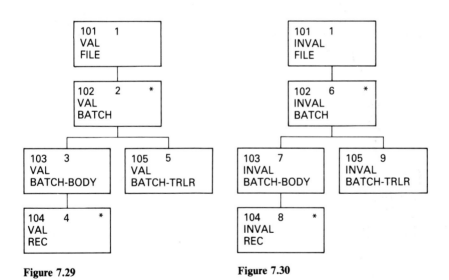

Figure 7.29   Figure 7.30

Step 2   Form a program structure diagram (see Fig. 7.31).

Posit a valid batch and quit if the batch trailer is incorrect. This has the favourable side-effect that the admit branch is entered with an invalid batch trailer, and therefore the structure of an invalid batch is redundant and can be omitted.

Step 3.1   List and allocate operations (see Fig. 7.31).

      1   Open all files.
      2   Close all files.
      3   Read record from INFILE.
      4   Add 1 to record total.
      5   Set record total to 0.

Step 3.2   List and allocate conditions (see Fig. 7.31).

      C1   End of INFILE.
      C2   Batch trailer.

Step 3.3   List and allocate quits and backtracking operations (see Fig. 7.31).

      !1   Quit P-VAL-BATCH if (batch trailer record total not = record total).
      !2   Set table of records to spaces.
      !3   Set subscript to 1.
      !4   Move input record to table element (subscript).
      !5   Add 1 to subscript.
      !6   Write table of records to valid file.
      !7   Write table of records to invalid file.

Although program component P-VAL-REC seems the obvious place to allocate an operation which writes a valid record, this would be an invalid allocation if it was followed by a quit to an invalid batch once the batch trailer had been read. As Write operations cannot be undone in the event of an invalid batch trailer, the only strategy which can be adopted to handle this intolerable side-effect is to *pretend* to write records to the valid file, but only *really* write them when a valid batch trailer has been read.

The easiest way to accomplish this is to store a record in an internal table instead of writing it (pretend), then write the whole table to the valid file on detection of a valid batch trailer (really). Backtracking operations

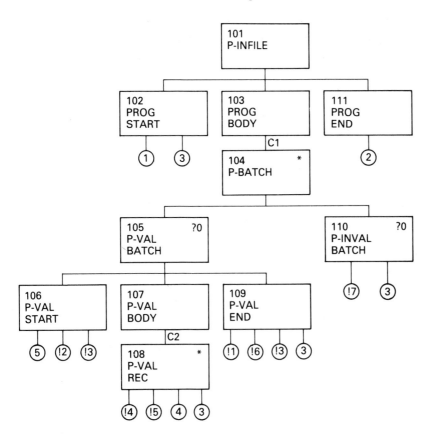

Figure 7.31

!2, !3, !4, !5, !6 and !7 accomplish this—desk check the program design to verify this.

Backtracking problems often require a great deal of thought, but any complexity lies in the nature of the problem not in the nature of its JSP solution. No solution to this problem could avoid the use of a table. The merit of the JSP approach is that it identifies an intolerable side-effect and shows the need for a table as part of an explicit strategy to cancel out that side-effect.

7.6 EXERCISES

1 The file INFILE contains three types of record: R1, R2 and R3. Records are valid only if they occur in groups of three, i.e. an R1 followed by an

R2 followed by an R3. In the following sample INFILE, valid records are underlined:

R1 <u>R1 R2 R3</u> R2 R3 R1 R2 <u>R1 R2 R3</u> R3

Design a program to output the total number of valid groups of records on the file.

Clue: a valid group of records is a sequence of R1, R2, R3; an invalid group is an iteration of invalid records.

2 Redesign the above program using multiple read-ahead instead of backtracking.

3 An update file contains batches of update records. The field UPD-TYPE on an update record indicates whether the record is an insertion ('*I*'), a deletion ('*D*'), an amendment ('*A*') or a rejection ('*X*'). Design a program to create a new update file from which all batches which contain rejections have been dropped. N.B. rejections may appear within a batch.

Clue: the program is similar to Example 7.5.2, except that batch invalidity may be detected at any point, not only at the end of a batch.

4 A character string held in a table contains up to forty characters terminated by a period. A valid character string contains two substrings, the first terminated by the number 0, the second by the number 9, e.g.

    VALID0STRING9.

Any characters occurring between the 9 and the period invalidate the string.
Design a procedure which validates the string and outputs the message 'VALID STRING' or 'INVALID STRING'.
Note that this exercise indicates how backtracking can be used to aid the design of syntax analysers, screen editors and compilers. Reference 20 contains further examples of these.

5 A direct-access file contains invoice records in customer number/invoice number sequence. A program is required to input a series of

customer numbers at a terminal (terminated by a customer number of all 9s) and output for each customer details of invoices, two records to a line. For example, if customer number 123456 has five invoices, output will be in the form:

invoice 1	invoice 2
invoice 3	invoice 4
invoice 5	

Clue: posit two records to a line, admit one record (quit if no more records).

Chapter 8

Inversion

When a program processes multiple data sets there are two techniques which can be applied to the design of the program: the correspondence technique and the inversion technique. The correspondence technique, presented in Chapter 5, combines multiple data structures into a single program structure. The inversion technique, presented in this chapter, keeps data structures separate, forms a procedure structure from each, allocates operations and conditions to each procedure structure, then combines the procedure structures into a single program structure. The technique involves two new sub-steps in the JSP design procedure:

2.2 Determine the interfaces between procedures.
3.4 List and allocate inversion operations.

8.1 THE TECHNIQUE OF INVERSION

When a program processes more than one set of data the program structure must be formed from all the data structures. There are two techniques which accomplish this:

1 The correspondence technique. Multiple data structures are combined into a single program structure by incorporating corresponding data components into the same program component.

2 The inversion technique. Data structures are kept separate, a procedure structure is formed from each data structure, operations and conditions are allocated to each procedure structure, and then the procedure structures are linked together by inversion.

Using the correspondence technique, we look for correspondences between two data structures and form a single program structure (see Fig. 8.1). Using the inversion technique, we form a procedure structure from each data structure, and then link them together to form the final program structure (see Fig. 8.2). Linking two procedures involves turning one into a subroutine of the other and passing data between them.

206

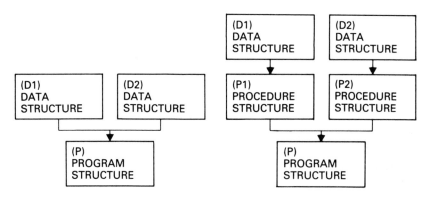

Figure 8.1   Figure 8.2

Suppose *D*1 in Fig. 8.2 is the data structure of an input file and *D*2 is the data structure of an output file. Procedure structures *P*1 and *P*2 are formed in the same way as program structures of programs which process a single data set: the procedure structure *P*1 is formed from the data structure *D*1, and the procedure structure *P*2 is formed from the data structure *D*2.

*P*1 is a procedure which reads the input file (*D*1) and passes data over to *P*2; *P*2 is a procedure which obtains data from *P*1 and writes the output file (*D*2). To link the two procedures, we can

either:

turn *P*2 into a subroutine and have *P*1 invoke it to write output.

or:

turn *P*1 into a subroutine and have *P*2 invoke it to read input.

Inversion is the process by which a procedure is turned into a subroutine. To turn *P*2 into a subroutine, invert *P*2; to turn *P*1 into a subroutine, invert *P*1.

Let us consider the linkage between *P*1 and *P*2 in greater detail. *P*1 reads an input record and passes it over to *P*2, which writes it to the output file and returns control to *P*1 to read another input record. Throughout the execution of the program, control is passed back and forth between *P*1 and *P*2 a number of times. It is as if *P*1 and *P*2 were two separate programs running in parallel, but of which only one is active at any one time. While *P*1 is active (i.e. reading a record), *P*2 waits; when control is passed to *P*2, *P*2 is active (i.e. writing a record) and *P*1 waits for control to be passed back.

*P*1 and *P*2 could be written as separate programs which have data passed between them in the form of a file. They could also be implemented as co-routines, or linked using a UNIX pipe or the concurrent programming facilities offered by machines such as the transputer or data flow machine. Inversion is a technique for linking them which turns one into a subroutine which is invoked by the other.

Whichever method is chosen to link *P*1 and *P*2, it must be decided what data will pass between them and when it will be passed, and to make the interface explicit it is best to define a link-area where the data to be passed across can be stored. In Pascal the link-area would take the form of a parameter list. In COBOL it would be declared (globally) in the Data Division. In Microsoft BASIC the explicit declaration of a link-area is not possible, but even if BASIC is to be the target source language the use of a link-area is still a useful design and documentation convention (see notes following Example 8.2.1 and Section 8.5 point 4). In *P*1 an operation is allocated which puts data into the link-area and passes control over to *P*2; in HOST we write 'Put LINK-AREA'. In *P*2 an operation is allocated which passes control over to *P*1 in order to get data into the link-area; in HOST we write 'Get LINK-AREA'.

Finally it must be decided which of the two procedures is to be the invoking procedure and which is to be the invoked procedure, and then the program design is complete. All that remains to be done is to turn the invoked procedure into a subroutine by using inversion. Inversion is therefore not a design technique at all but merely an implementation technique, and by using a PDL such as HOST the technicalities of inversion remain hidden from the programmer. The rules for coding inversion in HOST and converting it into BASIC and COBOL source code are as standard and capable of being automated as those for sequence, selection and iteration; sample BASIC and COBOL programs are presented for Example 8.2.1.

Designing programs using inversion requires two new sub-steps in the JSP design procedure: Step 2.2, which determines the interface between procedures, and Step 3.4, which lists and allocates inversion operations. Here is the full design procedure for programs which process two data sets using the inversion technique:

Step 1   Draw a data structure diagram of each data set.

Step 2.1   Form a procedure structure diagram from each data structure diagram.

Step 2.2   Determine the interface between procedures.

For each procedure:

Step 3.1   List and allocate operations.

Step 3.2   List and allocate conditions.

Step 3.3   List and allocate quits and backtracking operations.

Step 3.4   List and allocate inversion operations.

Rules for allocation of GET operations:

1   Allocate a GET at the start of the procedure.
2   Allocate a GET whenever an item of data is required from the link-area.

In other words, GET operations are allocated as per the read-ahead principle.

Rules for allocation of PUT operations:

1   Allocate a PUT whenever there is an item of data to be put into the link-area for processing by the other procedure.
2   Allocate a PUT at the end of the procedure unless one has already been allocated under Rule 1 (in order that the other procedure can undertake any end processing).
3   Before each PUT allocate an operation which moves the appropriate item(s) of data to the link-area.

8.2 PROGRAMS WHICH PROCESS TWO SEQUENTIAL DATA SETS

Example 8.2.1

This example is a redesign of Example 5.2.1 using the inversion technique instead of the correspondence technique. Refamiliarize yourself with the correspondence design before reading on.

A program is required to create a copy of the file INFILE1; the copy is to be called INFILE2. INFILE1 contains only one record type (INREC1).

 Step 1 Draw data structure diagrams of INFILE1 and INFILE2 (see Figs 8.3 and 8.4).

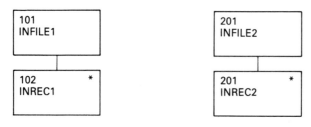

Figure 8.3   **Figure 8.4**

As the two data structure diagrams will eventually become procedure structure diagrams in the same program, they are numbered independently, using a root number of 101 for one and 201 for the other, in order to avoid duplicate component labels.

 Step 2.1 Form a procedure structure diagram from each data structure diagram (see Figs 8.5 and 8.6).

Note the use of PROC (an abbreviation of PROCEDURE) instead of PROG (an abbreviation of PROGRAM) in component names.

 Step 2.2 Determine the interface between procedures P-INFILE1 and P-INFILE2.

P-INFILE1 is a procedure which handles the processing of INFILE1, P-INFILE2 is a procedure which handles the processing of INFILE2. P-INFILE1 reads an INREC1 and puts it into a link-area in order that P-INFILE2 can get it and write it to INFILE2. In addition, P-INFILE1 must inform P-INFILE2 when end-of-file is reached. The link-area between the two procedures will therefore consist of two data items: an INREC1 and an EOF-SW. In COBOL this would be coded as:

```
01  LINK-AREA1.
    02  L1-SV       PIC 9 VALUE 1.
    02  L1-EOF-SW   PIC X VALUE '0'.
    02  L1-INREC1.
          . . . . . . . . . .
```

Note that the additional field L1-SV is used during inversion to generate source code, and is explained below along with source code transformation rules. The link-area is named LINK-AREA1 as a standard because programs using multiple inversion require more than one link-area (see Section 8.3).

For P-INFILE1

Step 3.1   List and allocate operations (see Fig. 8.5).

    1 Open INFILE1.
    2 Close INFILE1.
    3 Read record from INFILE1.

Step 3.2   List and allocate conditions (see Fig. 8.5).

    C1 End of INFILE1.

Step 3.3   List and allocate quits and backtracking operations.

    none required.

Step 3.4   List and allocate inversion operations (see Fig. 8.5).

    4 Move '1' to L1-EOF-SW.
    5 Move INREC1 to L1-INREC1.
    6 Put LINK-AREA1.

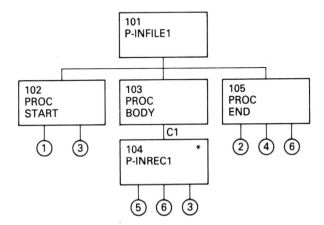

Figure 8.5

Operation 6 (Put LINK-AREA1) is allocated according to the two rules listed in Section 8.1:

1 Allocate a PUT whenever there is an item of data to be put into the link-area for processing by the other procedure.

2 Allocate a PUT at the end of the procedure unless one has already been allocated under Rule 1.

According to Rule 1, therefore, a Put is allocated to every program component in P-INFILE1 which requires a record to be put into LINK-AREA1 for processing (writing) by P-INFILE2. There is only one such component in P-INFILE1: P-INREC1. The sole function of P-INREC1 in this program is to Put a record into LINK-AREA1 and then read another one. According to Rule 2 a final Put is allocated to PROC-END.

The third rule concerning the allocation of PUTs states:

3 Before each PUT allocate an operation which moves the appropriate item(s) of data to the link-area.

According to this rule operation 5 is allocated to P-INREC1 (to move an INREC1 to LINK-AREA1 so that P-INFILE2 can write it) and operation 4 is allocated to PROC-END (to set L1-EOF-SW in LINK-AREA1 to '1' in order to inform P-INFILE2 to undertake any end processing, e.g. 'Close INFILE2').

For P-INFILE2

Step 3.1   List and allocate operations (see Fig. 8.6).

      1 Open INFILE2.
      2 Close INFILE2.
      3 Write INREC2 from L1-INREC1.

Step 3.2   List and allocate conditions (see Fig. 8.6).

      C1 L1-EOF-SW = '1'.

Step 3.3   List and allocate quits and backtracking operations.

      none required.

Step 3.4   List and allocate inversion operations (see Fig. 8.6).

      4 Get LINK-AREA1.

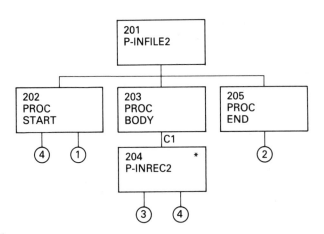

Figure 8.6

Operation 4 (Get LINK-AREA1) is allocated according to the two rules listed in Section 8.1:

1 Allocate a GET at the start of the procedure.

2 Allocate a GET whenever an item of data is required from the link-area.

Operation 4 is therefore allocated to PROC-START and to every other program component which requires to get a record from LINK-AREA1 in order to write it. In this procedure there is only one such component: P-INREC2. The sole function of P-INREC2 in this program is to write a record to INFILE2 and then Get another one from LINK-AREA1. The allocation of Get operations is as for the read-ahead principle, because in essence P-INFILE2 is 'reading' records from LINK-AREA1 instead of from a file.

The program design is now complete, and all that remains to be done to obtain a working program is to combine the two procedures into a single program and transform it into source code. To form a single program one procedure is turned into a subroutine of the other, using the inversion technique; one procedure becomes the main (invoking) procedure and the other procedure becomes an inverted subroutine invoked by the main procedure. It does not matter which procedure does the invoking and which is invoked, so let us opt to make P-INFILE1 the main procedure and

P-INFILE2 the subroutine. Note that flexibility of choice is facilitated by not allocating an explicit STOP RUN (COBOL) or END (BASIC) operation to either P-INFILE1 or P-INFILE2 (in favour of its generation during conversion to source code).

The inversion of P-INFILE2 can be indicated on its structure diagram by writing the name of the link-area from which it gets data alongside the root component number (see Fig. 8.7).

Figure 8.7

Note that it was in anticipation of inverting P-INFILE2 that it was drawn initially with a root component of 201 rather than 101, but this numbering standard is not a requirement. Numbering P-INFILE1 201 and P-INFILE2 101 would make no difference. The only important matter is that the invoking procedure (P-INFILE1) appears before the invoked procedure (P-INFILE2) when the program is coded (to enable program termination statements to be generated correctly).

The rules for coding inversion are given in Appendix D (Section 1, rule 1.7). HOST uses the inversion constructs Invert, Get and Put directly as statements, producing the following HOST program (inversion operations are underlined in order to highlight them):

LINK-AREA1 USED BY 201-P-INFILE2.

   101-P-INFILE1.
       Do 102-PROC-START.
       Do 103-PROC-BODY.
       Do 105-PROC-END.
   102-PROC-START.
       Open INFILE1.
       Read record from INFILE1.
   103-PROC-BODY ITER.
       Do 104-P-INREC1 until (end of INFILE1).
   104-P-INREC1.
       Move INREC1 to L1-INREC1.
       Put LINK-AREA1.
       Read record from INFILE1.

105-PROC-END.

    Close INFILE1.

    <u>Move '1' to L1-EOF-SW.</u>

    <u>Put LINK-AREA1.</u>

<u>201-P-INFILE2 INVERT USING LINK-AREA1.</u>

    Do 202-PROC-START.

    Do 203-PROC-BODY.

    Do 205-PROC-END.

202-PROC-START.

    <u>Get LINK-AREA1.</u>

    Open INFILE2.

203-PROC-BODY ITER.

    Do 204-P-INREC2 until (L1-EOF-SW = '1').

204-P-INREC2.

    Write INREC2 from L1-INREC1.

    <u>Get LINK-AREA1.</u>

205-PROC-END.

    Close INFILE2.

<u>201-P-INFILE2 INVERT-END.</u>

The statement 201-P-INFILE2 INVERT USING LINK-AREA1 indicates that P-INFILE2 is an inverted procedure which will use LINK-AREA1 as its interface with an invoking procedure. The USING clause is required for serial inversion (see Section 8.3).

The USED BY clause at the beginning of the program is required only by an automated HOST precompiler to enable it to transform HOST 'Put LINK-AREA1' statements into invocations of 201-P-INFILE2. The INVERT-END statement is similarly required to enable a HOST precompiler to generate end-of-procedure source code (see examples following). If the program is to be compiled by hand rather than by a HOST precompiler these statements are optional.

The HOST statements Invert, Invert-end, Get and Put are easily compiled into linear source code, preferably by a HOST precompiler, using the transformation rules given in Appendix D (Section 2, rule 2.6). Applying these rules to the above HOST program will produce the following source programs (source code for HOST inversion statements is underlined in order to highlight it).

BASIC:

```
100   REM P-INFILE1
110   GOTO 200
120   GOTO 300
130   GOTO 500
140   END
200   REM PROC-START
210   LET L1.SV=1
220   OPEN "I", #1, "INFILE1"
230   INPUT #1,...
240   GOTO 120
300   REM PROC-BODY
310   IF NOT EOF (1) GOTO 400
320   GOTO 130
400   REM P-INREC1
410   GOSUB 2100
420   INPUT #1,...
430   GOTO 300
500   REM PROC-END
510   GOSUB 2100
520   CLOSE #1
530   GOTO 140


2100   REM P-INFILE2 EOF (1), INREC1
2110   GOTO 2990
2120   REM EP1
2130   GOTO 2200
2140   GOTO 2300
2150   GOTO 2500
2160   GOTO 2999
2200   REM PROC-START
2210   OPEN "O", #2, "INFILE2"
2220   GOTO 2140
2300   REM PROC-BODY
2310   IF NOT EOF (1) GOTO 2400
2320   GOTO 2150
2400   REM P-INREC2
2410   PRINT #2,...
2420   LET L1.SV=2
```

```
2430   GOTO 2999
2440   REM EP2
2450   GOTO 2310
2500   REM PROC-END
2510   CLOSE #2
2520   GOTO 2160
2990   REM L1.SV-TEST
2991   ON L1.SV GOTO 2120, 2440
2999   RETURN
```

As Microsoft BASIC permits neither data declaration nor localization of variables to a procedure, the use of an explicitly defined link-area is not possible. The HOST conventions Get LINK-AREA1 and Put LINK-AREA1 (without prior Move statements) remain viable with regard to design, documentation and automated generation of source code, but in the source code procedure 201-P-INFILE2 may be allowed to reference EOF (1) and INREC1 directly. The separation of the two procedures is therefore not as complete as in COBOL (see also additional notes on COBOL code (1) following COBOL source program).

COBOL:

```
PROCEDURE DIVISION.
101-P-INFILE1-MAIN SECTION.
101-P-INFILE1.
    GO TO 102-PROC-START.
102-PROC-START EXIT.
    GO TO 103-PROC-BODY.
103-PROC-BODY-EXIT.
    GO TO 105-PROC-END.
105-PROC-END-EXIT.
    STOP RUN.
102-PROC-START.
    OPEN INPUT INFILE1.
    READ INFILE1 AT END MOVE '1' TO EOF-SW.
    GO TO 102-PROC-START-EXIT.
103-PROC-BODY.
104-P-INREC1-EXIT.
    IF NOT (EOF-SW = '1')
        GO TO 104-P-INREC1.
    GO TO 103-PROC-BODY-EXIT.
```

```
104-P-INREC1.
    MOVE INREC1 TO L1-INREC1.
    PERFORM 201-P-INFILE2 THRU 201-P-INFILE2-EXIT.
    READ INFILE1 AT END MOVE '1' TO EOF-SW.
    GO TO 104-P-INREC1-EXIT.
105-PROC-END.
    CLOSE INFILE1.
    MOVE '1' TO L1-EOF-SW.
    PERFORM 201-P-INFILE2 THRU 201-P-INFILE2-EXIT.
    GO TO 105-PROC-END-EXIT.


201-P-INFILE2.
    GO TO L1-SV-TEST.
201-P-INFILE2-EP1.
    GO TO 202-PROC-START.
202-PROC-START-EXIT.
    GO TO 203-PROC-BODY.
203-PROC-BODY-EXIT.
    GO TO 205-PROC-END.
205-PROC-END-EXIT.
    GO TO 201-P-INFILE2-EXIT.
202-PROC-START.
    OPEN OUTPUT INFILE2.
    GO TO 202-PROC-START-EXIT.
203-PROC-BODY.
204-P-INREC2-EXIT.
    IF NOT (L1-EOF-SW = '1')
        GO TO 204-P-INREC2.
    GO TO 203-PROC-BODY-EXIT.
204-P-INREC2.
    WRITE INREC2 FROM L1-INREC1.
    MOVE 2 TO L1-SV.
    GO TO 201-P-INFILE2-EXIT.
201-P-INFILE2-EP2.
    GO TO 204-P-INREC2-EXIT.
205-PROC-END.
    CLOSE INFILE2.
    GO TO 205-PROC-END-EXIT.
```

```
L1-SV-TEST.
    GO TO 201-P-INFILE2-EP1
    201-P-INFILE2-EP2
    DEPENDING ON L1-SV.
201-P-INFILE2-EXIT.
    EXIT.
```

A note on variable-state processing

Because different invocations of P-INFILE2 require different processing to be undertaken by P-INFILE2, P-INFILE2 is known as a *variable-state procedure* (as opposed to a *fixed-state procedure*): processing varies from invocation to invocation. On its first invocation (the 'Get LINK-AREA1' operation allocated to 201-PROC-START) P-INFILE2 opens INFILE2 and writes out a record; on second and subsequent invocations (the 'Get LINK-AREA1' operation allocated to 204-P-INREC2) P-INFILE2 simply writes out a record (unless end-of-file is detected, when condition C1 causes 205-PROC-END to close INFILE2). On each of the two types of invocation a different part of the procedure P-INFILE2 is executed. P-INFILE2 therefore has two states, two entry points and two Get operations.

Inversion is a technique for turning fixed-state procedures into variable-state procedures, and by studying the source code the mechanism of inversion, by which variable-state processing is accomplished, will become apparent. In essence, each chunk of code required by a particular invocation is given a separate entry point (i.e. 120 REM EP1 and 440 REM EP2 in the BASIC code, 201-P-INFILE2-EP1 and 201-P-INFILE2-EP2 in the COBOL code).

To keep track of which entry point is to be used at each invocation, P-INFILE2 keeps an internal counter known as its *state variable* (i.e. the variable which describes the current state/entry point of the procedure). This variable (in COBOL a PIC 9 field in LINK-AREA1: L1-SV) is initialized to 1 so that the first entry to the procedure will be at 120 REM EP1/201-P-INFILE-EP1. After processing a record the state variable is incremented to 2 so that the next entry will be at 440 REM EP2/201-P-INFILE2-EP2. The logic flow is directed to the appropiate entry point by an ON... GO-TO... statement in BASIC and a GO TO... DEPENDING ON... statement in COBOL.

The state variable is not a programmer-invented switch in the manner of a 'first-time-through' switch, but rather an explicit counter of the number of states of a variable-state procedure, derived explicitly and automatically from the allocation of Get operations and ultimately from the structure of the data with which the procedure is invoked. The state variable is used solely for implementation purposes, its generation and maintenance are standard and capable of automation, and its use is totally transparent to the programmer designing programs using JSP and coding in HOST. The only requirement of the COBOL programmer is that he define L1-SV in the link-area.

Additional notes on COBOL code

1 The use of a link-area to link the two procedures is not strictly necessary, as in BASIC. P-INFILE2 could reference P-INREC1 and EOF-SW directly rather than via LINK-AREA1, and then operations 4 and 5 would not be required. Enforcing the use of a link-area, however, makes the interface explicit, localizes variables, eases maintenance and enables procedures to be re-used in other programs (see Section 8.5). In other words, defining a link-area similar to a Linkage Section, which would have to be defined if P-INFILE2 were to be separately compiled, enables many of the advantages of the CALL statement to be realized.

2 The inverted procedure must be invoked as a whole, hence the generation of end paragraph 201-P-INFILE2-EXIT which enables the COBOL PERFORM... THRU... construct to be used. Alternatively, the procedure could be turned into a COBOL section and PERFORMed, or GOTOs could be used.

3 The Get operations within the inverted procedure become COBOL GOTOs. As with quit operations in backtracking, there is no other way to code them in COBOL (although see note 5). The design remains, as always, GOTO-less, and the use of a PDL such as HOST makes the use of GOTOs in COBOL an irrelevant matter.

4 The inverted procedure contains no generated STOP RUN statement after PROC-END processing; this is replaced by a branch to the end of the procedure.

5 The logic flow is directed to the appropriate entry point by a GO TO... DEPENDING ON.. statement. The logical place for this statement is at the beginning of the inverted procedure. It has been placed at

the end (and an extra GOTO generated at the start) to aid an automated HOST precompiler, which does not know how many Get operations (and hence entry points) are in the procedure until after it has parsed it. If the source language has a CASE-like statement (e.g. Pascal's CASE statement, COBOL 85's EVALUATE statement), the logic flow can be directed by the CASE statement rather than by GOTOs, but make sure that any GOTOs such as that in 205-PROC-END-EXIT, which would jump out of the CASE statement, can be handled by the source language compiler.

The inversion design for Example 8.2.1 is more complex than the correspondence design presented in Chapter 5, and for such a simple program the correspondence design would probably be preferable. However, the inversion design has a number of important advantages over the correspondence design (see Section 8.5) and these will become apparent once the examples in this and the following chapters have been studied.

Example 8.2.2

INFILE consists of a file header, a number of records which are either type $R1$ or type $R2$, and a file trailer. A program is required to print $R1$ records, and at end of report print how many $R1$ records and $R2$ records are on the file. The report additionally has a report heading on the first page.

Step 1   Draw data structure diagrams of INFILE and the report (see Figs 8.8 and 8.9).

Step 2.1   Form a procedure structure diagram from each data structure diagram (see Figs 8.10 and 8.11).

Step 2.2   Determine the interface between P-INFILE and P-INFILE-REPORT.

The report consists of four types of line: a report heading, an $R1$ detail line, an $R1$ total line and an $R2$ total line. In order to write an $R1$ detail line, P-INFILE-REPORT requires an $R1$ record, so P-INFILE must pass an $R1$ record across to it in LINK-AREA1. In order to write $R1$ and $R2$ total lines, P-INFILE-REPORT requires $R1$ and $R2$ totals. It knows nothing about type $R2$ records (which are not passed across by P-INFILE1), so it seems logical for P-INFILE to accumulate both totals and pass them across via LINK-AREA1, setting an L1-EOF-SW to '1' to indicate end-of-file. The report

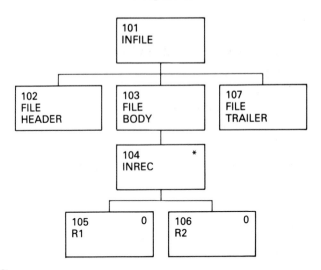

Figure 8.8

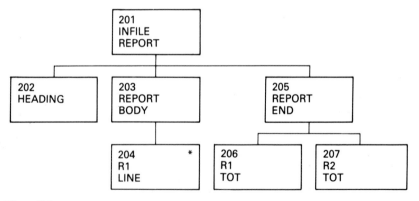

Figure 8.9

heading is a constant and P-INFILE-REPORT requires no information from P-INFILE in order to write it. LINK-AREA1 therefore consists of (in COBOL):

```
01  LINK-AREA1.
    02  L1-SV         PIC 9 VALUE 1.
    02  L1-EOF-SW     PIC X VALUE '0'.
    02  L1-INREC.
        ........
    02  L1-R1TOT      PIC...
    02  L1-R2TOT      PIC...
```

For P-INFILE

Step 3.1   List and allocate operations (see Fig. 8.10).

    1 Open INFILE.
    2 Close INFILE.
    3 Read record from INFILE.
    4 Add 1 to R1TOT.
    5 Add 1 to R2TOT.

Step 3.2   List and allocate conditions (see Fig. 8.10).

    C1 End of INFILE1.
    C2 R1.

Step 3.3   List and allocate quits and backtracking operations.

    none required.

Step 3.4   List and allocate inversion operations (see Fig. 8.10).

    6 Put LINK-AREA1.
    7 Move INREC to L1-INREC.
    8 Move R1TOT to L1-R1TOT.
      Move R2TOT to L1-R2TOT.
      Move '1' to L1-EOF-SW.

Note macro operation 8; the three operations which comprise operation 8 will always appear together and may therefore be specified as a single macro operation.

For P-INFILE-REPORT

Step 3.1   List and allocate operations (see Fig. 8.11).

    1 Open report.
    2 Close report.
    3 Write heading.
    4 Format and write R1LINE.
    5 Format and write R1TOTLINE.
    6 Format and write R2TOTLINE.

Step 3.2   List and allocate conditions (see Fig. 8.11).

    C1 L1-EOF-SW = '1'.

Step 3.3   List and allocate quits and backtracking operations.

    none required.

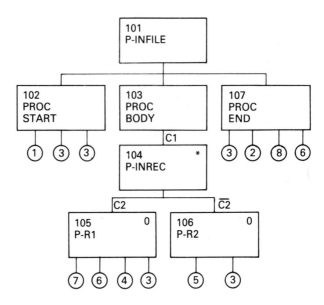

Figure 8.10

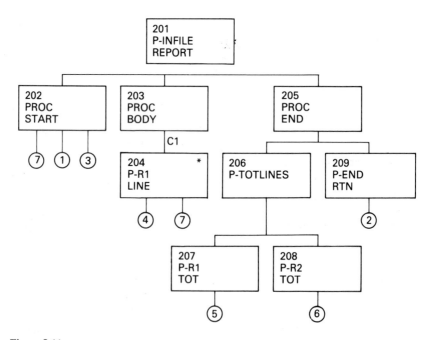

Figure 8.11

Step 3.4   List and allocate inversion operations (see Fig. 8.11).

7 Get LINK-AREA1.

As in Example 8.2.1, it is decided (arbitrarily) to invert the output procedure (P-INFILE-REPORT) (see Fig. 8.12).

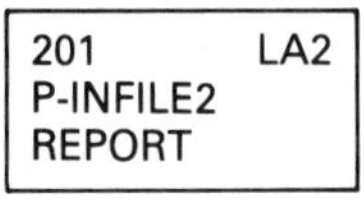

```
+-------------------+
| 201        LA2    |
| P-INFILE2         |
| REPORT            |
+-------------------+
```

Figure 8.12

The transformation of the program into HOST and source code is left as an exercise for the reader.

Example 8.2.3

An employee file contains employee records in department number/employee number sequence, i.e. employee number within department number. At the end of each department is a department trailer containing a total of the number of employees within that department.

A program is required to produce a report of employee records and department totals. Additionally, it is required to sequence check the file and check that the department totals are correct; if any invalidity is detected the program should output an appropriate error message and halt.

To cater for the possibility of premature program termination owing to an invalidity on the employee file, it is necessary to posit a valid file and admit an invalid one.

Step 1   Draw data structure diagrams of the employee file and report (see Figs 8.13 and 8.14).

Step 2.1   Form a procedure structure diagram from each data structure diagram (see Figs 8.15 and 8.16).

Step 2.2   Determine the interface between P-EMP-FILE and P-EMP-REPORT.

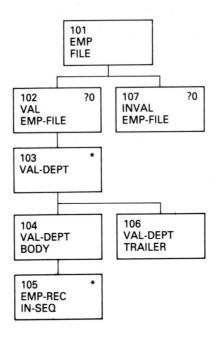

Figure 8.13

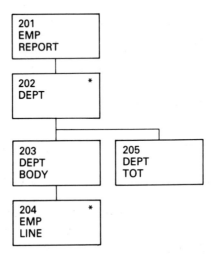

Figure 8.14

It seems logical that all validation of the employee file should be handled by P-EMP-FILE; P-EMP-REPORT need know nothing about it. All that needs to be passed across to P-EMP-REPORT are in-sequence employee records and valid department totals, together with an L1-EOF-SW to indicate end-of-file. LINK-AREA1 will therefore consist of (in COBOL):

```
01  LINK-AREA1.
      02  L1-SV            PIC 9 VALUE 1.
      02  L1-EOF-SW        PIC X VALUE '0'.
      02  L1-EMP-REC.
           03  L1-DEPT-NO  PIC...
           03  L1-EMP-NO   PIC...
           ............/.....
      02  L1-DEPT-TOT      PIC...
```

For P-EMP-FILE

Step 3.1 List and allocate operations (see Fig. 8.15).

    1 Open employee file.
    2 Close employee file.
    3 Read record from employee file.
    4 Add 1 to department total.
    5 Output error message.
    6 Move record key to current record key.
    7 Set department total to 0.

Step 3.2 List and allocate conditions (see Fig. 8.15).

    C1 End of employee file.
    C2 Department trailer.

Step 3.3 List and allocate quits and backtracking operations.

    !1 Quit P-VAL-EMP-FILE if (record key not > current record key
    Move 'SEQUENCE ERROR' to error message).
    !2 Quit P-VAL-EMP-FILE if (department total not = department trailer total
    Move 'INVALID DEPARTMENT TOTAL' to error message).

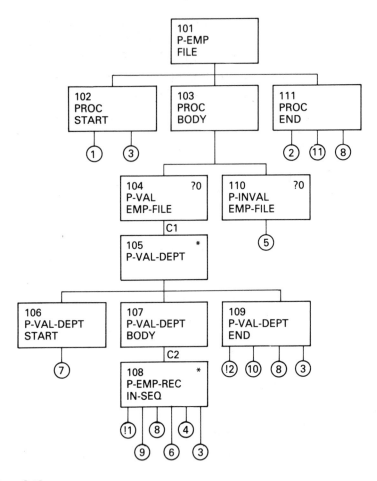

Figure 8.15

Step 3.4   List and allocate inversion operations (see Fig. 8.15).

     8 Put LINK-AREA1.

     9 Move employee record to L1-EMP-REC.

     10 Move department total to L1-DEPT-TOT.

     11 Move '1' to L1-EOF-SW.

For P-EMP-REPORT

Step 3.1   List and allocate operations (see Fig. 8.16).

     1 Open employee report.

2 Close employee report.

3 Write employee line from L1-EMP-REC.

4 Write department total line from L1-DEPT-TOT.

Step 3.2 List and allocate conditions (see Fig. 8.16).

C1 L1-EOF-SW = '1'.

C2 L1-EMP-NO = all 9s (i.e. department trailer).

Step 3.3 List and allocate quits and backtracking operations.

none required.

Step 3.4 List and allocate inversion operations (see Fig. 8.16).

5 Get LINK-AREA1.

This example, like Examples 8.2.1 and 8.2.2, processes two files, but this time it is decided (arbitrarily) to invert the input procedure rather than the output procedure; P-EMP-REPORT is to be the main procedure and P-EMP-FILE the subroutine (see Fig. 8.17).

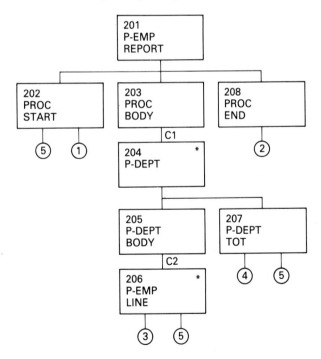

Figure 8.16

```
┌─────────────────────┐
│ 101            LA1   │
│ P-EMPFILE           │
│                     │
└─────────────────────┘
```

Figure 8.17

The USED BY statement is:

LINK-AREA1 USED BY 101-P-EMP-FILE.

and procedure 201-P-EMP-REPORT is coded *before* procedure 101-P-EMP-FILE USING LINK-AREA1.

The inversion of a procedure which reads a file in this way, in order to form a 'file handler' subroutine, is a common and useful application of inversion (see Section 8.5).

In Examples 8.2.1 and 8.2.2 the procedures containing Puts became main procedures and the HOST instruction Put became an invocation of the subroutine in source code; the procedures containing Gets became subroutines, and the HOST instruction Get was implemented using a GOTO in source code. In this example the procedure containing Gets becomes the main procedure and the HOST instruction Get becomes an invocation of the subroutine in source code; the procedure containing Puts becomes a subroutine, and the HOST instruction Put is implemented as a GOTO.

In other words, the transformation of Get and Put operations into source code depends upon whether they occur in an invoking procedure or a subroutine. In an invoking procedure both Get and Put become an invocation statement (e.g. a GOSUB in BASIC, a PERFORM in COBOL); in an inverted subroutine they both become a GOTO.

For example, component 202-PROC-START in the main procedure is coded in HOST as:

```
202-PROC-START.
        Get LINK-AREA1.
        Open employee report.
```

In BASIC this becomes:

```
GOSUB nnn (i.e. P-EMP-FILE)
OPEN "I", #2, "EMP-REP"
GOTO nnn (i.e. PROC-START-EXIT)
```

In COBOL this becomes:

```
202-PROC-START.
    PERFORM 101-P-EMP-FILE THRU 101-P-EMP-FILE-EXIT.
    OPEN OUTPUT EMP-REPORT.
    GO TO 202-PROC-START-EXIT.
```

Component 109-P-VAL-DEPT-END in the inverted procedure is coded in HOST as:

> Quit P-VAL-EMP-FILE if (department total not =
>   department trailer total
> Move 'INVALID DEPARTMENT TOTAL' to error message).
> Move department total to L1-DEPT-TOT.
> Put LINK-AREA1.
> Read record from employee file.

In BASIC this becomes:

```
IF DEPT.TOT<>DT.DEPT.TOT THEN
    LET ERRMESS$="INVALID DEPARTMENT TOTAL":
    GOTO NNN (i.e. P-INVAL-EMP-FILE)
LET L1.SV=3
GOTO NNN (i.e. P-EMP-FILE-EXIT)
REM EP3
INPUT #1,...
GOTO NNN (i.e. P-VAL-DEPT-END-EXIT)
```

In COBOL this becomes:

```
        109-P-VAL-DEPT-END.
          IF DEPT-TOT NOT=DT-DEPT-TOT
            MOVE 'INVALID DEPARTMENT TOTAL' TO ERR-MESS
            GO TO P-INVAL-EMP-FILE.
          MOVE DT-DEPT-TOT TO L1-DEPT-TOT.
          MOVE 3 TO L1-SV.
          GO TO 101-P-EMP-FILE-EXIT.
        101-P-EMP-FILE-EP3.
          READ EMP-FILE AT END MOVE '1' TO EOF-SW.
          GO TO 109-P-VAL-DEPT-END-EXIT.
```

8.3 PROGRAMS WHICH PROCESS THREE SEQUENTIAL DATA SETS

The programs in Section 8.2 process two sequential data sets. They are designed as two procedures, one procedure per data set, and then one procedure is inverted to become a subroutine of the other. Just as there is no reason why a program cannot have more than one subroutine, so there is no reason why it cannot have more than one inverted procedure; hence the inversion technique can be used to design programs which process any number of data sets. In this section one example of a program which processes three data sets is presented; the design of programs which process four or more data sets is a simple extension of the same technique.

If a program contains two procedures (*P*1 and *P*2) one of them must be inverted and use a link-area (i.e. LINK-AREA1) as its interface with the other. Whether *P*1 invokes an inverted *P*2, or *P*2 invokes an inverted *P*1, is irrelevant from the design point of view.

If a program contains three procedures (*P*1, *P*2 and *P*3) two of them must be inverted and two link-areas will be required (LINK-AREA1 and LINK-AREA2). Which procedures are inverted is again irrelevant from the design point of view, although some interfaces may be simpler than others. *P*1 may invoke *P*2 which in turn invokes *P*3, or *P*1 may invoke both *P*2 and *P*3, or *P*3 may be invoked by both *P*1 and *P*2, or perm any combination of invocations you can think of.

Example 8.3.1

This example is a re-design of Example 5.3.1 using inversion rather than the correspondence technique. Refamiliarize yourself with the correspondence design before reading on.

A program is required to process bank transactions keyed in at a terminal. The program is to be menu-driven and the menu gives the user three options:

1   Input a deposit.
2   Input a withdrawal.
9   Terminate program.

Deposits are to be written to a deposit file and withdrawals to a withdrawal file. Additionally, file trailers are to be appended to the deposit file and withdrawal file containing the total value of deposits and withdrawals respectively.

Step 1   Draw data structure diagrams of the input data stream and the deposit and withdrawal files (see Figs 5.9, 5.10 and 5.11).

Step 2.1   Form a procedure structure diagram from each data structure diagram (see Figs 8.18, 8.19 and 8.20).

Step 2.2   Determine the interface between P-SCREEN-INPUT, P-DE-POSIT-FILE and P-WITHDRAW-FILE.

The program consists of three procedures: one to process screen input, one to write the deposit file and one to write the withdrawal file. The simplest interface is to have P-SCREEN-INPUT process input transactions, passing deposit data across to P-DEPOSIT-FILE (using LINK-AREA1) and withdrawal data across to P-WITHDRAW-FILE (using LINK-AREA2). In addition P-SCREEN-INPUT must pass an end-of-data indicator to both procedures to inform them when to undertake appropriate end-of-procedure operations (e.g. 'Write file trailer'). The interfaces are therefore (in COBOL):

```
01   LINK-AREA1.
     02  L1-SV                  PIC 9 VALUE 1.
     02  L1-EOF-SW              PIC X VALUE '0'.
     02  L1-DEPOSIT-DATA.
         ........

01   LINK-AREA2.
     02  L2-SV                  PIC 9 VALUE 1.
     02  L2-EOF-SW              PIC X VALUE '0'.
     02  L2-WITHDRAWAL-DATA.
         ........
```

Other possible interfaces are discussed below.

For P-SCREEN-INPUT

Step 3.1   List and allocate operations (see Fig. 8.18).

1 Output user instructions.
2 Output menu.
3 Input option.

4 Output 'INVALID OPTION. PLEASE RE-ENTER'.
5 Input deposit data.
6 Input withdrawal data.

Step 3.2   List and allocate conditions (see Fig. 8.18).

C1 Option = 9.
C2 Option = 1.
C3 Option = 2.

Step 3.3   List and allocate quits and backtracking operations.

none required.

Step 3.4   List and allocate inversion operations (see Fig. 8.18).

7 Move '1' to L1-EOF-SW.

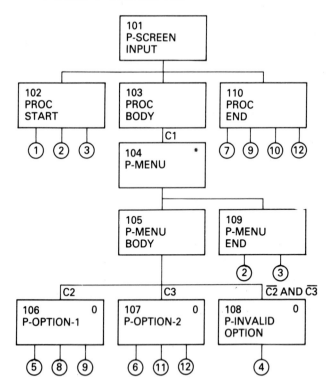

Figure 8.18

8 Move deposit data to L1-DEPOSIT-DATA.

9 Put LINK-AREA1.

10 Move '1' to L2-EOF-SW.

11 Move withdrawal data to L2-WITHDRAWAL-DATA.

12 Put LINK-AREA2.

For P-DEPOSIT-FILE

Step 3.1   List and allocate operations (see Fig. 8.19).

1 Open deposit file.

2 Close deposit file.

3 Write deposit record from L1-DEPOSIT-DATA.

4 Add 1 to deposit total.

5 Write deposit file trailer using deposit total.

Step 3.2   List and allocate conditions (see Fig. 8.19).

C1 L1-EOF-SW='1'.

Step 3.3   List and allocate quits and backtracking operations.

none required.

Step 3.4   List and allocate inversion operations (see Fig. 8.19).

6 Get LINK-AREA1.

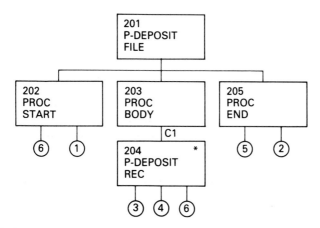

Figure 8.19

For P-WITHDRAW-FILE

Step 3.1   List and allocate operations (see Fig. 8.20).

    1 Open withdrawal file.
    2 Close withdrawal file.
    3 Write withdrawal record from L2-WITHDRAWAL-DATA.
    4 Add 1 to withdrawal total.
    5 Write withdrawal file trailer using withdrawal total.

Step 3.2   List and allocate conditions (see Fig. 8.20).

    C1 L2-EOF-SW = '1'.

Step 3.3   List and allocate quits and backtracking operations.

    none required.

Step 3.4   List and allocate inversion operations (see Fig. 8.20).

    6 Get LINK-AREA2.

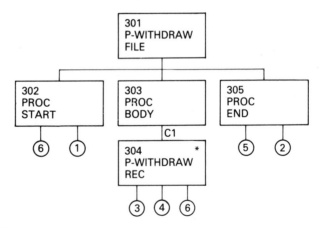

Figure 8.20

To combine the three procedures into a single program two of them must be inverted. It doesn't matter which, but as both the deposit and withdrawal files are formed from screen input data, it seems logical to invert P-DEPOSIT-FILE and P-WITHDRAW-FILE to P-SCREEN-INPUT (see Figs 8.21 and 8.22).

| 201   LA1 |
| P-DEPOSIT |
| FILE |

| 301   LA2 |
| P-WITHDRAW |
| FILE |

Figure 8.21   **Figure 8.22**

When a main procedure invokes two or more procedures in this way the program is said to exhibit *multiple inversion*. The procedures would be coded in HOST:

LINK-AREA1 USED BY 201-P-DEPOSIT-FILE.
LINK-AREA2 USED BY 301-P-WITHDRAW-FILE.
101-P-SCREEN-INPUT.

. . . .

201-P-DEPOSIT-FILE INVERT USING LINK-AREA1.

. . . .

301-P-WITHDRAW-FILE INVERT USING LINK-AREA2.

As an alternative implementation it may be decided to make P-DEPOSIT-FILE the main procedure, invoking P-SCREEN-INPUT inverted procedure, which in turn invokes P-WITHDRAW-FILE inverted procedure. In this implementation P-SCREEN-INPUT is both an invoked procedure (to P-DEPOSIT-FILE) and an invoking procedure (to P-WITHDRAW-FILE), and when procedures are linked in this way the program is said to exhibit *serial inversion*. The procedures would be coded in HOST:

LINK-AREA1 USED BY 101-P-SCREEN-INPUT.
LINK-AREA2 USED BY 301-P-WITHDRAW-FILE.
201-P-DEPOSIT-FILE.

. . . .

101-P-SCREEN-INPUT INVERT USING LINK-AREA1.

. . . .

301-P-WITHDRAW-FILE INVERT USING LINK-AREA2.

. . . .

In this implementation P-SCREEN-INPUT contains not only Gets from LINK-AREA1 (to be transformed into GOTOs) but also Puts to LINK-AREA2 (to be transformed into invocations of P-WITHDRAW-FILE). The USING clause enables the appropriate source code to be generated by a HOST precompiler.

Other possible interfaces

It is also possible, though more unlikely, to link the procedures as follows:

P-SCREEN-INPUT invokes P-DEPOSIT-FILE, which in turn invokes P-WITHDRAW-FILE. In this implementation P-SCREEN-INPUT would pass all transaction data to P-DEPOSIT-FILE (via LINK-AREA1). P-DEPOSIT-FILE would write deposit data to the deposit file and pass withdrawal data on to P-WITHDRAW-FILE (via LINK-AREA2). This is an unlikely implementation because P-SCREEN-INPUT might as well pass withdrawal data directly to P-WITHDRAW-FILE, but accepting it for purposes of illustration, consider what happens at end of screen input.

P-SCREEN-INPUT could pass an L1-EOF-SW to P-DEPOSIT-FILE, which in turn could pass an L2-EOF-SW to P-WITHDRAW-FILE, or again P-SCREEN-INPUT could pass an L2-EOF-SW directly to P-WITHDRAW-FILE. In this latter case, P-WITHDRAW-FILE would then be obtaining data from two sources: withdrawal data from P-DEPOSIT-FILE and an end-of-data indicator from P-SCREEN-INPUT.

It is for this reason that an inverted procedure is inverted to a link-area rather than to another procedure. P-WITHDRAW-FILE must obtain data from some other procedure, but whether that data is placed into LINK-AREA2 by P-SCREEN INPUT, P-DEPOSIT-FILE or both is irrelevant to P-WITHDRAW-FILE; an inverted procedure is inverted to its 'file' of input data, not to the procedures which generate that data (see also Example 9.4.1). This independence of an inverted procedure from other procedures, increased by the use of a link-area which makes all referenced variables local to the procedure, is one of the great benefits of inversion (see Section 8.5).

Note that if it was P-DEPOSIT-FILE rather than P-SCREEN-INPUT which was to pass the end-of-data indicator to P-WITHDRAW-FILE, then the allocation of inversion operations would need to be changed. This verifies that it would be a poor implementation. In Step 2.2 the simplest, most logical and most direct interface between the three procedures is chosen, and in Step 3.4 inversion operations are allocated accordingly. If an inversion implementation which does not match this allocation is then chosen, either the interface or the inversion implementation is incorrect. In essence, the interface chosen at Step 2.2 constrains the set of possible inversion implementations.

8.4 PROCESS SCHEDULING

In all the examples presented in this chapter, one procedure is chosen as a main procedure and the rest are inverted. An alternative implementation is to invert all procedures and design a *process scheduler* to invoke (i.e. schedule invocations of) them. In Example 8.2.1, for instance, both P-INFILE1 and P-INFILE2 could be inverted (using LINK-AREA1 and LINK-AREA2 respectively), and the scheduler shown in Fig. 8.23 used to invoke them.

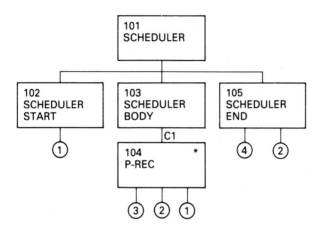

Figure 8.23

List of operations:

1 Get LINK-AREA1.
2 Put LINK-AREA2.
3 Move L1-INREC1 to L2-INREC2.
4 Move L1-EOF-SW to L2-EOF-SW.

List of conditions:

C1 L1-EOF-SW = '1'.

The logic of the scheduler is based on an iteration of record processing. For each record the scheduler:

(a) invokes P-INFILE1 (operation 1) to obtain an INREC1 (which P-INFILE1 puts into LINK-AREA1).

(b) moves the record from LINK-AREA1 to LINK-AREA2 (operation 3).

(c) invokes P-INFILE2 (operation 2) to write an INREC2 (which P-INFILE2 gets from LINK-AREA2).

At end of INFILE1 P-INFILE1 sets an L1-EOF-SW to '1' and the scheduler moves it to LINK-AREA2 (operation 4) to inform P-INFILE2 to close INFILE2.

The use of a scheduler is a top-heavy implementation for this example, but in general terms it has a number of advantages. For example, it enables the use of already existing common routines (see Section 8.5 point 7), removes any decision concerning which procedure is to be the main procedure, and is an extremely useful and powerful approach to online programs (see Chapter 9) and system implementation (see Chapter 10).

8.5 IN PRAISE OF INVERSION

In this section some benefits of using inversion are noted.

1 Inversion is a universal technique for the design of programs which process more than one data set. The programs in this chapter can all be designed using either the correspondence technique or the inversion technique, and for simple programs the inversion technique may be considered to be top-heavy, but the following chapter contains programs which cannot be designed using the correspondence technique.

2 Inversion aids modularization. Modularizing programs by splitting them into inverted procedures which process separate data sets is a good way of producing independent modules. Most other design methods can only offer rules of thumb by which to modularize a program, e.g. each module should process only one function, but there are no hard and fast rules as to what constitutes a function or how functional modularization can be achieved. In design using inversion, a module processes a single data structure, and there is no room for programmer interpretation (see also point 8 on program dismemberment).

3 Inversion simplifies the interface between procedures/modules. The interface between two modules should be as simple and as direct as possible. Each module should be a black box as far as other modules in the program are concerned; switches and other elements of control should not form part of the interface. This is difficult to achieve in other methods of program design except by trial and error or sometimes by judgment and experience. In design using inversion the interface between two modules always consists of data elements only, which the invoked module is required to process.

4 Inversion aids the localization of variables. The objective of localizing variables to a single procedure is to prevent other procedures from corrupting them. If a procedure can reference only those variables which it needs to reference, then modular independence is greater, modular interfaces are simpler and debugging and maintenance are simplified.

An inverted procedure which processes a single data set need never reference any variables used by another procedure. All operations on a data set are allocated to the procedure which processes that data set, and all variables operated on by those operations are referenced by that procedure only. In other words, all variables are local to a single procedure. If a variable used by another procedure is required, it can be obtained via a link-area; the link-area is the interface.

Note that not all languages enable the declaration of variables as local to a single procedure and the passing of variables between procedures using a link-area. Local declaration is possible in Pascal, and a link-area/interface can be defined in the form of a parameter list. In Microsoft BASIC all variables are undeclared and global to all procedures, and the use of a link-area as presented in this chapter can be no more than a useful design and documentation convention.

In COBOL data is declared in the Data Division, a global data area whose variables can be accessed (and corrupted) by any procedure in the Procedure Division. In Example 8.2.1, for instance, P-INFILE2 has no need of LINK-AREA1, containing L1-EOF-SW and L1-INREC1, because it can reference INFILE1 data directly in the Data Division. The use of a link-area, therefore, is not strictly necessary but is recommended as standard practice to increase modular independence and make interfaces more explicit and open to programmer inspection.

If modules are compiled separately and invocation of inverted procedures is done using the CALL statement, then the Data Divisions of each module cannot be corrupted by other modules, and the interface between modules must be specified explicitly by means of a Linkage Section. For this reason it is sometimes suggested that implementation of modular programming in COBOL should always be done using the CALL statement rather than the PERFORM statement. In COBOL 85 a facility has been included to enable procedures/modules to be coded and PERFORMed as nested programs, thereby permitting localization of variables without separate compilation.

5 Inversion aids run-time efficiency. In design using the correspondence

technique, all files are opened at PROG-START and closed at PROG-END. In design using inversion, a file is not opened until it is required, i.e. until the first invocation of the procedure processing it, and it is closed as soon as it is no longer required, thus minimizing the length of time for which file buffers and control blocks are required.

If the flow of control between main and inverted procedures increases memory requirements or causes paging problems on virtual memory machines, dismember the program text into more convenient load units as explained in point 8 following.

6 Inversion aids maintenance. The isolation of separate data structures and their associated operations into separate procedures means that it is easier to isolate an incorrect or omitted operation when debugging, and easier to add an operation to the correct place when enhancing a program, without causing unforseen interactions with the operations of other procedures.

7 Inversion aids the implementation of common routines. For instance, if a file is to be processed in more than one program, an inverted file handler routine should be written for it, which can then be copied or called into any program requiring to read the file. The file handler could include file corruption checks such as sequence checks and control total reconciliations, all of which would be transparent to and isolated from the main program, which would merely invoke the handler to obtain a record for processing. Using a process scheduler it is possible to use inverted routines for all input and output, as in the example in Section 8.4.

8 Inversion facilitates flexibility of implementation. This is probably the greatest benefit of the inversion technique. With normal methods of program design it is necessary at an early stage to make implementation decisions such as whether the program is to be batch or online and which devices it is to use. Inversion makes it possible to divorce logical design from physical implementation completely, to design the program first as a number of procedures, one per data set, and then decide how to implement it.

For example, inversion enables batch and online programs to be designed in almost exactly the same way. The main difference between a batch program and an online program from an implementation point of view is that whereas batch programs are fixed-state and process a whole file of records at one go, online programs are typically variable-state and process a stream of records or transactions one at a time over a long period, relinquishing control between times in order that other processing can be undertaken by the computer system.

Inversion is precisely the mechanism required in an online program to relinquish control and allow later re-entry at the same point, and this enables an online program to be treated as an inverted batch program. In other words, inversion enables all procedures to be designed as fixed-state and then converted to variable-state if so desired.

In Example 8.2.1 P-INFILE1 and P-INFILE2 could be coded as separate programs, with P-INFILE1 putting (i.e. writing) records to an intermediate file, and P-INFILE2 getting (i.e. reading) records from that file. Alternatively, P-INFILE2 could be inverted to P-INFILE1 (as in Example 8.2.1) such that P-INFILE1 invokes P-INFILE2 directly and the intermediate file is not required. As an inverted variable-state procedure P-INFILE2 is invoked many times to process a single record rather than once as a fixed-state batch program to process a whole file of records.

At one stroke, therefore, inversion unifies the design of batch and online programs which have traditionally required vastly different design methods. In JSP whether to make a program batch or online is a mere implementation consideration which can be automated. For example, it is possible to have a PDL precompiler option which translates Gets/Puts into either inversion source code (as in this manual) or Reads from/Writes to an interface file. JSP-COBOL, marketed by LBMS, is one precompiler which has such an option, making a batch or online implementation no more than a function of the compiler.

Moreover, each state of an inverted variable-state procedure is in essence a chunk of code entirely separated from other states, and this makes it possible to reduce memory requirements and increase efficiency in an online environment by making each state a separate load module. In other words, the entry points of an inverted procedure provide logical cut-off points at which to dismember a program text into smaller load units. To form a load unit for any state of a procedure, make a copy of the whole procedure and delete from it all code not reachable from that state's entry point.

Taking the concept of inversion to its logical limit, an entire application system can be viewed as a set of procedures inverted to the life-history of the data processed by the system, with 'master files' derived from a consideration of what data needs to be retained from one part of the life-cycle to the next. The possibilities opened up by this line of thought have led to the development of Jackson System Development (JSD), an exciting new approach to integrated systems development (see Chapter 10).

8.6 EXERCISES

Redesign the following programs from previous chapters using the inversion technique instead of the correspondence technique.

1 Example 5.2.2, inverting the output procedure.

2 Exercise 5.6.2, inverting the input procedure.

3 Example 7.3.1, using a scheduler.

Practise inversion on other examples and exercises from Chapters 5, 6 and 7, and use a variety of inversion implementations (i.e. invert an input procedure, invert an output procedure, use a scheduler).

Chapter 9

Structure Clashes

The previous chapter introduced the inversion technique as an alternative to the correspondence technique in the design of programs which process multiple data sets. The correspondence technique can be used only if correspondences can be found. If data structures clash there will be no correspondences and the correspondence technique cannot be used. This chapter examines the three types of structure clash and discusses their resolution:

1 *Ordering clash.*
2 *Boundary clash.*
3 *Interleaving clash.*

9.1 INTRODUCTION

In Section 5.5 we saw that one of the advantages of the inversion technique over the correspondence technique in program design is that the inversion technique is universally applicable whereas the correspondence technique is not. The correspondence technique falls down when there are insufficient correspondences between data structures; more specifically, the correspondence technique is inapplicable when data structures clash.

In this chapter you will learn how to recognize structure clashes with the aid of examples of some commonly occurring instances. No new program design techniques are required, although in one case an extension to the inversion technique is necessary.

There are three kinds of structure clash:

1 Ordering Clash.
2 Boundary Clash.
3 Interleaving Clash

The following sections examine each in turn.

245

9.2 ORDERING CLASH

An ordering clash occurs between two data structures when one data structure is in a different sequence from the other. The commonest example of an ordering clash is a sort program. For instance, suppose a file of customer records in ascending customer number sequence is to be sorted into descending customer number sequence. The data structure diagrams of the customer file and the sorted customer file are shown in Figs 9.1 and 9.2.

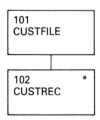

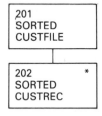

Figure 9.1   **Figure 9.2**

There is a correspondence between the two root components CUST-FILE and SORTED-CUSTFILE, but not between a CUSTREC and a SORTED-CUSTREC. Remember that for two data components to correspond they must occur:

1 The same number of times.
2 In the same order.
3 Under the same circumstances.

CUSTREC and SORTED-CUSTREC occur the same number of times (there are the same number on each file) and under the same circumstances (they belong to parent components which correspond), but they are not in the same order (CUSTRECs are in ascending order, SORTED-CUSTRECs are in descending order). If an attempt was made to combine the two components into a single program component, it would prove impossible to read a CUSTREC and write a different SORTED-CUSTREC within that same program component, as can be seen from the following sample files:

Customer file:
   1   2 5 11   12   49   60

Sorted customer file:
    60   49   12   11   5 2   1

When Customer 1 is read from the customer file, it cannot be processed at that point. It must be kept until all records have been read before it can be written to the sorted customer file because the output is required in reverse order. Customer 1 is the first record read but will be the last record written. It is not possible to design a single program component which both reads a CUSTREC and writes a SORTED-CUSTREC. The reading of the customer file cannot be synchronized with the writing of the sorted customer file. All the processing required for a single record cannot be combined into one procedure.

The solution is to write one procedure to process the customer file (reading records and writing them to a sort file), and another procedure to process the sorted customer file (reading records from the sort file and writing them to the sorted customer file). Between the two procedures a sort operation is required. Normally it is not necessary for a programmer to write his own sort programs, as sort operations are provided by computer manufacturers in the form of software utilities which handle input to and output from the sort file automatically.

In COBOL the procedures are implicit in the SORT verb:

```
SORT  SORT-FILE
         ON DESCENDING KEY CUST-NO
         USING CUSTOMER-FILE
         GIVING SORTED-CUSTOMER-FILE.
```

Sometimes, however, the procedures are required to undertake additional processing of records (e.g. accumulation of totals) during input to or output from the sort operation, and then they must be specified explicitly:

```
SORT  SORT-FILE
         ON DESCENDING KEY CUST-NO
         INPUT PROCEDURE P-CUSTFILE
         OUTPUT PROCEDURE P-SORTED-CUST-FILE.
```

in which case JSP should be used to design them.

If the customer file is small enough, the sort program can be coded using an internal table instead of a sort file and a sort operation. P-CUSTFILE puts records into the table, and when end-of-file is reached P-SORTED-CUSTFILE retrieves them in reverse order. The solution is similar to the sort file solution; the table, like the sort file, is an intermediate storage area, but unlike the sort file its records can be accessed directly and therefore do not require sorting.

As a second example of an ordering clash, consider a file which contains details of a two-dimensional table. Each record represents a row in the table, and each field on the record represents a column value in that row, e.g.

        Record 1   1   2   4   8
        Record 2   2   4   8   16
        Record 3   3   6   12   24

A program is required to print the table column by column, i.e. each printline will represent a column and each field on the printline will represent a row value in that column:

        Line 1   1   2   3
        Line 2   2   4   6
        Line 3   4   8   12
        Line 4   8   16   24

Again there is a synchronization problem; the first line cannot be printed until the last record on the file has been read. The data structure diagrams of the file and the report are shown in Figs 9.3 and 9.4.

 The root components TABLE-FILE and TABLE-REPORT correspond, but the lower-level components of the two data structures do not, and therefore there is an ordering clash. The solution is again either to store row records in a table then access column fields in the appropriate order, or to write column fields to a sort file (tagged by row number and column number) and sort them into the required sequence.

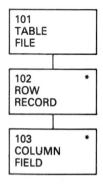

Figure 9.3

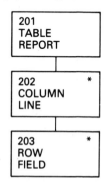

Figure 9.4

As a third example of an ordering clash, suppose an employee file whose records are in employee number sequence is to be printed in department number/employee number sequence (i.e. employee number within department number). The data structure diagrams of the employee file and the report are shown as Figs 9.5 and 9.6.

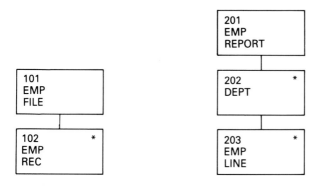

Figure 9.5   Figure 9.6

EMP-FILE corresponds with EMP-REPORT, but there are no lower-level correspondences. EMP-REC does not correspond with EMP-LINE because they are in a different order.

The solution is again to have two procedures linked by a sort file or a table. In all cases these are the only two solutions to an ordering clash. Inverting one procedure will not provide a solution because the sort output procedure cannot begin until the sort input procedure has ended; one procedure must follow the other rather than be a subroutine of it.

9.3 BOUNDARY CLASH

A boundary clash occurs between two data structures when their lower-level components do not correspond because they do not occur under the same circumstances. The standard exercise for the resolution of a boundary clash is the Telegram Analysis problem, first proposed by Henderson and Snowdon [9] and re-stated in *Principles of Program Design* [12]. What follows is a simplified version of this.

A file contains the texts of a number of telegrams. Each record on the file consists of a 'block' of words, where a block consists of a number of words followed by the text 'EOB'. The records are variable-length, and

EOB is therefore required as an end-of-block marker. Words are separated by a single space.

Each telegram consists of a number of words followed by the text 'ZZZ' to indicate end of telegram. A telegram may begin and end anywhere in a block; i.e. a telegram may span several blocks, or a single block may contain several telegrams. End-of-file is signified by a block containing only the text 'EOF'.

Sample Telegrams File:

```
BLOCK1   HAPPY BIRTHDAY ANGUS FROM EOB
BLOCK2   HAMISH ZZZ SUPPRESS LEADING ZEROES ZZZ EOB
BLOCK3   HI THERE ZZZ BEAM ME UP SCOTTIE ZZZ THE EOB
BLOCK4   THIRD FROG ON THE LEFT EOB
BLOCK5   IS CALLED HAROLD ZZZ EOB
BLOCK6   EOF
```

A program is required to print each telegram, one per printline. For purposes of simplification it can be assumed that no telegram is too large for one printline:

```
LINE1   HAPPY BIRTHDAY ANGUS FROM HAMISH
LINE2   SUPPRESS LEADING ZEROES
LINE3   HI THERE
LINE4   BEAM ME UP SCOTTIE
LINE5   THE THIRD FROG ON THE LEFT IS CALLED HAROLD
```

The data structure diagrams of the telegrams file and the telegrams report are shown in Figs 9.7 and 9.8.

When looking for correspondences it is tempting to note a correspondence between WORD on TEL-FILE and WORD on TEL-REPORT. Certainly all the WORDs on TEL-FILE appear on TEL-REPORT in the same order, so there is no ordering clash. But they do not occur under the same circumstances because their parent components do not correspond. BLOCK-BODY does not correspond to TEL-LINE-BODY. In the above sample file, for instance, there are six BLOCKs but only five TEL-LINEs. The number of WORDs in a BLOCK is not the same as the number of WORDs in a TEL-LINE: there are four WORDs in the first BLOCK but five in the first TEL-LINE.

It would be impossible to form a single program structure diagram from the two data structure diagrams. If we designed a program

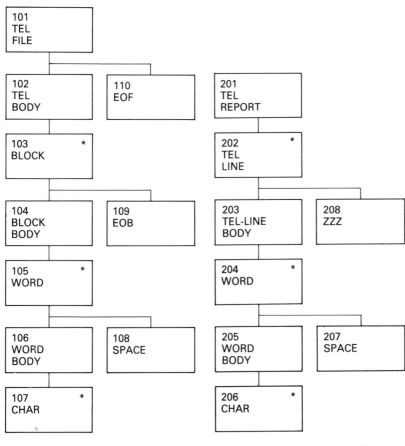

Figure 9.7   Figure 9.8

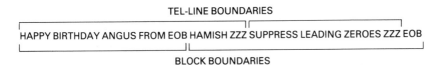

Figure 9.9

component P-WORD, which processed both a WORD in a BLOCK and a WORD in a TEL-LINE, until what condition would P-WORD be iterated? Until end-of-BLOCK (EOB) or end-of-TEL-LINE (ZZZ)?

Because a BLOCK does not consist of an integral number of TEL-LINEs, nor a TEL-LINE consist of an integral number of BLOCKs, it is impossible to synchronize the processing of the two. We say there is a boundary clash between a BLOCK and a TEL-LINE because their boundaries do not coincide. This can be illustrated with the above sample file, showing the different boundaries of a BLOCK and a TEL-LINE by using brackets (see Fig. 9.9).

The solution to a boundary clash is to avoid it. Instead of attempting to form a *single* program structure from two clashing structures, form two procedure structures and invert one of them. By keeping the two structures separate the synchronization problem is avoided because the solution is asynchronous.

Unlike with an ordering clash, an inversion solution is possible here because the output is in the same order as the input. It is therefore possible for an input procedure (P-TEL-FILE) to pass data to an output procedure (P-TEL-REPORT) for immediate processing, instead of having to store it on a sort file or in a table until end-of-file is reached.

In order to link the two procedures P-TEL-FILE and P-TEL-REPORT, it must be decided what data will be passed across from P-TEL-FILE to P-TEL-REPORT via the link-area. A telegram cannot be passed across because P-TEL-FILE has no data component for a telegram; the obvious component to pass across is WORD, which P-TEL-REPORT can then assemble into a telegram line. CHARs could be passed across, but if the interface occurs at the highest possible data level there will be less linkage, i.e. P-TEL-REPORT will be invoked once per WORD rather than one per CHAR. If WORD is chosen as the interface P-TEL-REPORT need know nothing about the composition of WORD, i.e. data components beneath WORD in TEL-REPORT can be omitted.

P-TEL-FILE must also inform P-TEL-REPORT when end-of-file is reached and when end-of-telegram is reached. End-of-file can be signified by setting an L1-EOF-SW to '1' as per usual. End-of-telegram could be signified by setting an L1-EOT-SW to '1', but P-TEL-FILE would then have to reset this to '0' at start-of-telegram. It seems preferable for P-TEL-FILE simply to pass across the end-of-telegram text 'ZZZ', and it was in anticipation of this solution that the data component ZZZ was included in Fig. 9.8. End-of-file could similarly be signified by passing across the end-of-file text 'EOF', but it was decided in Fig. 9.8 to maintain L1-EOF-SW as a standard and not introduce an EOF data component.

Having determined the interface between P-TEL-FILE and P-TEL-REPORT, the remainder of the design procedure is straightforward, and is left as an exercise for the reader.

The most common example of a boundary clash occurs when a paged report of a file is required. In Example 5.2.2, for instance, a report of an employee file was required; refamiliarize yourself with this example before reading on.

Using the correspondence technique correspondences between EMP-FILE and EMP-REPORT, the two DEPT components, and EMP-REC and EMP-LINE were noted, and a program structure diagram was formed. Now suppose it is required to print only ten EMP-LINEs per page with a heading at the top of every page. The data structure diagram of the employee file, shown in Fig. 5.6, is repeated in Fig. 9.10, and the new data structure diagram of EMP-REPORT is shown in Fig. 9.11.

There is now no correspondence between EMP-REC and EMP-LINE; there are ten EMP-LINEs to a PAGE but there may be more or less than ten EMP-RECs to a DEPT. EMP-REC and EMP-LINE no longer occur under the same circumstances because their parent components DEPT and PAGE do not correspond. The boundaries of PAGE and DEPT do not coincide, as can be seen from a sample file of employee numbers (see Fig. 9.12).

In Section 5.5 two alternative solutions to the paging problem were

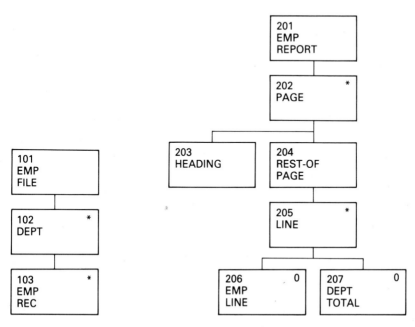

Figure 9.10   **Figure 9.11**

DEPARTMENT BOUNDARIES

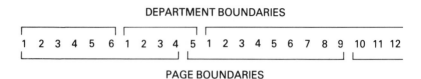

PAGE BOUNDARIES

Figure 9.12

suggested, in which the structure of the report was replaced by a line-group structure or an equivalent macro operation. In essence both solutions incorporate a reduced and altered report structure in order to avoid inversion. By so doing the overheads of inversion are avoided at the cost of the independence of the file and report procedures and the maintainability of the program. A selection for new page must be included at every point in the program structure where a line is to be printed, and amendments to the report structure are not so easily handled.

Consider an amendment to print page footings. This is easily incorporated into the inversion design by allocating an operation to an end-of-program component in the report structure, but to incorporate it into either of the designs presented in Section 5.5 would necessitate an additional selection for end-of-page and a first-time-through switch (to ensure a footing is not printed before the first heading), at every point where a line is to be printed. If inversion is not to be used to resolve the paging problem, the programmer should be aware of the consequences.

As a final point on boundary clashes, it should be noted that paging does not *always* cause a boundary clash. Consider a program which is required to produce a report of the file in Fig. 9.13, one record per line and twenty lines per page; Fig. 9.14 shows the structure of the report. There is a boundary clash between RECORD and LINE because their parent components do not correspond; there are twenty LINES to a PAGE but there may be more or less than twenty RECORDS to a FILE. But the program should not contain a boundary clash, because there is no reason why RECORDs cannot be grouped into batches of twenty for processing purposes. The correct logical data structure diagram of FILE for this program is shown in Fig. 9.15, and it can be seen that there is now no boundary clash with the data structure of REPORT: all three components on each diagram correspond.

In this program records can be viewed logically as batches of twenty because no other structure is imposed upon them within the file. In the

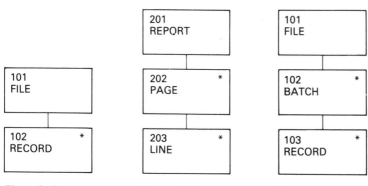

Figure 9.13   Figure 9.14   Figure 9.15

previous example, however, employee records are already structured in departments, and it is this which causes the boundary clash. Make sure that any boundary clash which arises during program design is not caused simply by an inadequate logical data structure diagram.

9.4 INTERLEAVING CLASH

An interleaving clash is a special form of an ordering clash and is best understood by means of an example.

Example 9.4.1

A firm has decided to introduce flexi-time and employees have been issued with clock cards. The clocking procedure has been computerized such that clock-in times and clock-out times are automatically transmitted to the computer system in the form of time records. One of the programs in the payroll suite is required to produce a daily report for management of clock-in and clock-out times together with hours worked, in clock-out sequence.

Here is a sample clock-in/clock-out sequence for four employees.

EMP NO		TIME
2	(IN)	8.00
1	(IN)	9.00
4	(IN)	9.15
3	(IN)	10.00

3	(OUT)	14.00
1	(OUT)	16.30
2	(OUT)	17.00
4	(OUT)	19.00

Here is the format of a time record (in COBOL):

```
01   TIME-REC.
     02   T-EMP-NO       PIC 9(6).
     02   T-TIME         PIC 99V99.
```

Here is the report required:

EMP NO	IN	OUT	HOURS
3	10.00	14.00	4.00
1	9.00	16.30	7.30
2	8.00	17.00	9.00
4	9.15	19.00	9.45

Step 1   Draw data structure diagrams of the file of time records and the report of hours worked (see Figs 9.16 and 9.17).

There is a correspondence between the two root components, but that is all. Time records are in chronological sequence, but employee lines are

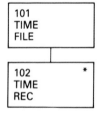

Figure 9.16

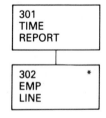

Figure 9.17

in clock-out sequence. It would be impossible to synchronize the processing of a clock-in record with that of an employee line because an employee line is written only when a clock-out record is read.

One way to resolve the clash would be to treat it as an ordering clash and sort the file of time records into the required sequence. However, this is a special kind of ordering clash, in which the data for one employee is interleaved with the data for other employees. Using the above sample file this can be shown graphically by linking clock-in and clock-out records for each employee by brackets (see Fig. 9.18).

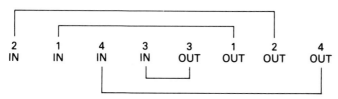

Figure 9.18

For each employee's time records the data structure diagram shown in Fig. 9.19 is true.

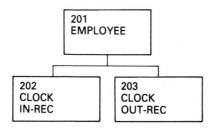

Fig. 9.19

An employee's time records consist of a clock-in record followed by a clock-out record. The structure clash is not an ordering clash but an interleaving clash.

If this hidden data structure is introduced alongside the data structures of TIME-FILE and TIME-REPORT, a very attractive solution to the interleaving clash can be designed using the powerful technique of parallel inversion, which has implications far beyond the bounds of this relatively simple example.

Step 2.1 Form a procedure structure diagram from each data structure diagram (see Figs 9.20, 9.21 and 9.22).

Step 2.2 Determine the interface between P-TIME FILE, P-EMPLOYEE and P-TIME-REPORT.

Let us first of all consider the simple case where there is only one employee. P-TIME-FILE is a file handler which will read time records and pass them across one at a time to P-EMPLOYEE; the link-area between the two (LINK-AREA1) will consist of an L1-TIME REC. P-EMPLOYEE will process the first record passed across as a clock-in record and the second as a clock-out record, and after receiving the second it will invoke P-TIME-REPORT to calculate time worked and print an employee line. The link-area between P-EMPLOYEE and P-TIME-REPORT (LINK-AREA2) will therefore consist of an employee number, a clock-in time and a clock-out time.

In addition P-TIME-REPORT must receive a final invocation in order to know when to close the report file, so P-TIME-FILE will pass across to it an L2-EOF-SW of '1' at end-of-file. P-TIME-REPORT is therefore invoked from both P-EMPLOYEE and P-TIME-FILE. P-EMPLOYEE need know nothing about end-of-file; it merely receives records and passes appropriate information on to P-TIME-REPORT. Before receiving the clock-out record from P-TIME-FILE, P-EMPLOYEE will need to store the clock-in time to prevent it being overwritten in L1-TIME-REC.

It follows that because P-EMPLOYEE knows nothing about end-of-file, it cannot be the main procedure, and it would seem logical to invert both it and P-TIME-REPORT, making P-TIME-FILE the main procedure.

For the simple case where there is only one employee, procedure P-EMPLOYEE is in practice redundant because P-TIME-FILE can pass time records directly to P-TIME-REPORT. P-EMPLOYEE is required only when there are many employees whose records are interleaved. Consider the case where there are four employees. If P-EMPLOYEE is the procedure for one employee, then in theory for four employees four P-EMPLOYEE procedures are required: P-EMPLOYEE-1, P-EMPLOYEE-2, P-EMPLOYEE-3 and P-EMPLOYEE-4, each one processing one employee's time records.

Processing the sample file presented above, P-TIME-FILE reads 2(IN) and passes it across to P-EMPLOYEE-2, which stores employee 2's clock-in time. P-TIME-FILE then reads 1(IN) and passes it across to P-EMPLOYEE-1, which stores employee 1's clock-in time. Similar processing is undertaken for 4(IN) and 3(IN).

P-TIME-FILE then reads 3(OUT) and passes it across to P-EMPLOYEE-3; P-EMPLOYEE-3 passes clock-out time (from this record) and employee 3's stored clock-in time across to P-TIME-REPORT, which calculates time worked and prints a line. Similar processing is undertaken for 1(OUT), 2(OUT) and 4(OUT), and then P-TIME-FILE detects end-of-file and passes an L2-EOF-SW of '1' to P-TIME-REPORT to close the report file.

This is a fine solution in theory, but in practice it would be necessary to write as many P-EMPLOYEE procedures as there were employees. However, the structure and operations of each P-EMPLOYEE procedure are identical; the only procedure-dependent data are the state variable and the employee data. If this data is separated out from the procedure text and stored elsewhere, then it becomes possible to use one P-EMPLOYEE procedure to process all employees.

The data specific to any one of the above P-EMPLOYEE procedures (i.e. its set of local variables) is known as the procedure's *state vector*, and the process of separating it out from the procedure text is known as *state vector separation*. The result of state vector separation is to produce a single P-EMPLOYEE procedure text and a list or file of state vectors, one per employee; in DP terminology this would commonly be called an employee master file, and the state vector would be called an employee record.

Each state vector consists of the variables local to an employee, i.e. the state variable, employee number, clock-in time and clock-out time; in COBOL:

```
01  EMP-REC.
    02  E-EMP-NO      PIC 9(6).
    02  E-SV          PIC 9.
    02  E-IN-TIME     PIC 99V99.
    02  E-OUT-TIME    PIC 99V99.
```

Once employee-dependent data has been separated out in this way, all employees may use the one single P-EMPLOYEE procedure in parallel; the program text is said to be *re-entrant*. In essence the procedure is *multi-threaded*, and the program is said to exhibit *parallel inversion*. In the above sample file, for instance, processing of a second employee begins before processing of the first employee has finished; this is made possible because P-EMPLOYEE is a variable-state procedure and processing of the first employee can be suspended at any entry point, with his data stored in a state vector until required again. State vectors are held in a table or, more commonly, on a direct-access file—the employee master file, whose record format is therefore obtained as a by-product of parallel inversion.

For the simple case where there is only one employee, procedure P-EMPLOYEE is redundant because P-TIME-REPORT can handle any necessary processing. P-TIME-REPORT, however, cannot be multi-threaded because some of its operations must be performed once only (e.g. 'Open time report'). The multi-threaded procedure P-EMPLOYEE is therefore required in order to handle the interleaving clash.

When invoking the multi-threaded procedure P-EMPLOYEE it is

necessary to retrieve the appropriate state vector (i.e. EMP-REC) before invocation and pass it across in the link-area, then update it after invocation. P-TIME-FILE therefore reads a time record, uses the employee number on that record to obtain the appropriate EMP-REC, places the EMP-REC into LINK-AREA1 and invokes P-EMPLOYEE, then restores an updated EMP-REC. This will become clearer following consideration of the detailed program design. Here are the COBOL link-areas (P-EMPLOYEE uses LINK AREA1 and P-TIME-REPORT uses LINK-AREA2):

```
01  LINK-AREA1.
    02  L1-EMP-REC.
        03  L1-E-EMP-NO        PIC 9(6).
        03  L1-E-SV            PIC 9.
        03  L1-E-IN-TIME       PIC 99V99.
        03  L1-E-OUT-TIME      PIC 99V99.
    02  L1-TIME-REC.
        03  L1-T-EMP-NO        PIC 9(6).
        03  L1-T-TIME          PIC 99V99.
01  LINK-AREA2.
    02  L2-SV                  PIC 9        VALUE 1.
    02  L2-EOF-SW              PIC X        VALUE '0'.
    02  L2-EMP-NO              PIC 9(6).
    02  L2-IN-TIME             PIC 99V99.
    02  L2-OUT-TIME            PIC 99V99.
```

For P-TIME-FILE

Step 3.1   List and allocate operations (see Fig. 9.20).

        1   Open time file and employee file.
        2   Close time file and employee file.
        3   Read time record from time file.

Step 3.2   List and allocate conditions (see Fig. 9.20).

        C1   End of time file.

Step 3.3   List and allocate quits and backtracking operations.

        none required.

Step 3.4   List and allocate inversion operations (see Fig. 9.20).

        4   Move '1' to L2-EOF-SW.

5 Put LINK-AREA2.
6 Move time record to L1-TIME-REC.
7 Put LINK-AREA1.
8 Obtain appropriate EMP-REC.
9 Update appropriate EMP-REC.

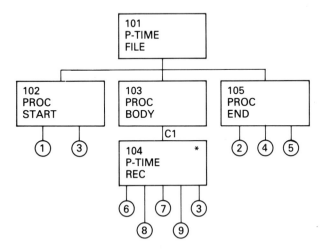

Figure 9.20

Note that the logical structure diagram for this procedure does not need to distinguish between clock-in and clock-out records—that will be handled by P-EMPLOYEE, according to the setting of the state vector. In essence P-TIME-FILE is nothing more, nothing less than a process scheduler (see Section 8.4). Its sole function is to read the file of time records and schedule either P-EMPLOYEE (using the file of state vectors or EMP-RECs) or P-TIME-REPORT (at end-of-file). As a further refinement the reading of the time file could be isolated into an inverted file handler which could check for file corruption.

Operation 8 uses the employee number on a time record to obtain the appropriate state vector (i.e. EMP-REC) and place it into LINK-AREA1 for passing across to P-EMPLOYEE. If there were only a small number of state vectors they could be held in an internal table, in which case operation 8 would involve a table search. More normally, as in this example, the number of state vectors (i.e. employees) is large and they are held on a direct-access file such as a COBOL indexed-sequential file, in which case operation 8 involves a Read operation using employee number as a key.

If the employee number is not found a new EMP-REC is created and added to the file (i.e. a clock-in record has just been read), with a state variable initialized to 1. If the employee number is found then the EMP-REC already exists (i.e. a clock-out record has just been read). The EMP-REC is placed into LINK-AREA1 and passed across to P-EMPLOYEE along with the time record (operation 6). In COBOL operation 8 on an indexed-sequential file could be coded as:

```
8   MOVE T-EMP-NO TO E-EMP-NO.
    MOVE '0' TO NF-SW.
    READ EMP-FILE INVALID KEY MOVE '1' TO NF-SW.
    IF NF-SW = '1'
       MOVE SPACES TO EMP-REC
       MOVE 1 TO E-SV.
    MOVE EMP-REC TO L1-EMP-REC.
```

Operation 9 is a Write operation on the file of EMP-RECs which updates the EMP-REC of an employee after processing by P-EMPLOYEE. In COBOL operation 9 could be coded as:

```
9   MOVE L1-EMP-REC TO EMP-REC.
    IF NF-SW = '1'
       WRITE EMP-REC
    ELSE
       REWRITE EMP-REC.
```

For P-EMPLOYEE

Step 3.1   List and allocate operations.

```
1   Move L1-T-TIME to L1-E-IN-TIME.
2   Move L1-T-TIME to L1-E-OUT-TIME.
```

Step 3.2   List and allocate conditions.

none required.

Step 3.3   List and allocate quits and backtracking operations.

none required.

Step 3.4   List and allocate inversion operations (see Fig. 9.21).

3   Get LINK-AREA1.

4   Move L1-E-EMP-NO to L2-EMP-NO.
    Move L1-E-IN-TIME to L2-IN-TIME.
    Move L1-E-OUT-TIME to L2-OUT-TIME.

5   Put LINK-AREA2.

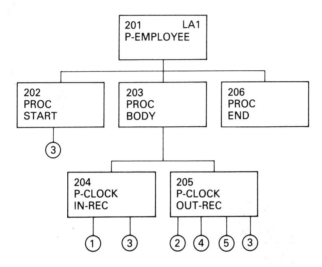

Figure 9.21

Note

All the operations in this procedure concern the updating of the state vector (operations 1 and 2) or communication with other procedures (operations 3, 4 and 5), and it would be possible to allocate them all to P-TIME-FILE and to do away with procedure P-EMPLOYEE altogether. This is commonly what happens in non-JSP design, when selections are added to the file-handling procedure to determine what kind of record has been read (see Example 3.4.2).

The advantage of using a multi-threaded P-EMPLOYEE procedure is that its design, in common with all JSP design, is based on the data structure of an employee. No new selections, switches or other program variables need to be introduced. The allocation of P-EMPLOYEE operations to P-TIME-FILE in this example would be relatively straightforward only because the example is a trivial one.

Consider what would happen if an employee could clock-in and clock-out several times a day, if data validation were required or if additional record types were introduced. These modifications are easily catered for by amendments to P-EMPLOYEE, but if they were to be incorporated into P-TIME-FILE the result would be an increasingly complex and unmaintainable program structure laden with switches and bearing no resemblance to the structure of the data being input.

P-EMPLOYEE's structure remains simple because it is based on the structure of a single employee; interleaving of employee data is handled by a state variable whose generation and maintenance are absolutely automatic. Moreover, the incorporation of P-EMPLOYEE's operations into P-TIME-FILE would be feasible only if the program were to be implemented as a batch program, whereas parallel inversion enables the program to be designed as batch or online (see Section 9.5). As an online program procedure P-TIME-FILE would be required to be no more than a process scheduler, receiving input and scheduling (inverted) procedures as appropriate.

Note that operations 2 and 3 allocated to 205-P-CLOCK-OUT-REC are not strictly required as there is to be no re-entry to the procedure following the processing of an employee's clock-out record. However, it may be considered useful to hold the clock-out time on the employee file (e.g. for processing by another program) and to have the state vector updated (e.g. to enable verification that a clock-out record has been processed).

For P-TIME-REPORT

Step 3.1 List and allocate operations (see Fig. 9.22).

1 Open time report.
2 Close time report.
3 Format and write employee line.
4 Calculate time worked = L2-OUT-TIME—L2-IN-TIME.
5 Write report heading.

Step 3.2 List and allocate conditions (see Fig. 9.22).

C1 L2-EOF-SW = '1'.

Step 3.3 List and allocate quits and backtracking operations.

none required.

Step 3.4   List and allocate inversion operations (see Fig. 9.22).

6   Get LINK-AREA2.

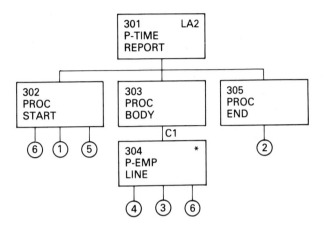

Figure 9.22

On first acquaintance the resolution of an interleaving clash may cause some conceptual difficulty; if so, this example will repay further study on your part. Desk-check the program using the sample file given. Parallel inversion, like every other aspect of JSP, conforms to a rigid set of rules and once the rules have been learned designing programs becomes the application of a skill rather than an exercise in trial and error.

9.5   IN PRAISE OF PARALLEL INVERSION

In mastering parallel inversion you have come a long way from the design of simple batch programs which process a single sequential file. At one stroke parallel inversion unites the design of batch programs and multi-threaded online programs. How often has a novice programmer been told by his more experienced colleagues that in order to design large online programs where data may be interleaved from several sources at once, the first step is to forget all he knows about batch programming? If program design is based on data structure, however, it makes no difference whether input is in the form of a batch file or an online data stream.

Example 9.4.1, for instance, illustrates the design of a program which processes a file of time records and produces a report, but to turn it into an online program which runs throughout the day and processes time records as soon as they arrive merely requires an amendment to the I/O operations allocated, e.g. changing Read operations to Input operations. Further, in order to prevent the program from hogging the machine throughout the day, all three procedures could be inverted to a process scheduler (e.g. a teleprocessing monitor) which would invoke them only when required.

As a batch solution the program design presented for Example 9.4.1 is top-heavy; a simpler design, as suggested at the beginning of Section 9.4, would be to treat the interleaving clash as an ordering clash and sort the file of time records into the required sequence. The sort strategy is not suitable as an online solution, however, when time records must be processed as soon as they are input and before further time records are input.

Parallel inversion leads the programmer into the design of complex interactive programs as a natural extension of the inversion technique. Using parallel inversion you will be able to approach the design of such programs in a skilled and methodical manner, confident of their correctness, reliability and maintainability. Here are some examples of programs which are commonly regarded as complex creations whose design requires much trial and error and years of experience, yet which fall easily to the technique of parallel inversion:

—A program which reports on the usage of a time-sharing system, e.g. number of users and time used, number of jobs run and average run-time.

    The JSP design would be similar to Example 9.4.1. One procedure would input login and logout times and job start and end times, passing data across to a multi-threaded user procedure and a multi-threaded job procedure, both of which would in turn pass data across to an inverted routine.

—An expansion to Example 6.1.1, which processes customer transactions at a bank's cash dispensing terminals, where inputs from one terminal may be interleaved with inputs from another.

    The program would consist of two procedures, one to input transaction data and one (multi-threaded) to process that data. The input procedure would require the addition of a queuing algorithm to cater for simultaneous input. The multi-threaded procedure would have a similar structure to Fig. 6.3, but note that the iteration of transaction data would refer to transactions at one terminal only rather than to all (interleaved) transactions. The iteration of transaction data would continue forever; when shutdown occurs the input handler would simply stop invoking this procedure. Cancellation of a transaction would be handled by backtracking, as in Example 7.4.1. A system reporting procedure could be added as a further inverted routine.

—Incorporation of online queuing mechanisms. In a program which processes input from many sources it may be necessary to add a queuing algorithm to cater for simultaneous input, as noted above. If processing is interleaved it may be necessary to prevent the processing of one transaction from overtaking the processing of another by the addition of a further queuing algorithm. (If one processing thread is not allowed to overtake another the program text is said to be serially reusable rather than re-entrant.)

In Example 9.4.1, for instance, if it is required to print the report in clock-in rather than clock-out sequence, it is necessary to add a queuing algorithm to the program. In the program as designed in Section 9.4 a second employee may clock in after a first and clock out before him, in which case the processing of the second employee overtakes that of the first and a line is printed on the report for the second employee. But if the report is required in clock-in sequence a line for the second employee cannot be printed until after the first employee has clocked out. In other words, the second employee must queue up for processing, which requires the maintenance of a direct-access file of queuers, chained in clock-in sequence.

Using JSP the incorporation of the queuing algorithm is a simple matter. Operation 1 in P-EMPLOYEE, which stores the clock-in time in the state vector, must additionally chain the employee number to the end of the file of queuers. Operation 4, which invokes P-TIME-REPORT when an employee has clocked out, must be changed to flag the employee as clocked-out on the file of queuers, and cause to be passed across to P-TIME-REPORT data for all employees who are at the start of the queue and are flagged as clocked-out.

—Any interrupt-driven routine. The addition of interrupts in an online system (e.g. supervisor interrupts, shutdown, error detection and recovery), is easily catered for by backtracking.

The design of a routine which is driven entirely by interrupts (e.g. a teleprocessing monitor, a real-time process control system), on the other hand, is no different from the design of any other procedure, because in such routines interrupts can be treated like any other input data stream. A simple interrupt handler is nothing more than a process scheduler which receives requests, schedules actions (via multi-threaded subroutines), sends interrupt-complete replies etc. Errors are handled by backtracking. Reference 18 (reprinted in 6) contains an example of the design of an interrupt-driven microcode routine to drive the ICL 2903/4 communications coupler. Reference 7 contains an example of the design of a real-time process control system, including multiplexors and hardware drivers, which responds to changes in the state of the external world.

As a final thought on parallel inversion, consider again Example 9.4.1 as a program running all day which is de-activated and re-activated by a scheduler as and when required. A direct analogy can be made between this program and any application system (e.g. a payroll system, a stock control system) whose programs are activated only when there is data to be processed, and it is an attractive idea to design such a system as a set of inverted procedures.

The data structures of this system would describe the entire life-history of the data to be processed, no matter how many years it might take that data to arrive (e.g. consider the time-span of an insurance policy from policy start to policy end). By basing the system procedures on these life-history data structures and inverting the procedures to a computer run-time scheduler, appropriate procedures would be executed only at required times. This approach to systems design has resulted in the development of JSD, a system development method which brings the same benefits to system development that JSP brings to program development (see Chapter 10).

In conclusion, there is a commonality of design between batch programs, online programs and application systems which JSP is the only design method to exploit usefully, enabling the skills learned in one area to be transferred to others. With the aid of JSP the programmer (trainee or experienced) can approach the development of all types of program in a standard and methodical manner which is based on principles of software engineering and which can be extended to encompass the complete system development process.

9.6 EXERCISES

Which of the following three problems involves a structure clash, and
what sort of structure clash?

1 A file of playing cards is held on magnetic tape in the sequence Hearts,
Clubs, Diamonds, Spades—Ace to King in each suit. A program is
required to produce a report of the file.

(a) Suppose there is one record per card and it is required to print
four cards per printline.

(b) Suppose there is one record per suit and it is required to print four
cards per printline.

(c) Suppose there is one record per suit and it is required to print
court cards (i.e. Jack, Queen, King) three to a printline.

(d) Suppose there is one record per card and it is required to print all
red cards one to a line, followed by all black cards one to a line.

2 A file of customer records is held on punched cards. A customer record
contains a variable number of fixed-length transaction fields, may begin
and end anywhere on a card and may span two or more cards. For each
customer print a line of information on a report.

3 A file consists of data concerning births, marriages and deaths. A record
on the file consists of a name, a code and a date; the code is either 1
(birth), 2 (marriage) or 3 (death). The file is in chronological sequence and
is to be printed in name/code sequence.

4 Complete the design of the Telegram Analysis program presented in
Section 9.3.

5 Redesign the program for Example 7.4.1 to cater for many cash
dispensing terminals, where the data from one may be interleaved with
that from another.

Practise parallel inversion using the examples outlined in Section 9.5, e.g.
a time-sharing system usage program.

Chapter 10

Jackson System Development

This chapter presents a brief introduction to Jackson System Development (JSD) which extends the principles and techniques of JSP into the realm of systems analysis and design. The six steps of the JSD procedure are illustrated by the design of a simple example system.

10.1 INTRODUCTION

The case for a more methodical approach to all areas of systems development was made in Chapter 1; traditional systems development strategies have resulted in a software crisis from which only software engineering can extricate us. JSP is only one tool in the software engineer's kitbag, and there are many areas of systems development which lie outside the domain of JSP and to which other methods and techniques must be applied.

Of special concern to the program designer are the areas of systems analysis and design, which produce the input to JSP, i.e. a program specification. JSP can do little to verify the correctness of a specification. The formation of a program structure diagram from explicitly defined data structure diagrams can do much to unearth omissions, ambiguities and inaccuracies in a specification, but many systems design errors will pass through undetected into live code.

Following on from the success of JSP in the late 1970s work began in earnest to extend the method into the realm of systems analysis and design. This was fuelled by a number of concerns, notably:

—The continuing intractability of the systems analysis and design process. More bugs are inserted at this stage than at any other. Studies show that the systems analysis phase which results in the production of a system specification accounts for 56% of all errors detected [4], and of the remaining errors 61 to 64% occur during system and program design [5].

—The cost of correcting errors introduced during systems analysis and design. The earlier that bugs can be fixed during the systems

270

development life cycle, the greater the cost benefits. Fixing a bug after implementation can cost up to 15 to 16 times as much as fixing it during systems analysis and design [5].

—Widespread experience of the use of JSP in live DP environments, and a realization of how the JSP approach to program development could be applied to complete systems.

Work by Jackson and his colleagues at MJSL in the area of complete system development resulted in 1982 in the publication of *System Development* [13]. In this book Jackson argued the need for a radical new approach to system development and proposed a development method which has since become known as Jackson System Development (JSD). Over the following year a number of JSD systems were implemented, experience of JSD in live DP environments grew, some refinements to the method were made in the light of this, and an updated version of the method was published [6]. In 1985 Speedbuilder, the first piece of software to support and automate JSD, was unveiled by MJSL, and today JSD has taken its place alongside JSP as a proven software engineering method.

JSD is as different from traditional development as JSP is from traditional program development. Non-JSD system development revolves around the production and implementation of a specification which describes the functions of the system. It is typically in verbose and ambiguous English narrative form, or it may use some graphical notation such as a data flow diagram.

Whichever form the specification takes, it is based on system function, it details inputs, processes and outputs, and it cannot help but confuse the first two steps of software engineering: problem definition and solution design. The very nature of a functional specification makes it impossible to divorce the definition of inputs, processes and outputs from the design of a solution which incorporates them.

Indeed, it is only because the solution design is implicit in the specification that the design of the system becomes possible. System design proceeds by decomposing the overall functional specification into sub-functions, which are then packaged into program specifications. Any error in the system specification is perpetuated in the program specifications.

The result of the functional approach to system development is a system which exhibits all the symptoms of the software crisis as detailed in Chapter 1: lateness, costliness, unmaintainability, unreliability, unusability. The parallel with the functional approach to program development is almost exact: a functional design is individualistic by nature, is chosen from the set of possible functional designs on no methodical basis and is difficult to maintain in the face of functional amendments.

JSP improves upon functional program development by using an explicit data-driven approach which makes functional amendments straightforward and which is based on structures which exist in the data outside the programmer's imagination. In a similar manner JSD adopts a data-driven approach to system development which begins by modelling the real world components of the user's problem environment outside the system and only adds system function later.

The JSD procedure consists of six steps:

Step 1   Entity/Action Step
Step 2   Initial Model Step
Step 3   Interactive Function Step
Step 4   Information Function Step
Step 5   System Timing Step
Step 6   System Implementation Step

Steps 1 and 2 form the problem definition phase of software engineering; they define the user's problem environment, free of any functions that may be performed in that environment, using entity life-history diagrams (which are similar to data structure diagrams in JSP). Steps 3 and 4 form the solution design phase of software engineering; they define the functions to be performed in the user's environment, by adding functional operations to entity life-history diagrams (in a manner similar to allocating operations in JSP). Steps 5 and 6 form the solution implementation phase of software engineering; they transform the designed system into source code using techniques such as state vector separation and inversion, all of which can be automated.

The following section expands on each of these six steps and illustrates them with a simple example. It must be stressed, however, that the presentation is in the form of an overview only, and the reader should not expect the same level of exposition as in previous chapters on JSP. Knowledge of JSP concepts will be assumed.

10.2   THE JSD PROCEDURE

Step 1   Entity/Action Step

This step involves defining entities and actions which are of interest in the user's real world environment. An action is an event in the real world which affects the environment. The term 'entity' in JSD has a different meaning from its common usage as a logical record on a file or database. In JSD an entity is something in the real world which performs or suffers actions. 'Date' is not an entity, therefore, because it does not perform or suffer actions; 'Error report' is not an entity because it does not exist in the real world, it is a system output. 'Produce error report' is not an action because it does not take place in the real world, only in a computer system.

In a banking environment entities of interest might be: Bank, Bank manager, Customer, Account; actions of interest might be: Open account, Close account, Withdraw, Deposit. In a stock control environment entities of interest might be: Stock item, Order; actions of interest might be: Place order, Cancel order, Issue stock, Receive stock. In a library environment entities of interest might be: Book, Reader; actions of interest might be: Lend, Catalogue, Return.

Which entities and actions are of interest and which are not is determined in consultation with the user using all the techniques available to the systems analyst: interviews, questionnaires, observation, record searching etc. In a banking enviroment, for example, only entities and actions concerned with the business of banking are of interest. 'Enter bank' and 'Scratch nose' may be considered to be actions performed by a customer, but unless the user is interested in counting the number of customers entering the bank or in listing customers' personal habits, these actions are not of business interest.

In essence Step 1 defines a model of the user's business environment. In contrast to the functional approach to system development, any system based on this model will be able to support the complete set of functions consistent with the business environment, in the same way that a program structure diagram supports a set of program functions in JSP. The model is a map on which many functional journeys can be made (and changed).

The end point of the initial phase of Step 1 is a list of entities and actions. The list is usually quite small and its derivation straightforward, but care must be taken, as in all systems analysis tasks, to make sure that it is complete. In a banking environment, for instance, the entities Customer and Account may appear to be synonymous at first, and only after further investigation may it emerge that a customer can have several accounts and that the entities are distinct from each other. In practice the first four steps of JSD involve an iterative procedure in which entities and actions may emerge at a later stage of design and require incorporation into the list produced at Step 1.

An action is defined in terms of its attributes (i.e. its local variables, the data of which it consists), which are listed alongside it. The attributes of action Lend in a library environment might include: reader identification, book identification, copy number. The attributes of action Deposit in a banking environment might include: account number, deposit amount.

An entity is defined in terms of its actions, which always occur in some sort of order. In a library environment, for example, the entity Book might be defined by the action 'Enter library' followed by an iteration of 'Loan' which is in turn a sequence of 'Issue' and 'Return'. In a banking environment the entity Account might be defined by the action 'Open account' followed by an iteration of 'Movement', which is either a 'Deposit' or a 'Withdrawal', followed by the action 'Close account'. A life-history diagram is drawn for each entity to show the time-ordering of its actions, using the same notation as a data structure diagram in JSP.

The life-history diagram shows the entire life-history of an entity, which may be a period of years. Other data modelling techniques begin with a static picture of entities and actions, for example in the form of a data flow diagram or a database, which binds the model to a specific function at a specific point in time and which cannot easily incorporate change. Most DP environments are dynamic, and the output required from DP systems is often of a historical nature, e.g.

When was the last deposit made to this account?
How many hours has this employee worked this month?
What is the annual turnover for this department?

The dynamic life-history model of JSD easily caters for such requirements, which are added to life-history diagrams during Step 4 in the same way as operations are added to program structure diagrams in JSP. Other aspects of data modelling are also incorporated into JSD in a manner which will be familiar to the student of JSP. Interleaving of actions (e.g. a customer interleaves movements on several accounts) is catered for by inversion as in Example 9.4.1. Premature termination of an entity's life (e.g. a library book is lost, or a stock order is placed but cancelled before the stock is issued) is catered for by backtracking as in Example 8.2.3.

Example 10.2.1   Car Hire System

The business of a car hire company concerns the hiring of cars to customers. Cars are picked up and returned by customers, and customers are invoiced for each hire.

After systems analysis the list of entities, actions and attributes shown in Table 10.1 is produced.

Table 10.1

Entity	Action	Attributes
Car	Buy	Registration number, make, model, year
	Sell	Registration number
	Pick up	Registration number, customer name, date
	Return	Registration number, date
Customer	Start	Customer name, address
	Receive invoice	Customer name, address, registration number, make, model, date, period of hire, amount
	Pay invoice	Customer name, amount

The life-history diagram of each entity is shown in Figs 10.1 and 10.2.

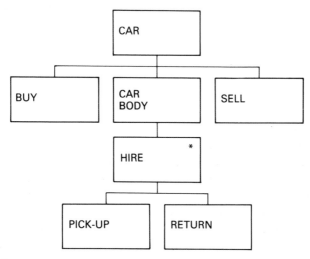

Figure 10.1

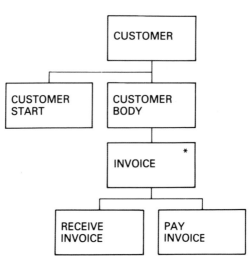

Figure 10.2

Note that for purposes of simplification the analysis undertaken for this example system is incomplete (and inadequate) in order that entities, actions and attributes can be kept to a minimum. The design of a viable car hire system which would cater for all the functions normally associated with the business of hiring cars would exceed the bounds of this chapter (see Section 10.3), and the example is intended solely as an illustration of the JSD procedure.

Step 2   Initial Model Step

This step completes the definition of the JSD model of the user's environment by connecting it to the real world. To accomplish this, operations which communicate actions to the model from the real world are allocated to the entity life-history diagrams. Whenever an action occurs in the real world (e.g. a 'Car return' or a 'Customer start' in the car hire example), a transaction is input to the model and an operation is allocated to receive that transaction.

In the car hire example the input operation has been allocated to the entity life-history diagrams as operation 1 ('Get transaction') according to the read-ahead principle (see Figs 10.3 and 10.4). Operations and conditions other than operation 1 are added during Steps 3 and 4 and are discussed below.

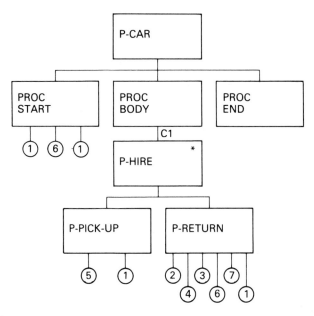

Figure 10.3

Operations and conditions for Fig. 10.3:

List of operations:
1. Get transaction.
2. Access customer's state vector.
3. Create and put 'Receive invoice' transaction.
4. Create and write invoice.
5. Set on-hire switch on.
6. Set on-hire switch off.
7. Put car details.

List of conditions:
    C1 Sell.

Operations and conditions for Fig. 10.4:

List of operations:
1. Get transaction.

List of conditions:
    C1 Forever.

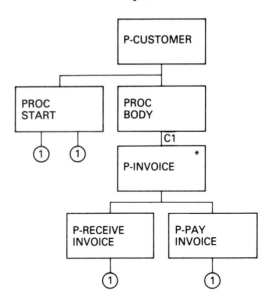

Figure 10.4

By allocating input operations to each entity life-history diagram, each entity becomes a system process which simulates the corresponding real world process (hence the changing of component names in Figs 10.3 and 10.4, e.g. CAR to P-CAR). Whether the 'Get transaction' operation is to be coded as a Read from a file or as an inverted Get from an input-handling scheduler is of no concern at this stage of logical system design; the Get will be transformed into appropriate source code during implementation at Step 6. Nor is it of concern that there may be a long elapsed time between arrival of transactions.

If the system were to be implemented at this stage it would simulate the real world car hire system but would produce no outputs. It is like a program after Step 2 of JSP, a skeletal structure on which functional operations can be hung as required and changed as required. It is in this sense that JSD is data-driven rather than functional. As in JSP, any changes consistent with the real world environment are easily incorporated because the computer system is based on an explicit real world model. In non-JSD systems the real world model is implicit and only partly represented, viewed narrowly from a single functional viewpoint, and changes inconsistent with that function are not easily incorporated. The parallel with JSP and non-JSP maintenance (see example in Section 1.2) is exact.

System processes and their interfaces with the real world and each other are shown diagrammatically in the form of a system specification diagram (SSD). Fig. 10.5 shows the SSD for the car hire example after Step 2. Rectangles represent system processes, circles represent data streams and arrows represent direction of data flow. CAR represents the data stream of actions Buy, Sell, Pick-up and Return; CUS represents the data stream of actions Customer start, Receive invoice and Pay invoice. The SSD tells us little at this stage of design but it provides a basis on which to build functions during Steps 3 and 4.

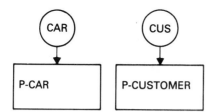

Figure 10.5

Step 3   Interactive Function Step

Steps 3 and 4 are conducted in parallel and concern the allocation of functions to the model in a manner similar to the allocation of operations to a program structure diagram in JSP. Step 3 adds to the model interactive functions, i.e. functions which generate further input transactions, and Step 4 adds to the model functions which generate system outputs.

For instance, in the car hire example it is decided to automate the invoicing of customers. This involves the addition of the information function 'Produce a customer invoice' and the interactive function 'Generate a Receive invoice transaction'. Although the generated 'Receive invoice' transaction and the customer action 'Receive invoice' may not occur at the same time in the real world, they may be considered to occur simultaneously unless it is required to incorporate the postal system into the model.

Consideration of system functions begins, therefore, by allocating operations which generate a 'Receive invoice' transaction. The transaction should be generated (along with the production of the invoice—see

Step 4) when a car is returned from hire, and hence the required operations are allocated to component P-RETURN in process P-CAR. In Fig. 10.3 operations 2 and 3 perform the necessary processing. Operation 2 accesses the customer's state vector to obtain name and address for printing on the invoice; this could be coded as a direct-access Read of a customer file (see Step 6). Operation 3 creates the 'Receive invoice' transaction; this is shown as a Put operation and could be coded as an invocation of P-CUSTOMER.

The addition of the function to the model is shown on the SSD in Fig. 10.6. P-CAR passes to P-CUSTOMER 'Receive invoice' transactions (RIN), which are removed from data stream CUS; a circle denotes data stream connection. P-CAR also accesses P-CUSTOMER's state vector to obtain customer address (ADR); a diamond indicates state vector connection.

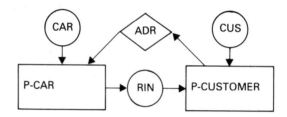

Figure 10.6

Sometimes state vector connection is also required at Step 2 to connect the model to the real world; e.g. a process control system may inspect real world variables rather than have them input in the form of a data stream of transactions.

Step 4   Information Function Step

This step adds to the model functions which generate system outputs. In the car hire example it is decided that the system should perform three information functions:

1 Produce customer invoices.
2 Respond to enquiries about whether a particular car is on hire or not.
3 Produce a weekly report of car hire details.

Function 1   Produce customer invoices

The operation to create and write a customer invoice must be allocated to the same program component which generates the 'Receive invoice' transaction, i.e. P-RETURN in process P-CAR (see operation 4 in Fig. 10.3). The data stream of invoices is also added to the SSD (INV in Fig. 10.9). The joining of the two output data flow lines from P-CAR indicates that the two data streams are output at the same time.

Function 2   Process hire enquiries

As a hire enquiry may occur at any time during the running of the system, the operations required to process an enquiry cannot be embedded in either P-CAR or P-CUSTOMER in the same way as the operations concerned with invoice production. In other words, there is a structure clash between the processing of cars and customers and the processing of enquiries. The clash is solved, as in the examples in Chapter 9, by creating a separate system process to handle enquiries and linking it to appropriate existing processes by inversion.

The design of the enquiries process is obtained from a consideration of its input and output data structures, using JSP principles; it is structured simply as an iteration of enquiries and its life-history diagram is shown in Fig. 10.7.

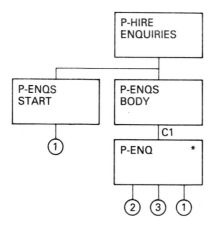

Figure 10.7

List of operations:

1   Get transaction (i.e. enquiry).
2   Access car's state vector.
3   Output reply.

List of conditions:

C1   Forever.

Operation 1 gets an enquiry, operation 2 accesses P-CAR's state vector and operation 3 outputs a reply to the screen. Note that the read-ahead principle is not strictly required for the allocation of operation 1. Operation 2 could be coded as a direct-access read of a file of state vectors (see Step 6), and the state vector must include a data switch which indicates whether the car is on hire or not. Consequently operations 5 and 6 are added to process P-CAR to set the switch on and off at appropriate points (see Fig. 10.3).

As transactions for process P-HIRE-ENQUIRIES and process P-CAR may arrive (interleaved) at any time, the interface between the two processes will be handled by a process scheduler which will receive all transactions and schedule appropriate processes (see Step 6). Hence operation 1 in both processes will be coded as an inverted Get operation, but such considerations are of no concern at this stage; they are elaborated here for purposes of exposition only.

In process P-HIRE-ENQUIRIES the iteration of P-ENQ continues forever—as long as enquiries are input they will be processed; at system shutdown the scheduler simply stops invoking the process.

The enquiries process is added to the SSD as shown in Fig. 10.9. It forms a new process which is connected to the real world by an input data stream of enquiries (ENQ) and an output data stream of replies (RPY), and to process P-CAR by state vector connection (HSW).

Function 3   Produce hire report

Like the enquiries process, the structure of the report process clashes with existing system processes and its operations cannot be embedded in them, e.g. the operation to write a heading at start of page. Therefore a separate process is set up (using JSP principles) and connected to appropriate existing processes by data stream or state vector connection. The hire report process is shown in Fig. 10.8.

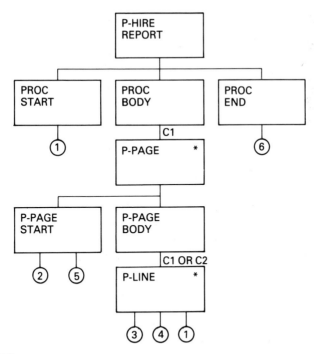

Figure 10.8

List of operations:

1 Get transaction (i.e. hire details).
2 Write page heading.
3 Format and write hire details line.
4 Add 1 to line count.
5 Set line count to 0.
6 Write report totals.

List of conditions:

C1 End of week.
C2 Line count > 19.

If the process is to be implemented as online, operation 1 will be coded as an inverted Get operation and the iteration of P-PAGE will continue until an end-of-week transaction is input. If the process is to be implemented as an end-of-week batch program (more likely, although a decision does not have to be made at this stage), then operation 1 will be coded as a file Read operation (with associated 'Open file' and 'Close file' operations added) and the iteration of P-PAGE will continue until end-of-file. In this case the end-of-week transaction will be replaced by an end-of-week execution request to the system operator.

The hire report process is added to the SSD as shown in Fig. 10.9. It forms a new process which is connected to the real world by an input data stream which indicates end-of-week (EOW—an online trans-action or a batch execution request) and an output report data stream (REP), and connected to process P-CAR by a data stream of hire details (HIR). In process P-CAR is added an operation (operation 7 in Fig. 10.3) which puts hire details to this data stream. The joining of the two input data flow lines to P-HIRE-REPORT indicates a merge process, i.e. EOW determines the cut-off point for which HIR details are to appear on a report. The crossed-lines annotation to the HIR data flow indicates a many-to-one relationship, i.e. P-CAR writes many HIR transactions to one report.

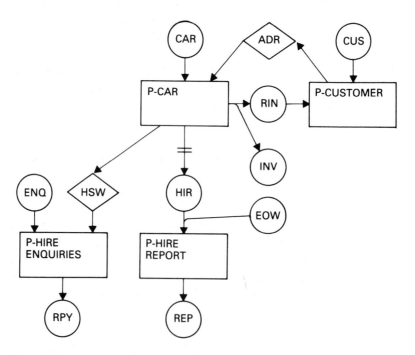

Figure 10.9

Further functions can be added to the system as required, either *embedded* (as per Function 1) or *imposed* (as per Functions 2 and 3).

Step 5   System Timing Step

This step considers or reconsiders system timing constraints, which are documented as a set of notes for implementation or as annotations to the SSD. In the care hire example it is decided that all processes must respond to transactions immediately, except the hire report process, which produces output at end-of-week only and can be implemented as a batch program.

Step 6   System Implementation Step

There is a growing recognition within DP that the traditional demarcation line between systems analysts and programmers, actualized in the form of a program specification, is an inapplicable one; the true demarcation line should be between user-oriented analysts and computer-oriented designers. JSD endorses this approach.

Steps 1 to 5 produce a fully specified and designed system and may be undertaken by user-oriented analysts who require no knowledge of machine considerations. Step 6 involves the implementation of the system and should be undertaken by machine-oriented system designers who require a detailed knowledge of how to fit the specification to the machine.

Commonly implementation is considered at a much earlier stage of system development, even if only implicitly. In some cases the system is specified in terms of batch or online programs, in others it is specified in terms of the available hardware; all such physical constraints limit the system's applicability, portability and maintainability by forcing the specification into an implementation mould. In JSD the system is specified to fit the real world, then transformed to fit the machine.

In principle a system such as the car hire system is directly executable after Step 5. All that is required is one dedicated micro per entity instance (i.e. for every car and every customer), and a copy of the relevant process on each micro, running for the entire life-history of the entity.

Implementation problems arise only when all processes and all entity instances are to be processed on one machine, interleaved not only with each other but also with components of other systems. The problem is therefore one of scheduling, and the JSD solution is as presented in Chapter 9; parallel inversion and process scheduling.

A process scheduler is required to accept transactions from the real world and invoke the appropriate (inverted) process. A scheduler for the car hire example system is shown in Fig. 10.10.

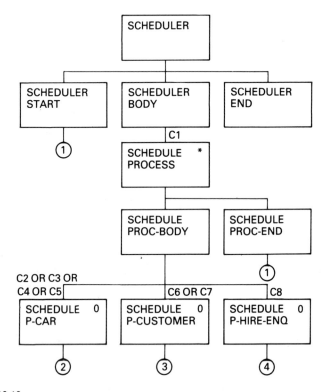

Figure 10.10

List of operations:

    1 Input transaction.
    2 Invoke P-CAR.
    3 Invoke P-CUSTOMER.
    4 Invoke P-HIRE-ENQUIRIES.

List of conditions:

    C1   Shutdown.
    C2   Buy.
    C3   Sell.
    C4   Pick-up.
    C5   Return.
    C6   Customer start.
    C7   Pay invoice.
    C8   Enquiry.

An invocation of P-HIRE-REPORT is not included as a scheduler operation because it has been decided to execute that process as a separate stand-alone end-of-week program. The Invoke operation in HOST would be a Put to an appropriate link-area, coded as a suitable source language procedure invocation statement.

Process P-CAR processes (interleaved) transactions for many cars, so it is coded according to the rules for parallel inversion, with state vectors separated out into a direct-access CAR-FILE. The contents of a state vector (i.e. car record) are determined by consideration of what action attributes need to be saved from one invocation of P-CAR to the next in order that P-CAR can perform the functions required of it. Operation 1 ('Get transaction') is coded as an inverted Get operation, receiving input from the scheduler. Operation 7 ('Put hire details') is coded as a Write macro-operation to a file of hire details ('Open hire file', 'Write hire record', 'Close hire file').

Process P-CUSTOMER processes (interleaved) transactions for many customers, and is also coded according to the rules for parallel inversion, with state vectors separated out onto a direct-access CUSTOMER-FILE. Operation 2 in P-CAR accesses this file. Operation 1 in P-CUSTOMER ('Get transaction') is coded as an inverted Get operation, receiving input from both the scheduler and process P-CAR.

Process P-HIRE-ENQUIRIES processes enquiries one at a time and is inverted to the scheduler. State vector separation is not required because enquiries are not interleaved. Operation 1 ('Get transaction') is coded as an inverted Get operation receiving input from the scheduler. Operation 2 accesses the CAR-FILE.

Process P-HIRE-REPORT is a stand-alone program executed at end-of-week. Operation 1 ('Get transaction') is coded as a 'Read record from hire file' operation, and 'Open file' and 'Close file' operations are allocated to components PROC-START and PROC-END respectively. Condition C1 is coded as 'End-of-file'. File open and close operations are implementation-dependent; they cannot and should not be allocated until batch/online and file/database decisions have been made at Step 6.

As P-CAR and P-CUSTOMER are multi-threaded procedures, 'Obtain state vector' and 'Update state vector' operations must be allocated to the scheduler, along with open and close operations for the car and customer files. In Fig. 10.10 these operations have been taken as implicit and omitted for purposes of exposition of this example only. The scheduler thus deals with all data management of state vector files, although it is also possible to distribute the obtaining and updating of state vectors to the start and end of the appropriate inverted processes, in order to avoid the input of state vector keys to the scheduler. Otherwise a process never updates its state vector; all processing of state vector fields is done in a work area (in HOST a link-area).

The implementation can be shown diagrammatically in the form of a system implementation diagram (SID—see Fig. 10.11).

On this diagram an invocation of an inverted subroutine is indicated by parallel lines.

If the procedures which form the online part of the system cause memory or paging problems owing to their size or interaction, they should be dismembered and re-organized into efficient load modules (see Section 8.5, point 8).

10.3   RETROSPECT

Like JSP, JSD is a data-driven approach to software development which builds functions onto a model of the real world. In JSP the real world consists of the data which is input to and output from the program; in JSD the real world consists of entities and actions in the user's business environment which are communicated to the system in the form of data. The Jackson approach to program and system development considers function to be of secondary concern to getting the underlying model correct.

Unlike other approaches to systems development, the model which JSD uses is explicit rather than implicit and dynamic rather than static. The processes in the system specification diagram in Fig. 10.9 should be considered as running in parallel and forever, just like the processes in the

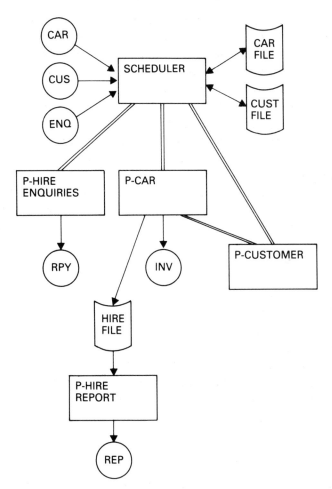

Figure 10.11

real world which they simulate. Any attempt to design a system which begins with a static model, such as a data flow diagram or a database, will be based on a view of the system at one point in time and will be function-bound, implementation-bound and difficult to maintain.

Maintenance to a JSD system is more straightforward. New functions are incorporated either as embedded operations in existing processes or as new imposed processes. In the car hire example system the following functions are easily added:

—Process enquiries concerning which car makes and models are available for hire. The enquiry process could be menu-driven, with various enquiry options, and access paths to make and model in the car file would be required (e.g. a secondary index on an indexed-sequential file).

—List the outstanding invoices at end of month. A monthly stand-alone program would be required to read the customer file and list unpaid invoices. A paid switch would be required for each customer, set on and off by process P-CUSTOMER.

—List all cars older than five years. Another stand-alone program would be required to read the car file and compare purchase dates against current date.

—List number of hires and average mileage per hire for each car. Pick-up and Return mileages would require to be input and stored on the car file, and P-CAR would write a record to a hire history file for each Return. This file would then be sorted and processed.

—Validation of input. The entity life-history diagrams describe the order in which input should arrive, and incorporating validation using backtracking is no great problem.

As an exercise you may wish to consider the incorporation of these processes into the car hire system, or to consider other functions which could be added. It is instructive to note that there are some functions which cannot be added to the model because the model has been intentionally simplified for purposes of exposition and illustration.

For example, it has been assumed that a customer can hire only one car at once, and that he must pay one invoice before hiring another car and receiving another invoice (i.e. component P-INVOICE in process P-CUSTOMER is an iteration of P-RECEIVE-INVOICE followed by P-PAY-INVOICE). Moreover, there is no check within P-CAR that a first invoice has been paid before a second hire begins (which would require an access of the customer's invoice-paid switch). If a customer may hire several cars at once, with pick-ups and returns interleaved (e.g. the customer may be a business firm), then a separate multi-threaded hire process would be required.

Another function which the model does not support is an enquiry as to whether a customer has a car on hire, because actions Pick-up and Return have not been included in process P-CUSTOMER. The model is therefore incomplete and inadequate but serves its purpose as a simplified illustration of the JSD procedure.

Implementation considerations in JSD come last of all. The state vectors for P-CAR and P-CUSTOMER could be normalized and implemented using a database equally as well as direct-access files. But system design should not begin with that database. If a database already exists, then the system should still not be designed for that database—logical design must precede physical design. Only at Step 6 should the designed system be considered in terms of the existing database, and any mismatches and inconsistencies will be extremely instructive.

Here is a list of some major differences between JSD and non-JSD systems development:

—JSD is a data-driven rather than functional approach to system development. It begins with a function-independent model of the user's real world and only adds functions to this model at a later stage.

—The JSD model is dynamic rather that static. It reflects the entire life history of an entity rather than its current state (e.g. in a database).

—JSD is not top-down. It begins with an analysis of entities and actions and from them builds a model which is a network of interconnecting parallel processes.

—JSD concentrates on logical system specification and only considers physical implementation as a final step.

—JSD considers functions independently of each other, following each one through to its detailed specification in terms of operations before turning to another. This is in contrast to top-down design, which begins with an abstraction of the complete set of interrelated functions.

—Design of a system process is based on an entity's life-history diagram (in the case of an embedded process) or a process's input and output data structures (in the case of an imposed process). As in JSP, there is no place for switches, GOTOs and programmer variability (see also discussion of procedure P-EMPLOYEE in Example 9.4.1).

—The implementation of a JSD specification can be automated given appropriate software.

These differences have been explored earlier in this chapter and in previous chapters on JSP. The interface between JSD and JSP is perhaps not as clear-cut as the experienced JSP programmer would initially wish. JSD is not a bolt-on front end to JSP. JSD parallels the JSP development of programs at the system level—model, function, implementation; in other words, the elements of the JSP procedure are distributed throughout the whole JSD procedure. The equivalent of the data structure diagram appears at Step 2, allocation of operations and conditions occurs at Steps 3 and 4, inversion occurs at Step 6. The JSP programmer will find that he has much to contribute, therefore, to the entire systems development process.

The presentation of JSD in this chapter must of necessity leave many questions unanswered owing to limitation of space. It is intended as a brief introduction only, and the interested reader should consult references 13 and 6 for further information. It is the author's contention that each characteristic of JSD outlined in the above list is an advantage that JSD has over almost all other approaches to system development. The future of system development lies in formalization (of specification) and automation (of implementation), supported by appropriate software tools. JSD points the way to this future.

Appendix A

OPERATIONS IN COBOL AND BASIC

English	Meaning	COBOL	BASIC
Add	Add	ADD	LET
Amend	Alter data	MOVE	LET
Calculate	Calculate	COMPUTE	LET
Close	Close file	CLOSE	CLOSE #
Exit database	Exit database	Database dependent	Database dependent
Fetch	Obtain data from database	Database dependent	Database dependent
Format	Fill with data	MOVE	LET
Get	Obtain data from (inversion)	PERFORM/GO TO	GOSUB/GOTO
Input	Input data from terminal	ACCEPT	INPUT
Invoke database	Invoke database	Database dependent	Database dependent
Move	Move data	MOVE	LET
Open	Open file	OPEN	OPEN #
Output	Output data to terminal	DISPLAY	PRINT
Put	Put data to (inversion)	PERFORM/ GO TO	GOSUB/GOTO
Quit	Quit posit branch (backtracking)	GO TO	GOTO
Read	Read record from file	READ	INPUT #
Set	Assign value	MOVE	LET
Subtract	Subtract	SUBTRACT	LET
Write	Write record to file	WRITE	PRINT #

Appendix B

OPERATIONS AND CONDITIONS CHECKLISTS

Operations Checklist

1   Input data from terminal.
2   Output data to terminal.
3   Open file.
4   Close file.
5   Read record from input file.
6   Format output record.
7   Write record to output file.
8   Zeroize a total.
9   Add to a total.
10   Output or write a total.
11   Initialize and increment variables, e.g. subscripts, counters.
12   Store a variable in a work-area for later processing.
13   Set up a reference criterion for a condition.
14   Process a record/variable (e.g. calculate, amend).
15   Set up key for direct-access.
16   Set a switch on/off, e.g. for COBOL direct-access Read.
17   Allocate quits and backtracking operations.
18   Allocate inversion operations Get and Put (plus associated moves to link-area).
19   Obtain/update state vector in parallel inversion.
20   Terminate program (if not generated by PDL precompiler).

Add further operations to the checklist as you think necessary

ALLOCATE OPERATIONS TO ELEMENTARY COMPONENTS ONLY

Conditions Checklist

1 Allocate a condition to every selected and iterated component.
2 List conditions as they appear on the program structure diagram from left to right, leg by leg, higher-level before lower-level conditions.
3 The negation of a condition may be used to reduce the size of the conditions list. C1 is the negation of C1.
4 Use simple, not compound, conditions in the conditions list. Conditions may be compounded during allocation, e.g. C1 AND C2.
5 If a nested iteration is not performed a fixed number of times and is not ended by a special input record, carry down the end-of-iteration condition(s) from the higher-level iteration(s).

Appendix C

COMPONENT LABELS

The component labels used in this book consist of a component number and a component name.

Component names

Component names are for the benefit of people not computers. Computers would work quite happily with component numbers, but the human mind finds more meaningful data easier to grasp. Component names, therefore, are an aid to program understanding, and should be meaningful and consistent.

A name which has no meaning is worse than useless. A root component for a Customer File print program which was named 'STOCKPRINT' would not endear the author to someone who had to maintain it. A verbose name such as PROCESS-CUSTOMER-FILE-PRINT would also irritate: the author would get tired of writing it and the reader would find that its length increased visual scanning time of the program text. The ideal to aim for is meaningfulness with conciseness, e.g. PRINT CUSTFILE.

Use meaningful abbreviations, e.g. CUST for CUSTOMER, REC for RECORD, EMP for EMPLOYEE. Learning to abbreviate meaningfully is something of an art, but remember: write your program for others, not for yourself. The component names for diagrams in this manual have been restricted to two lines of ten characters; judge for yourself whether you consider them all meaningful.

Names should be consistent in that it should be possible to trace a component from a data structure diagram through a program structure diagram to source code. The latter step is simple—a component name on a program structure diagram becomes a HOST paragraph name and a source language paragraph name or comment, but the initial incorporation of a data component into a program structure diagram may require more thought. The simplest way of turning a data component into a program component is to put 'P' (for 'PROCESS') in front of it, e.g. CUST-REC becomes P-CUST-REC. But sometimes other more meaningful names

296

are appropriate, e.g. PRINT, CHECK, VALIDATE, UPDATE; use your initiative.

It is also permissible to have a more indirect connection between data component names and program component names, provided the connection is meaningful and apparent. Thus the processing of data component FILE-HEADER may be subsumed into program component PROG-START, and the data component FILE-TRAILER may be subsumed into program component PROG-END.

When programs are formed from two or more data structure diagrams using the correspondence technique, a program component is often formed from two or more data components. When this happens the program component name should reflect the processing of all its constituent data components, and a meaningful indirect name may be most appopriate.

Component Numbers

Unlike component names, component numbers do not greatly aid the comprehension of a program structure diagram, nor are they integral to the JSP design method. Many interactive diagram generators (e.g. MJSL's PDF) work quite happily without a numbering system. However, numbering components does have advantages:

Advantages of a Component Numbering System

—A number provides a short-hand method of referring to a component without having to call it by name. This may be of use to a data dictionary or an interactive JSP diagrammer.

—If a component occurs more than once on the same diagram, each occurrence can be labelled uniquely by a component number.

—Program component labels should be easy to locate in a program text which is used for debugging and maintenance, and the only way to ensure this is to number them in some way and code them in a standardized (usually ascending) sequence.

—A good numbering system will reflect the structure of the program and aid debugging and maintenance.

The numbering system adopted in this manual numbers components of a structure diagram from left to right, leg by leg, higher levels before lower levels. The root component is numbered 101 and this is incremented by 1 to obtain each subsequent component number: 102, 103, etc. Each component number becomes a paragraph number within HOST.

This numbering system ensures that paragraphs are listed in execution sequence (to aid debugging), that child sub-components (i.e. subroutines) are always further down the program listing and that, so far as possible, parent and child components are kept close together.

Additional notes

If a new component is added during maintenance and a utility which renumbers components automatically is not available, number the new component using a fourth digit. To insert a component between component 106 and component 107, for instance, number it 1061.

If a diagram becomes too large for a sheet of paper, split it into two (see Appendix E) and number components of the second diagram 201, 202, etc. If you really must design large programs which require more than nine diagrams, use letters after that.

Appendix D

CODING RULES

Section 1   Program Structure Diagram Into HOST

This section lists the rules for converting a program structure diagram with allocated operations and conditions into HOST. For comparison purposes, equivalent Structure Text constructs are shown alongside HOST constructs.

Rule 1.1 Program Components

Each program component (i.e. box on a diagram) is represented in HOST by a paragraph name consisting of the component number and name.

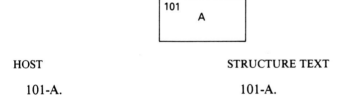

HOST   STRUCTURE TEXT

   101-A.   101-A.

Figure D.1

The hierarchical organization of program components is indicated by coding them in component number sequence.

Rule 1.2 Elementary Components

An elementary component is represented by a paragraph name followed by the operations, if any, of which it consists.

299

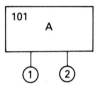

HOST

    101-A.
        operation 1
        operation 2

STRUCTURE TEXT

    101-A seq
        operation 1;
        operation 2;
    101-A end

Figure D.2

Rule 1.3 Sequence

A sequence component is represented by a paragraph name followed by a
DO... statement for each sub-component of which it consists.

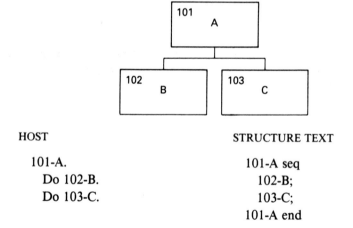

HOST

    101-A.
        Do 102-B.
        Do 103-C.

STRUCTURE TEXT

    101-A seq
        102-B;
        103-C;
    101-A end

Figure D.3

Rule 1.4 Selection

A selection component is represented by a paragraph name and the literal
'SEL', followed by a DO... IF... statement for each sub-component of
which it consists.

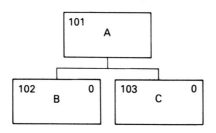

HOST

   101-A SEL.
     Do 102-B if (C1).
     Do 103-C if (C2).

STRUCTURE TEXT

     101-A select C1
       102-B;
     101-A alt C2
       103-C;
     101-A end

Figure D.4

Rule 1.5 Iteration

An iteration component is represented by a paragraph name and the literal 'ITER', followed by a DO... UNTIL... statement for the sub-component of which it consists.

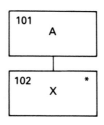

HOST

   101-A ITER.
     Do 102-X until (C1).

STRUCTURE TEXT

     101-A ITER while not (C1)
       102-X;
     101-A end

Figure D.5

Rule 1.6 Backtracking

A program component which consists of a posit sub-component and an
admit sub-component is represented by a paragraph name and the literal
'POSIT', followed by a DO... POSIT statement for the posit sub-
component and a DO... ADMIT statement for the admit sub-component. A quit is represented by a QUIT... IF... statement.

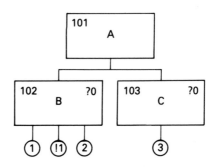

HOST	STRUCTURE TEXT
101-A POSIT.	101-A posit 102-B
Do 102-B POSIT.	102-B seq
Do 103-C ADMIT.	operation 1;
102-B.	101-A quit (!1)
operation 1.	operation 2;
Quit 102-B if (!1).	102-B end
operation 2.	101-A admit 103-C
103-C.	103-C seq
operation 3.	operation 3;
	103-C end
	101-A end

Figure D.6

Rule 1.7 Inversion

As inversion is purely an implementation technique for transforming
designed programs into source code, rules for its representation in
diagrammatic form are inapplicable. If inversion is to be automated using
a HOST compiler, it should be formally coded in HOST as per the following
example. Suppose that 101-A is a main (invoking) procedure putting data
to 201-B and 301-C which are inverted (invoked) procedures.

LINK-AREA1 USED BY 201-B.
LINK-AREA2 USED BY 301-C.

101-A.
. . . .
Put LINK-AREA1.
Put LINK-AREA2.
. . . .

201-B INVERT USING LINK-AREA1.
. . . .
Get LINK-AREA1.
. . . .
201-B INVERT-END.

301-C INVERT USING LINK-AREA2.
. . . .
Get LINK-AREA2.
. . . .
301-C INVERT-END.

Note that allocation of Get and Put operations depends on the interface between procedures (see main text).

Section 2   HOST into COBOL and BASIC

This section lists the rules for automated conversion of HOST into linear COBOL and BASIC. Rules for other programming languages are easily derived.

Rule 2.1 Root Component

Before the root component paragraph in COBOL generate the statements:

PROCEDURE DIVISION.
(Root-component-name)-MAIN SECTION.

At the end of the root component paragraph in COBOL generate the statement:

STOP RUN.

At the end of the root component in BASIC generate the statement:

END

Rule 2.2 Sequence

HOST	COBOL	BASIC	
101-A.	101-A.	100	REM A
Do 102-B.	GO TO 102-B.	110	GOTO 200
Do 103-C.	102-B-EXIT.	120	GOTO 300
	GO TO 103-C.	130	. . . .
	103-C-EXIT.		
. . . .	. . . .	. . . .	
102-B.	102-B.	200	REM B
operation 1.	operation 1.	210	operation 1
103-C.	GO TO 102-B-EXIT.	220	GOTO 120
operation 2.	103-C.	300	REM C
	operation 2.	310	operation 2
	GO TO 103-C-EXIT.	320	GOTO 130

Rule 2.3 Selection

HOST	COBOL	BASIC	
101-A-SEL.	101-A.	100	REM A
Do 102-B if (C1).	IF C1	110	IF C1 GOTO 200
Do 103-C if (C2).	GO TO 102-B.	120	IF C2 GOTO 300
	IF C2	130	. . .
	GO TO 103-C.		
	102-B-EXIT.		
	103-C-EXIT.		
. . . .	. . . .	. . . .	
102-B.	102-B.	200	REM B
operation 1.	operation 1.	210	operation 1
103-C.	GO TO 102-B-EXIT.	220	GOTO 120
operation 2.	103-C.	300	REM C
	operation 2.	310	operation 2
	GO TO 103-C-EXIT.	320	GOTO 130

Rule 2.4 Iteration

HOST	COBOL	BASIC	
101-A ITER.	101-A.	100	REM A
Do 102-X until (C1).	102-X-EXIT.	110	IF NOT C1
	IF NOT C1		GOTO 200
	GO TO 102-X.		
. . . .	. . . .	. . . .	
102-X.	102-X.	200	REM X
operation 1.	operation 1.	210	operation 1
	GO TO 102-X-EXIT.	220	GOTO 100

Rule 2.5 Backtracking

HOST	COBOL	BASIC	
101-A POSIT.	101-A.	100	REM A
Do 102-B POSIT.	GO TO 102-B.	110	GOTO 200
Do 103-C ADMIT.	102-B-EXIT.	120	....
	103-C-EXIT.		
....	....	....	
102-B.	102-B.	200	REM B
operation 1.	operation 1.	210	operation 1
Quit if (!1).	IF !1	220	If !1 GOTO 300
operation 2.	GO TO 103-C.	230	operation 2
103-C.	operation 2.	240	GOTO 120
operation 3.	GO TO 102-B-EXIT.	300	REM C
	103-C.	310	operation 3
	operation 3.	320	GOTO 120
	GO TO 103-C-EXIT.		

Rule 2.6 Inversion

INVERT/INVERT-END

HOST: 201-B INVERT USING LINK-AREA1.

  AT START OF PROCEDURE:

COBOL	BASIC	
201-B.	2100	REM B PARAMETERS
GO TO L1-SV-TEST.	2100	GOTO 2990
201-B-EP1.	2120	REM EP1

  AT END OF ROOT COMPONENT:

COBOL	BASIC	
GO TO 201-B-EXIT.	21nn	GOTO 2999

HOST: 201-B INVERT-END.

COBOL	BASIC	
L1-SV-TEST.	2990	REM L1-SV-TEST
GO TO 201-B-EP1	2991	ON L1.SV GOTO 2120,...
201-B-EP2	....	
....	2999	RETURN
201-B-EPn		
DEPENING ON L1-SV.		
201-B-EXIT.		
EXIT.		

where n is the total number of Gets/Puts in the inverted procedure and L1-SV is a variable (in COBOL a PIC 9 field in LINK-AREA1) initialized to 1 (see main text).

GET/PUT

In a main (invoking) procedure:

HOST	COBOL	BASIC
Get LINK-AREA1. Put LINK-AREA1.	PERFORM 201-B THRU 201-B-EXIT.	GOSUB 2100

In an inverted (invoked) subroutine:

first occurrence:

HOST	COBOL	BASIC
Get LINK-AREA1. Put LINK-AREA1.	nothing generated. as per subsequent occurrences.	nothing generated as per subsequent occurrences.

subsequent occurrences:

HOST	COBOL	BASIC
Get LINK-AREA1. Put LINK-AREA1.	MOVE n TO L1-SV. GO TO 201-B-EXIT. 201-B-EPn.	L1.SV=n GOTO 2999 REM EPn

where n is 2 for the second Get/Put in the inverted procedure, 3 for the third etc.

Note on first occurrence:

Each Put represents an entry point in an inverted procedure. Each Get also represents an entry point, but as the first Get is always allocated to start of procedure (according to the read-ahead principle) nothing needs to be generated for it, any source code required being generated by the Invert statement.

Appendix E

LARGE DIAGRAMS

Large programs require large diagrams which may not fit on a single page. This is a problem for any diagrammatical tool of program design and this appendix examines three solutions.

A first solution is to draw smaller boxes and write smaller text inside them. This is an obviously limited solution because there is a limit to how small we can write or read comfortably, but it is one which is adopted by far too many text books.

A second solution is to use a larger sheet of paper, sellotaping sheets together if necessary. This is a disarmingly simple but useful approach, and is in theory limited only by the amount of paper and sellotape available.

The 'larger sheet of paper' approach is one solution adopted by graphics utilities which draw structure diagrams on a VDU screen. A diagram is drawn on a virtual screen of which the actual screen is only a part; a window facility enables the actual screen to be moved around the virtual screen to see other parts of the diagram. This solution may become unwieldy with very large diagrams, however, and it is also untenable for a text-book writer who must work with a fixed page-size.

A third solution is to divide or dismember a diagram into sub-diagrams. Here are a few pointers on diagram dismemberment, using the diagram in Fig. E.1 for discussion purposes.

1 If a diagram is too deep, remove a branch by dismembering it at a parent component. In Fig. E.1 branch D could be placed in a separate sub-diagram; box D should be shown on both diagrams for cross-reference purposes. Alternatively, to reduce the diagram depth by 1 level, branch E and branch I could be dismembered into separate sub-diagrams.

2 If a diagram is too wide, removing branches of the diagram according to the rules for depth dismemberment will often also reduce width, e.g. the removal of branch I in Fig. E.1. On rare occasions the diagram may be too wide because a sequence or selection contains a large number of children. In this case, try to organize some of the children into a group, replace them by a single group component and drop them down to the next level of the diagram as children of the group component; then if the diagram is still too wide use depth dismemberment rules.

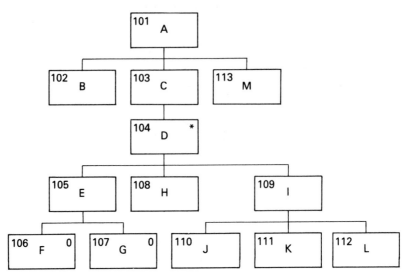

Figure E.1

3 Use a component numbering system which reflects diagram dismemberment. In Fig. E.1 component *D* is numbered 104; if branch *D* is dismembered it should be given a number of 201 on the sub-diagram to denote its new position as the root of that diagram. In addition the number 201 should be incorporated into the name of component 104 on the parent diagram (i.e. 201-D) for cross-reference purposes. In HOST a sub-diagram becomes a subroutine invoked by a DO statement, e.g. DO 201-D.

The numbering system can be extended to cater for more than nine sub-diagrams by the use of letters of the alphabet, but if you ever reach that level of dismemberment, perhaps the program is too large and you should consider dividing it into two smaller programs.

Diagram dismemberment is a useful optimization strategy for common routines. If a branch occurs more than once on a diagram, dismember all occurrences into a single sub-diagram and invoke it (in HOST) using a DO statement.

In the main text examples of program dismemberment are given in Examples 6.2.1, 6.3.1 and 7.4.1.

Appendix F

OUTLINE SAMPLE SOLUTIONS

To conserve space solutions are shown in outline form only using an abbreviated component labelling and diagrammatic notation.

2.7.1

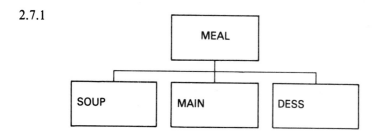

2.7.2

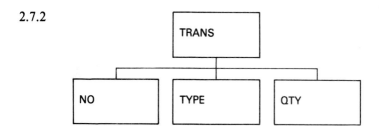

2.7.3

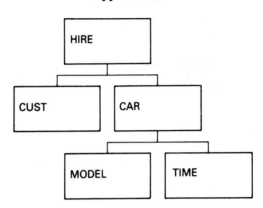

2.7.4

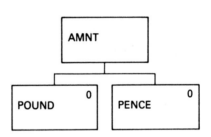

2.7.5

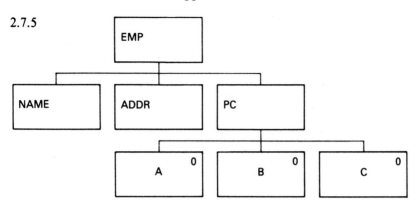

2.7.6

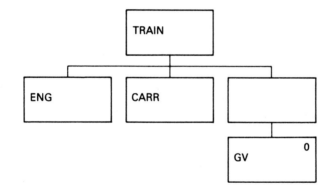

2.7.7

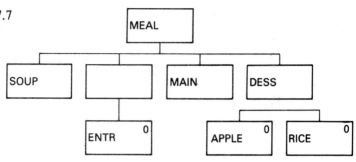

2.7.8

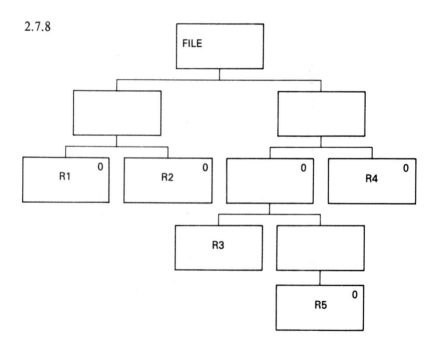

2.7.9

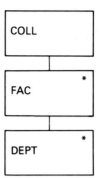

2.7.10

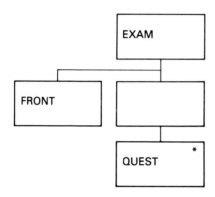

2.7.11

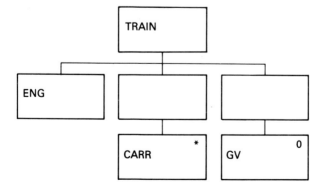

2.7.12

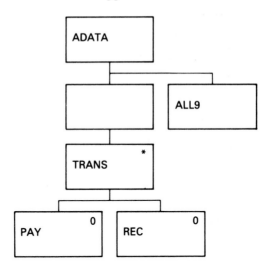

2.7.13

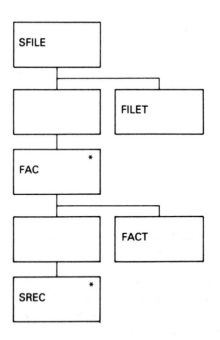

2.7.14

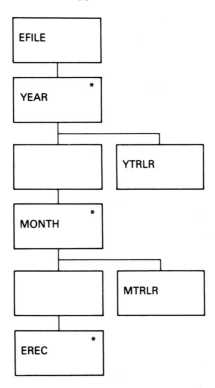

3.3.1

6. Add cost to cost total (P-QTY-END).
7. Output cost total (PROG-END).

3.3.2

6. Add invoice amount to paid total (P-PAID).
7. Output warning message.

PROG-END becomes a sequence of P-POSS-MESSAGE followed by P-END-RTN (to which operations 5 and 2 are allocated). P-POSS-MESSAGE consists of selected component P-MESS (to which operation 6 is allocated). Condition for P-MESSAGE:

C3   Unpaid total > paid total.

3.5.1

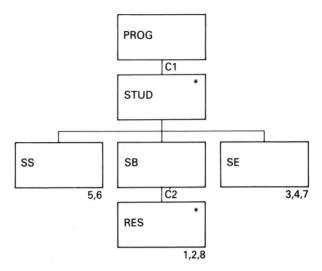

1. Input result.
2. Add result to result total.
3. Calculate average result = result total / 6.
4. Output average result.
5. Set result total to 0.
6. Set COUNT2 to 1.
7. Add 1 to COUNT1.
8. Add 1 to COUNT2.

C1. COUNT1 > 30.
C2. COUNT2 > 6.

3.5.2

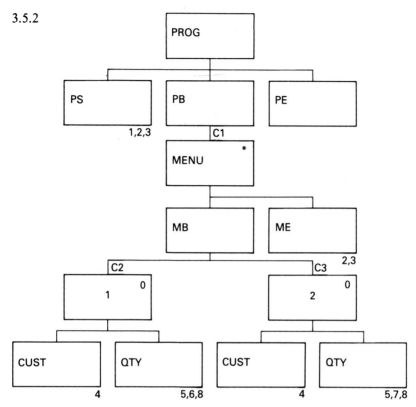

1. Output user instructions.
2. Output menu.
3. Input option.
4. Input customer number.
5. Input quantity.
6. Calculate cost = quantity × 99 × 0.9.
7. Calculate cost = quantity × 99.
8. Output cost.

C1. Option = 9.
C2. Option = 1.
C3. Option = 2.

3.5.3

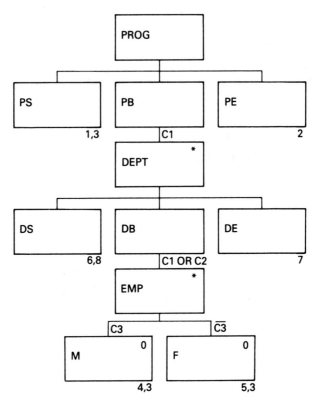

1. Open employee file.
2. Close employee file.
3. Read record from employee file.
4. Add 1 to male total.
5. Add 1 to female total.
6. Set male total and female total to 0.
7. Output male total and female total.
8. Move department number to current department number.

C1. End of employee file.
C2. Department number not = current department number.
C3. REC-TYPE = 'M'.

3.5.4

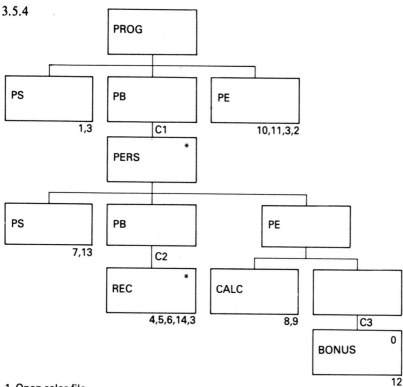

1. Open sales file.
2. Close sales file.
3. Read record from sales file.
4. Add sales (COUNT) to person sales total.
5. Add 1 to person total.
6. Add sales (COUNT) to file sales total.
7. Set person sales total to 0.
8. Calculate average person sales = person sales total / 12.
9. Output average person sales.
10. Calculate average file sales = file sales total / person total.
11. Output average file sales.
12. Output 'BONUS'.
13. Set COUNT to 1.
14. Add 1 to COUNT.

C1. File trailer.
C2. COUNT > 12.
C3. Average person sales > 1000.

3.5.5

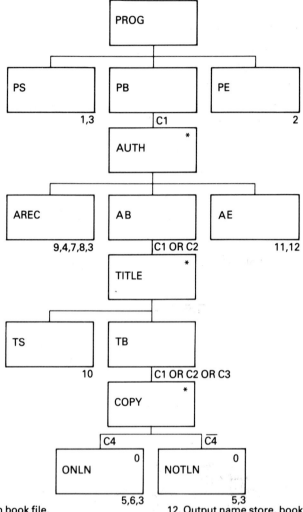

1. Open book file.
2. Close book file.
3. Read record from book file.
4. Move author's name to name store.
5. Add 1 to book total.
6. Add 1 to loan total.
7. Set book total to 0.
8. Set loan total to 0.
9. Move author number to current author number.
10. Move title number to current title number.
11. Calculate loan average = book total / loan total × 100.
12. Output name store, book total, loan average.

C1. End of book file.
C2. Author number not = current author number.
C3. Title number not = current title number.
C4. LOAN-INDIC = '1'.

5.6.1

As per Fig. 3.16 with the following amendments:

'Open cost file' allocated to PROG-START.
'Write cost record' allocated to P-QTY-END, replacing operation 5.
'Add cost to total cost' allocated to P-QTY-END.
'Write file trailer using total cost' allocated to PROG-END.
'Close cost file' allocated to PROG-END.

5.6.2

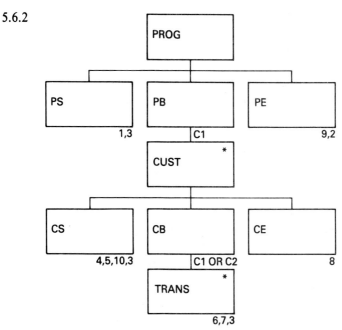

1. Open files.
2. Close files.
3. Read record from customer file.
4. Set customer total to 0.
5. Move customer number to current customer number.
6. Add invoice amount to customer total.
7. Add invoice amount to file total.
8. Format and write customer record using header store and
   customer total.
9. Format and write file trailer using file total.
10. Move header information to header store.

C1. End of customer file.
C2. Customer number not = current customer number.

5.6.3

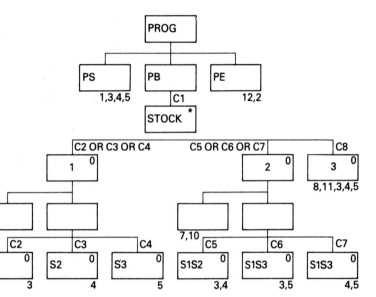

1. Open files.
2. Close files.
3. Read record from stock file 1;
        at end-of-file move all 9s to stock key 1 (SK1).
4. Read record from stock file 2;
        at end-of-file move all 9s to stock key 2 (SK2).
5. Read record from stock file 3;
        at end-of-file move all 9s to stock key 3 (SK3).
6. Format and write 'STOCK ITEM ON ONE FILE ONLY' printline.
7. Format and write 'STOCK ITEM ON TWO FILES ONLY' printline.
8. Format and write 'STOCK ITEM ON ALL THREE FILES' printline.
9. Add 1 to one-file total.
10. Add 1 to two-file total.
11. Add 1 to three-file total.
12. Format and write totals printlines.

C1. SK1 = SK2 = SK3 = all 9s.
C2. SK1 < (SK2 AND SK3).
C3. SK2 < (SK1 AND SK3).
C4. SK3 < (SK1 AND SK2).
C5. (SK1 = SK2) < SK3.
C6. (SK1 = SK3) < SK2.
C7. (SK2 = SK3) < SK1.
C8. SK1 = SK2 = SK3.

5.6.4

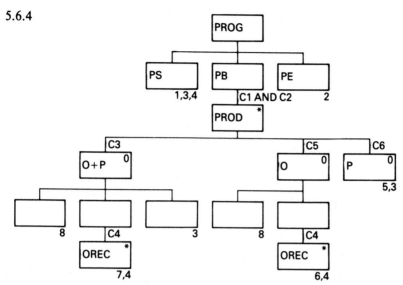

1. Open files.
2. Close files.
3. Read record from product file;
     at end-of-file move all 9s to product number.
4. Read record from orders file;
     at end-of-file move all 9s to order key.
5. Format and output 'NO ORDERS' message.
6. Format and output 'NO PRODUCT' message.
7. Format and output 'ORDER OK' message.
8. Move order key to current order key.

C1. Product number = all 9s.
C2. Order key = all 9s.
C3. Product number = order key.
C4. Order key not = current order key.
C5. Product number > order key.
C6. Product number < order key.

5.6.5

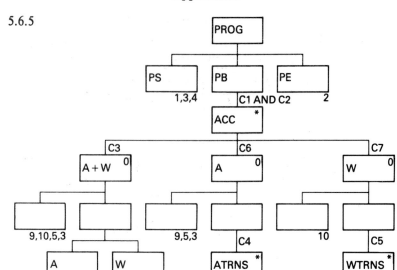

1. Open files.
2. Close files.
3. Read record from accounts file;
        at end-of-file move all 9s to account key.
4. Read record from weekly transactions file;
        at end-of-file move all 9s to weekly account key.
5. Write C/F account header from B/F account header.
6. Write C/F transaction from B/F transaction.
7. Write C/F transaction from weekly transaction.
8. Write error transaction printline.
9. Move account key to current account key.
10. Move weekly account key to current weekly account key.

C1. Account key = all 9s.
C2. Weekly account key = all 9s.
C3. Account key = weekly account key.
C4. Account key not = current account key.
C5. Weekly account key not = current weekly account key.
C6. Account key < weekly account key.
C7. Account key > weekly account key.

6.4.1 206-P-CUST-BODY becomes a selection between P-ORDER-ON-DB and P-ORDER-NOT-ON-DB (+ operation to output error message).
306-P-CUST-BODY becomes a selection between P-INVOICE-ON-DB and P-INVOICE-NOT-ON-DB (+ operation to output error message).
307-P-INVOICE becomes a selection between P-PAID and P-NOT-PAID, with operation 17 allocated to P-PAID only.

6.4.2

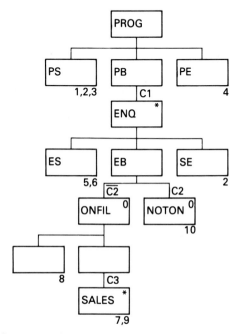

1. Output user instructions.
2. Input salesperson code.
3. Open sales file.
4. Close sales file.
5. Set INVAL-SW to '0'.
6. Read salesperson file INVALID KEY MOVE '1' TO INVAL-SW.
7. Output sales (subscript).
8. Set subscript to 1.
9. Add 1 to subscript.
10. Output 'NOT ON FILE'.

C1. Salesperson code = 999999.
C2. INVAL-SW = '1'.
C3. Subscript > 12.

6.4.3

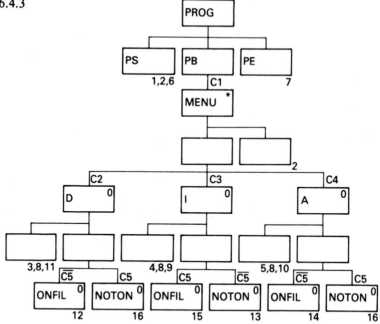

1. Output user instructions.
2. Input option.
3. Input delete key.
4. Input insert key + data.
5. Input amend key + data.
6. Open car file.
7. Close car file.
8. Set INVAL-SW to '0'.
9. Format and write car record.
10. Read, amend and rewrite car record.
11. Read and delete car record.
12. Output 'DELETED'.
13. Output 'INSERTED'.
14. Output 'AMENDED'.
15. Output 'ON FILE'.
16. Output 'NOT ON FILE'.

C1. Option = 9.
C2. Option = 1.
C3. Option = 2.
C4. Option = 3.
C5. INVAL-SW = '1'.

6.4.4

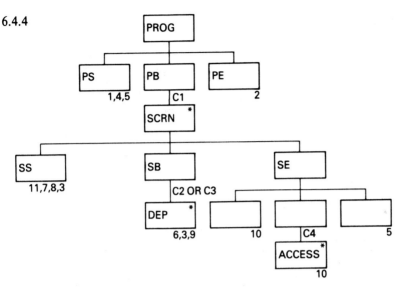

1. Open departures file.
2. Close departures file.
3. Read record from departures file.
4. Input time from user.
5. Move time to time store.
6. Format and output departure line.
7. Set COUNT to 1.
8. Set departures file access point using time store.
9. Add 1 to COUNT.
10. Input time from clock.
11. Output screen heading.

C1. Time store = 00.00.
C2. COUNT > 10.
C3. End of departures file.
C4. Time not = time store.

7.6.1

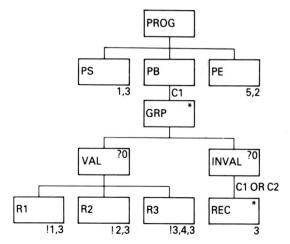

1. Open INFILE.
2. Close INFILE.
3. Read record from INFILE.
4. Add 1 to valid total.
5. Output valid total.

C1. End of INFILE.
C2. R1.

!1. Quit valid if (end of INFILE or not R1).
!2. Quit valid if (end of INFILE or not R2).
!3. Quit valid if (end of INFILE or not R3).

7.6.2

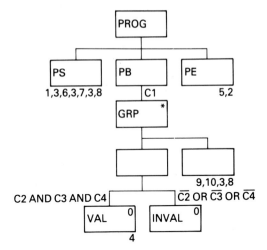

1. Open INFILE.
2. Close INFILE.
3. Read record from INFILE.
4. Add 1 to valid total.
5. Output valid total.
6. Move record to store 1.
7. Move record to store 2.
8. Move record to store 3.
9. Move store 2 to store 1.
10. Move store 3 to store 2.

C1. End of INFILE.
C2. Store 1 = R1.
C3. Store 2 = R2.
C4. Store 3 = R3.

7.6.3

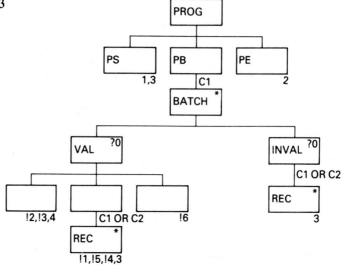

1. Open files.
2. Close files.
3. Read record from B/F update file.
4. Move batch number to current batch number.

C1. End of B/F update file.
C2. Batch number not = current batch number.

!1. Quit valid if (rejection).
!2. Move spaces to table.
!3. Set subscript to 1.
!4. Add 1 to subscript.
!5. Move B/F update record to table element (subscript).
!6. Write C/F update records from table.

7.6.4

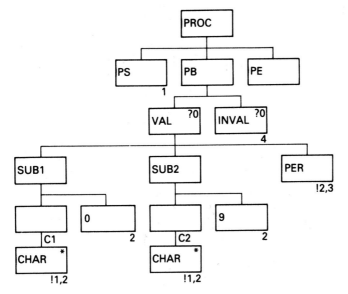

1. Set subscript to 1.
2. Add 1 to subscript.
3. Output 'VALID STRING'.
4. Output 'INVALID STRING'.

C1. Character (subscript) = '0'.
C2. Character (subscript) = '9'.

!1. Quit valid if (character (subscript) = '.').
!2. Quit valid if (character (subscript) not = '.').

7.6.5

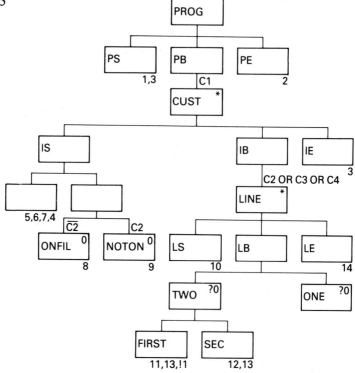

1. Open invoice file.
2. Close invoice file.
3. Input invoice number.
4. Read invoice file INVALID KEY MOVE '1' TO INVAL-SW.
5. Set INVAL-SW to '0'.
6. Set EOF-SW to '0'.
7. Move input customer number to invoice file key.
8. Move customer number to current customer number.
9. Output customer not found message.
10. Move spaces to output-line.
11. Move invoice record to first half of output-line.
12. Move invoice record to second half of output-line.
13. Read record from invoice file (i.e. sequential Read).
14. Output output-line.

C1. Input customer number = all 9s.
C2. INVAL-SW = '1'.
C3. EOF-SW = '1'.
C4. Customer number not = current customer number.

!1. Quit complete-line (i.e. TWO) if (EOF-SW = '1' or
      customer number not = current customer number).

8.6.1

Two procedures: P-EMP-FILE, P-EMP-REPORT.

P-EMP-FILE passes an EOF-SW and an employee record to P-EMP-REPORT, which formats and writes printlines and accumulates totals.

8.6.2

Two procedures: P-CUST-FILE, P-SUMMARY-FILE.

P-CUST-FILE passes an EOF-SW, customer header information and customer total invoice amount to P-SUMMARY-FILE. P-SUMMARY-FILE need know nothing about transactions; it writes summary customer records and accumulates file total invoice account.

8.6.3

Four procedures: SCHEDULER, P-TRANS-FILE, P-VAL-FILE, P-ERROR-REPORT. The scheduler obtains a transaction record from P-TRANS-FILE, passes a valid record to P-VAL-FILE and an invalid record to P-ERROR-REPORT. Backtracking is handled by the scheduler. At end-of-file the scheduler obtains an EOF-SW from P-TRANS-FILE and passes it on to P-VAL-FILE and P-ERROR-REPORT.

9.6.1

(a) No clash. A line is an integral number (4) of records.
(b) Boundary clash. A line is not an integral number of records, nor a record an integral number of lines.
(c) No clash. There is a one-to-one relationship between line and record; only some of the information on a record is printed.
(d) Ordering clash. The report is in a different sequence from the file.

9.6.2

Boundary clash. A line is not an integral number of records, nor a record an integral number of lines.

9.6.3

Interleaving clash. Records are already in code sequence for each name, but records for one name are interleaved with those for other names.

9.6.5

Two procedures: P-CUST-TRANS, P-TERMINAL.

P-CUST-TRANS is an iteration of transaction inputs; it accepts an input, obtains terminal state vector, invokes P-TERMINAL and updates terminal state vector.

P-TERMINAL is an iteration (forever) of customer transactions (as per Figs

7.8 to 7.11). P-TERMINAL's state vector consists of terminal identification, state variable, attempt counter, account number, PIN and withdrawal amount.

This solution can be enhanced by a queuing algorithm to cater for simultaneous input, and by an inverted report procedure. The program can be simulated at a single terminal by keying in an explicit terminal number to represent terminal identification (i.e. point of origin).

References

1 Baber, R. L. *Software Reflected*, North-Holland, 1982.
2 Beizer, B. *Software Testing Techniques*, Van Nostrand, 1983.
3 Boehm, B. W. That maintenance iceberg, *Datamation*, May 1973.
4 Boehm, B. W. Software engineering, *IEEE Transactions on Computers*, **C-25**, 12, Dec. 1976, 1226–41.
5 Bohm, C. and Jacopini, G. Flow diagrams, Turing machines and languages with only two formation rules, *Communications of the ACM*, **9**, 5, May 1966, 361–71.
6 Cameron, J. *JSP and JSD: The Jackson Approach to Software Development*, IEEE Computer Society Press, 1983.
7 Cohen, A. *Structure logic and program design*, John Wiley and Sons, 1983.
8 Glass, R. L. *Software Reliability Guidebook*, Prentice-Hall, 1979.
9 Henderson, P. and Snowdon, R. An experiment in structured programming, *BIT* 12, 1972, 38–53.
10 IBM technical report TR002762.
11 International Survey and Report on Structured Programming Practice, Infotech International, 1976.
12 Jackson, M. A. J. *Principles of Program Design*, Academic Press, 1975.
13 Jackson, M. A. J. *System Development*, Prentice-Hall, 1982.
14 Martin, J. *Application Development Without Programmers*, Prentice-Hall, 1982.
15 Martin, J. *Program Design Which is Provably Correct*, Savant Research Studies, 1982.
16 McCabe, T. J. A complexity measure, *IEEE Transactions on Software Engineering*, 1976, 308–20.
17 McCracken, D. Revolution in programming—an overview, *Datamation*, **19**, 12, Dec. 1973, 50–52.
18 Palmer, P. F. Structured programming techniques in interrupt-driven routines, *ICL Technical Journal*, Nov. 1979, 247–64.
19 Pressman, R. S. *Software Engineering: A Practitioner's Approach*, McGraw-Hill, 1982.
20 Shneiderman, B. *Software Psychology*, Winthrop, 1980.
21 Structured Design Method—Central Government Mandatory Standard 18: parts 1, 2 and 3, Central Computer and Telecommunications Agency, 1983.
22 Yourdon, E. and Constantine, L. *Structured Design*, Yourdon Press, 1978.
23 Yourdon, E. *Classics in Software Engineering*, Yourdon Press, 1979.

Index

action 272–274
admit construct 167, 170–203, 302
array *see* tables
Assembler 84–85, 96, 103
attribute 274
automation *see* JSP, automation of

backtracking 93–94, 164–203, 302, 305
  coding constraint 93
  in JSD 274
  nested 191–194
  side-effects 194–203
  technique of 164–171
  testing of 112
BASIC 61, 68, 86–89, 131
  backtracking 176, 184
  coding from HOST 101–102, 303–306
  coding constraints 93–94
  direct-access files 143, 145
  hierarchical code 86
  inversion 208, 216–217, 230–231,
    241
  linear code 89
  mixed code 88
  nested code 87
  nested selection 92
  operations in 293
Boolean 166
boundary clash 249–255
boundary value analysis 106–107
branch (instruction) see GOTO
branch (of tree) 26, 307
BREAK 178

CALL 220, 241
CASE 94, 103, 221
child 27, 307
COBOL 61, 68, 84, 87–89, 95–97, 99, 131
  backtracking 176–177, 184
  coding constraints 90–94
  coding from HOST 102–103, 303–306
  direct-access files 141, 152–153, 262
  hierarchical code 97

inversion 208, 217–219, 231, 241,
  262
  linear code 89
  mixed code 88
  nested code 88
  operations in 293
COBOL 68 88, 92–93
COBOL 74 88, 92–93
COBOL 85 88, 92,
  94, 221, 241
coding 82–105, 299–306
collating 125
component labels 35, 296–298
components names 35, 296–297
component numbers 297–298
conditions 50, 72–73, 78
  checklist 295
  evaluation problems 164–171
control break 75
control structures
  restricted 9–11, 25
correspondence 114–138, 245
  limitations of 136–138
  rules of 115, 123–124

data analysis 34, 41–43, 75
data base *see* database
data components 25–27
data flow diagram 271
data flow machine 208
data sets 25
  direct-access 144–161
  matching 125–136
data processing 1–9, 13
data specification 34, 41–42
data structure diagrams 25–43
  large 99, 307–308
data driven design 14, 21–23, 272, 288,
  291
database 153–161, 291
diagrams
  see data structure diagrams *and*
    program structure diagrams

direct-access files 144–145, 147–153
dismembering 307–308
DO 98, 105

elementary components 27, 299–300
embedded function 285, 291
END–IF 88, 92
end-of-file 68, 131
entity 272–274
equivalence partitioning 106–107
EVALUATE 94, 221
exercises
  backtracking 203–205
  correspondence 138–140
  direct-access data sets 162–163
  deriving test data 113
  designing programs 80–81
  inversion 244
  structure clashes 269
  sequence 44
  sequence and selection 44
  sequence, selection and iteration
    44–45
  solutions 309–334

files *see* data sets
fixed-state procedure 219, 243
flowchart 8, 22–23
FOR/NEXT 59
functional decomposition *see* top-down
  design
functional design 11, 21–23, 74–75, 271

GET (in HOST) 209, 213, 220, 230, 303,
  306
GOSUB 88, 103
GOTO 10–11, 25, 75, 94, 102–103, 166,
  170, 177–178, 220

Hamish 168–171
hierarchical code 86–87, 92–94
hierarchical decomposition *see* top-down
  design
Higher Order Software 13
Hierarchically Organized Structured
  Text *see* HOST
HOST
  backtracking 175
  coding from program structure
    diagram 97–101, 299–303
  conversion into BASIC and COBOL *see*
    BASIC *and* COBOL

inversion 208, 214–215, 230–231,
  237
HOSTAGE 101, 105
identification criterion 73
IF/ELSE 92–93
implementation 242–243, 285–288
imposed function 285, 291
indentation of code 92, 100
indexed-sequential files 141, 261
interleaving clash 255–265
interrupt-driven routine 267–268
INVALID KEY 142–143
inversion 93–94, 115, 206–244,
  302–303, 305–306
  benefits of 240–244
  coding constraint 94
  in JSD 274
  multiple 237
  parallel 259, 265–268, 286
  serial 237
  technique of 206–209
  testing of 112
INVERT/INVERT-END 215, 303, 305
iteration 10, 25, 50, 73, 304
  components 35–41, 301
  nested 38, 73, 93, 295
  testing of 107–111
  words implying, in data
    specification 42

Jackson, Michael A.J. 19, 97, 131, 271
Jackson Structured Programming *see*
  JSP
Jackson System Development *see* JSD
JSD
  entity/action step 272–276
  information function step 280–285
  initial model step 276–279
  interactive function step 279–280
  system implementation step 285–288
  system timing step 285
JSP
  automation of 21, 83–85, 90,
    103–104, 106
  benefits of 20–21
  overview 6–7, 13–24
  steps of 14, 25, 46–50, 171, 208–209
JSP-COBOL 105, 243
leaf 26
leg (of tree) 26
life-history diagram 274
linear code 88–89, 92–94
link-area (in inversion) 208–209, 220,
  241
local variables 241

machine code 84
maintenance 2, 21, 83, 242
MAJIC 84
matching 125–136
merging 125–131
mixed code 88, 94
mixed-type components 33, 37
modular programming 9
modularization 11–13, 95, 240
    see also top-down design
multi-threaded procedure 259

nested code 87–88, 92–94
nesting 10, 29, 32, 38, 73, 87–88,
    90–94, 100

object code 95
operations 9, 25, 47–50, 72
    checklist 294
ordering clash 246–249

paging 148–149, 253–255
parent 27, 86, 332
Pascal 68, 77, 87, 94, 145, 178, 208,
    221, 241
PDF *see* Program Design Facility
PDL *see* Program Design Language
PDL generator 96
PDL precompiler 96, 104–105
PERFORM 59, 93, 95, 103, 153, 178, 220,
    241
posit construct 167, 170–203, 302
premature program termination 167,
    225–231
process scheduling 238–240, 286
PRODIGY 84
program components 47, 299
Program Design Facility (PDF) 84
Program Design Language (PDL)
    94–105, 178
    see also HOST *and* Structure Text
program structure diagrams 47, 83,
    94–95, 115
    coding in HOST 299–303
    large 99, 307–308
pseudocode 22–23
psychological set 95, 99
PUT (in HOST) 209, 212, 230, 303, 306

queuing 266–267
quit construct 167, 170–203, 302

random files 141
READ 68, 75, 131, 142, 191
    conditional 88, 93
read-ahead principle 62–63, 66, 75, 145,
    183, 194, 213, 276
    multiple 200
REDEFINES 145, 152
re-entrant procedure 259
reference criterion 73
relative files 141
reliability 2–3, 20
root (of tree) 12, 26, 86, 303, 308

scheduler *see* process scheduling
SEARCH 190–191
selection 10, 25, 50, 304
    components 31–35, 300–301
    nested 90–92
    testing of 108–111
    words implying, in data
        specification 41
sequence 10, 25, 304
    components 28–30, 300
    nested 29
    testing of 110
    words implying, in data
        specification 41
sibling 27
side-effects of backtracking *see*
        backtracking
software crisis 1–3, 270–271
software engineering 4–7, 270, 272
software psychology 100
SORT 247
sort program 137, 246–249
source code 95
source code generator 85
Speedbuilder 271
standardization
    of coding 84, 94
    of design 82
state variable 219–220
state vector 259
stepwise refinement *see* top-down design
structure clashes 137, 245–268
    see also boundary clash, interleaving
        clash, ordering clash
structure diagrams 20
    see also data structure diagrams *and*
        program structure diagrams
Structure Text 97–99, 299–302
Structured Design 13
Structured programming 9–13
subroutines 86–87
    in inversion 208

switches 75, 165–166, 191
syntax processing 167, 204
system development 1, 3–5, 270–271, 288, 291–292
system implementation diagram 288
system specification diagram 279
systems analysis 270
systems design 6, 270

tables 145–153
  searching 167, 187–191
testing 6–7, 20, 83, 105–113
time-sharing system 266

top-down design 11–13, 21–23, 27
transputer 208
tree 12, 23, 26–27
updating of sequential file 133–136
UNIX 208
USED BY 215, 303
USING 215, 237, 303, 305

validation 122, 164–167, 172–174, 178–187, 194, 200–203
VALUE 77, 152
variable-state procedure 219–220, 243